HITLER'S PAWN

Postcard photo of Herschel Grynszpan,
shortly before assassination

HITLER'S PAWN

THE BOY ASSASSIN
AND THE HOLOCAUST

WITHDRAWN

STEPHEN KOCH

COUNTERPOINT
Berkeley, California

Hitler's Pawn

Copyright © 2019 by Stephen Koch
First hardcover edition: 2019

Library of Congress Cataloging-in-Publication Data
Names: Koch, Stephen, 1941– author.
Title: Hitler's pawn : the boy assassin and the Holocaust / Stephen Koch.
Description: First hardcover edition. | Berkeley, California : Counterpoint, c [2019] |
    Includes bibliographical references and index.
Identifiers: LCCN 2018018729 | ISBN 9781640091443
Subjects: LCSH: Grynszpan, Herschel Feibel, 1921–approximately 1943. | Jewish
    refugees—France—Biography. | Assassins—France—Paris—Biography. | Vom Rath,
    Ernst, 1909–1938—Assassination.
Classification: LCC DS134.42.G79 K63 2019 | DDC 940.53/18420092 [B]—dc23
LC record available at https://lccn.loc.gov/2018018729

Jacket design by Sarah Brody
Book design by Jordan Koluch

COUNTERPOINT
2560 Ninth Street, Suite 318
Berkeley, CA 94710
www.counterpointpress.com

Printed in the United States of America
Distributed by Publishers Group West

10 9 8 7 6 5 4 3 2 1

For Franny

CONTENTS

Preface 3

1   *La Paix! La Paix! La Paix!* 5

2   The Child 14

3   Hunted 23

4   Dispossession .33

5   The Assassin's Night 43

6   The Assassin's Day 59

7   Hitler's Luck 74

8   Arrest and Fame 90

9   Two Speeches 101

10   The Whole World Hears 111

11   Grief and Grandiosity 121

12   The Phony War 138

13   "I'm Herschel Grynszpan! Arrest Me!" 149

14   Herschel the Captive 160

15   The Homosexual Strategy. 179

16   Victory Unaware. 192

17   Oblivion. 202

EPILOGUE   Two Brothers 212

Acknowledgments. .219

APPENDIX   Herschel Grynszpan's Testament,
           Dictated in Code, April 24–29, 1942. 221

A Note on Sources 223

Visuals. 229

Bibliography 231

Notes. 235

Index. 253

HITLER'S PAWN

Preface

On November 7, 1938, Herschel Grynszpan, an impoverished seventeen-year-old Polish Jew living in Paris, obsessed with Nazi persecution of his family in Germany and brooding on protest, revenge, and his own insignificance, bought a small handgun, carried it on the Paris Métro to the German embassy, and, never before having fired a weapon in his entire life, shot down the first German diplomat he saw. When the wounded official died two days later, Adolf Hitler and Joseph Goebbels used his death as their pretext for the great state-sponsored wave of anti-Semitic violence and terror known as the Kristallnacht, the pogrom many consider to be an initiating event of the Holocaust. Overnight, a perfect political nobody found himself world famous, a face on front pages everywhere, and a pawn in the machinations of great power.

But the pogrom of November 9, 1938, was not the end. It became Herschel Grynszpan's destiny to play a role in the Second World War and the Holocaust unlike that of anyone else in the world. Until 1940, Herschel's impending murder trial in France—never held—made him an icon in the battle of ideas between anti-Nazis and profascists in Europe and America. Hoping to save the boy's life by using his trial to unmask Nazi anti-Semitic outrages, the great anti-Nazi journalist Dorothy Thompson founded a defense fund for him and hired the best lawyers in France to defend him. There was embattled controversy. Various conspiracy theories—other than Hitler's own—flourished. Sexual and political rumors swirled around him. The Germans accused him of being a British agent. Some influential anti-Nazis even suspected he might be an agent of the Gestapo, set up to provoke the Kristallnacht.

When France fell in 1940, Herschel was forced into an entirely new role. Hitler dispatched an elite squad of the Gestapo to Paris to find Herschel Grynszpan, arrest him, and bring him to Germany alive. After a bizarre chase, the boy—still a teenager—was captured and flown in secret to Berlin, where he was held prisoner as the defendant in a massive show trial the Nazis designed to be a front for the mass murders that were about to begin. Its purpose: to prove that "the Jews" had started the Second World War—sparked by Herschel's crime.

When the maturing Herschel realized that the Nazis were planning to use him against his people once again, he set out to use all his ingenuity to prevent this trial from ever taking place. Preparations for the trial were sinister, elaborate, advanced, and developed at the highest levels of the regime. Hitler was kept constantly informed. It became a duel of wits between one imprisoned Jewish youth and Joseph Goebbels and the Führer himself.

Yet Herschel's story has been *almost* forgotten, shrouded in the boy's own insignificance and twisted in myth and conspiratorial fantasy. His name appears for a few lines in any respectable history of the European war. Histories of the Kristallnacht usually grant him a chapter or two. There have been a few books about him in various languages (see "A Note on Sources"). Most are virtually unknown. Some are excellent. Some are fiction or dubious mixtures of fact and fiction. Some are scholarly but in places erroneous. Several are mired in false information or out-of-date research. For decades, mystification persisted. Herschel Grynszpan's crime was a simple one, but it was only in 2013—seventy-five years after the shots were fired—that definitive clarity was finally achieved.

This is his story.

La Paix! La Paix! La Paix!

Fondling another glass of *bon vin rouge*, the exhausted premier of France tried without success to relax into his plane's plush seat. He was flying home from Germany after signing what history would come to condemn as the Munich Pact. It was October 1, 1938, as the two-engine, twenty-eight-seat Air France luxury airliner flew westward into the declining European afternoon. This was not the premier's first glass of red for the day, nor would it be his last. Édouard Daladier was normally an abstemious man, but some suspected that he had signed the actual agreement itself—then seen as the salvation of civilization—in a state of less-than-perfect sobriety. The premier was desperately unhappy.[1]

Daladier was a stubby, deceptively tough-looking politician from the South of France. He had a wide, square, stolid face, and within twenty-four hours, countless newsreels would show the world that he was the shortest leader among the four at the meeting he had just left: shorter than Hitler and Benito Mussolini, and much shorter than the British prime minister, Neville Chamberlain. With his thick neck, heavy head, and implacable brow, Daladier's political nickname was "the Bull of Vaucluse." He *looked* tough—fearless, decisive—and that look had helped elect him.

Looks deceived. Daladier was an intelligent man, and in contrast to

Neville Chamberlain, he was not wrong about Hitler. Chamberlain believed that it might be possible to treat Hitler as a normal politician. Daladier did not. His assessment of the Nazi threat to his country and the world was lucid to the point of clairvoyance. He knew who Hitler was. Knowing that, he also knew that he had just played a losing hand in Munich. The night before, he had signed away part of the stature and power of France. He had signed because he was indecisive and doubted that France could face down Hitler with a threat serious enough to frighten the tyrant. He was afraid that a second world war would begin on his watch.[2]

"If I'd had three or four thousand more aircraft," he later said, "Munich would never have happened."[3] If he had had three or four thousand more aircraft, France would have responded to Hitler's threat to invade Czechoslovakia with a declaration of war.

Either to toast or to drown the illusion of peace, Daladier took another sip.

The premier's five-hour flight from Munich was nearing its end; the Air France aircraft had been back in French air space for the last ninety minutes. Daladier knew what was coming. He would step off his plane and walk across the tarmac to the thicket of microphones, newsreel cameras, and clamoring reporters. There he would make some sort of statement. The welcoming committee would include the usual dignitaries, led by the foreign minister of France, Georges Bonnet, who would step forward to greet Daladier with unfeigned joy.

It was joy because Bonnet was as delighted with the Munich Pact as Daladier was troubled. As the prime appeaser of appeasers, Bonnet was convinced that France would be the sure loser in any confrontation with Germany. He was one of the sly masterminds behind all that had just happened in Munich.

After making his statement, the premier would step into an open car, where he would sit beside his beaming foreign minister during the ride back into Paris.

And clustered at a distance, neatly confined behind the airport's police lines, there would be the public, delirious with either rage or joy. Had they come to idolize him or assassinate him? Daladier merely muttered the question, and his aides were shocked to realize that the premier's query about his possible assassination on the ride home was not quite a joke. He was unsure whether the French public would see Munich as a defeat or a victory. He genuinely feared the fury of the people. What if they saw, as he did, that in the depths of the night before, he had subjected his country to a defeat without a battle?

The premier was as divided and paralyzed as the nation he led, a nation close to civil war over the great choice of the thirties: democracy or dictatorship, power or decadence, daring or defeat, confronting Hitler or doing what the premier had just done in Munich: saving the illusion of peace with a real surrender.

Édouard Daladier had been an infantry grunt in the First World War. He had seen the bleeding guts of his comrades spilled into the filth of the trenches. With memories like that in his mind, he was returning from Munich with the cold comfort of being the man who had *not* started a second world war.

Yet.

What made Daladier want to anesthetize his pain with *le vin rouge* was that he had no illusions about the threat France was facing. Chamberlain fondly believed that if they met the German dictator's more . . . well, *plausible* demands, the Nazi would relent in his aggression and begin to act like a normal politician. Daladier did not. Daladier had been in London in what he was sure would be a last-ditch effort to form an alliance with the British, seeking a joint strategy. The restless PM sat bored and irritated while Daladier told him the simple truth: "I tell you, this man is seeking a domination of the continent in comparison with which the ambitions of Napoleon were feeble. Today, it is the turn of Czechoslovakia. Tomorrow it will be Poland or Romania. When Germany has obtained all the oil it needs, she will turn to the west. Certainly, we have to multiply our efforts to avoid war. But that will not be obtained unless Britain and France stick together, intervening in Prague for new concessions but declaring at the same time that they will safeguard the independence of Czechoslovakia. If, on the contrary, the western powers capitulate again, they will only precipitate the war they wish to avoid."[4]

It was crystalline foresight—and yet Daladier had signed away western Czechoslovakia rather than honor an earlier treaty to defend that small country against Germany because the premier underestimated French power and overestimated German power.

Was he right? The facts were foggy. He was pretty sure Britain would not follow him if he took France into war over Czechoslovakia.[5] And his worst fear was to precipitate yet another world war. That is why, when it came to be his turn to be premier and he had to choose a foreign minister for his cabinet, he rejected a lucid anti-Nazi and appointed Bonnet the appeaser against his better judgment. He chose a man who so fervently believed in "peace at any price" that gossip scattered unproven claims that Bonnet and his wife were all but German agents.[6] In 1938, Bonnet was secretly negotiating further concessions to the Nazis, far beyond the Munich Pact. Because, he said, he wanted peace.

And that is what Daladier, in his desperation, also wanted. Peace.

A steward approached: "Ten minutes, sir." Daladier downed what was left in his glass and closed his eyes, trying to marshal whatever composure it would take for him to step up to those microphones and then climb into that waiting car. Daladier pulled back the curtain to the porthole beside his seat. He looked down on his country more seriously. The undulant green-and-gold cubism of French farmland—so beautiful he could barely gaze his fill—was becoming the tangled maze of the great city, a considered chaos of tracks and roads and slums and warehouses. There

Paris lay: capital of the nation that yesterday he had so very reasonably, so very sensibly, betrayed.

Using the tray in front of him, Daladier took a piece of paper, uncapped his pen, and without trembling wrote out his statement for the nation. The words came slowly to this taciturn man. The statement wouldn't take more than a few minutes; it would be broadcast on French national radio from the airport.

These words were the heart of the statement: *I return with the profound conviction that this accord is indispensable to the peace of Europe. We achieved it thanks to a spirit of mutual concessions and close collaboration.*[7]

Long-term, Daladier knew that talk about the pact being indispensable to the peace of Europe was a lie. Short-term, if it wasn't the exact truth, it was . . . close enough. It was the best he could do. All of it was the best he could do. The whole thing was the best he could do. He capped his pen.

The plane had begun gently to lose altitude.

Red-faced and stolid, the Bull of Vaucluse was never easy to read, but nothing on his face indicated the satisfaction and joy that would suffuse Bonnet when the two met on the runway. But as the premier who had made Bonnet foreign minister lit a cigarette, his silent certainty remained: *I tell you, this man is seeking a domination of the continent in comparison with which the ambitions of Napoleon were feeble . . .*

The plane deepened its descent, and Daladier's aides were mildly surprised when the premier asked a steward to deliver a message to the pilot: *Delay landing. Tell him to circle the airport.*[8]

The premier needed time.

Below, the crowd had broken through the police barriers. From the premier's porthole it looked as though a vast bubble filled with humanity had burst, sweeping past the police and inundating the area around the gate. It was almost impossible to see the tarmac for the human swarm. *If I had three or four thousand more aircraft, I would not have signed.* Did that crowd down there know that yesterday their country had ceased to be a great power? Did

they know that what the journalists called France's "continental position"—
that is, its role as the leading power of Europe—had been signed away?[9]

In a few moments the plane adjusted its descent into the slight sideways
tilt of circling.

The steward came back, saying that the pilot wanted to know how long
he should circle Le Bourget.

*Until he's told to stop. Tell him the premier needs just a little more time
to . . . prepare.*

As the steward walked back toward the cockpit, Daladier lit another
cigarette and, twisted by uncertainty, sank into his stoic silence.

His plane circled Le Bourget once . . . twice . . . three times . . . four
times . . . five times—maneuvers of hesitation that looked exalted and tri-
umphant to the crowd below. Looking up, it was possible to mistake those
circles as demonstrations of delight: five exuberant airborne victory laps.

Ten minutes later, the premier of France summoned the steward: *Tell
the pilot to land now.* He said it the way a condemned man might tell the
executioner he was ready.

Some kind of rhythmic chant below was not quite audible under the
juddering roar of the two engines. Daladier was rigid; staring out as they
were about to land, he kept his hand on the curtain, as if uncertain whether
to show his face or hide it. The plane hit the tarmac with a shuddering bump
and slowed to gently taxiing speed. The premier did not extinguish his cigarette but stared out the window at the crowd of humanity, trying to read the
masses he had been elected to lead.

At length the plane stopped at the gate; the roar of the engines—which
for some reason seemed even louder on the ground than in the air—sputtered
and ceased. And the chant of the crowd could be heard: *La paix! . . . La
paix! . . . La paix!*

Daladier rubbed out his cigarette in the now-full brass ashtray attached
to his seat. He frowned as the stairs for deplaning were rolled to the air-
plane's side.

Do we open the door now? a steward wanted to know. Daladier rose and with a nod headed to the exit. The wheel sealing the aluminum portal was spun, and the door swung open. The bewildering roaring singsong now reached him in a roar:

La paix! . . . La paix! . . . La paix!

They were cheering.

In the many decades since the Second World War ended, the Munich Agreement has been seen as one of the most disgraceful blunders in modern diplomatic history, a work of cowardice and treachery viewed with such universal contempt that it is at first difficult to grasp the mass enthusiasm that greeted it. Of course, factions that already recognized the Hitlerian threat—the Nazis' victims, Jews and the anti-Nazi intelligentsia, some of the press, and much (though not all) of the left—opposed the pact. But it is difficult to overstate its popularity with the masses. Words falter trying to catch the mood, but newsreels of Daladier's return to Le Bourget airport on October 1, 1938, show what is hard to tell. This is frenzy.[10]

This is understandable only when one grasps how much the democratic world feared that a second world war in 1938 might bring civilization to an end. For comparison, people in the twenty-first century might consider their fear of a nuclear Armageddon. With its leaders' return from Munich, Europe imagined it had just been saved. In both Paris and London, a vast part of the whole population began to pour into the streets; it was as if joy overflowed. This was the joy of the masses, of people in every home and on every street, cheering their salvation. Four mere walls could not contain them; there was nothing anyone wanted to do except joyfully embrace the victory of "peace" over the war in which, as everyone knew, millions would die.

Not only citizens were overjoyed; leaders around the world welcomed the news from Munich. When his plane landed, Chamberlain waved a document in which Hitler promised nonaggression, and told the world that Germany and Britain had "agreed never to go to war with one another again." Later that day Chamberlain announced that the agreement meant "peace in our time." President Franklin Roosevelt sent him an exuberant telegram—"*Good man!*"—and King George VI invited him directly to Buckingham Palace to receive "the recognition of the lasting gratitude of your fellow countrymen throughout the British Empire."[11]

The palace was only five miles from Heston airport, but it took hours for the prime minister's car to creep through the wild throngs that swarmed every street along the way, going at most a few miles an hour as the celebrating people ran out to touch the passing car, kiss the windows of the limousine, leap onto the running boards, or pelt the somber official car with flowers. Reaching the palace, there came the moment of royal glory as Chamberlain was led out onto the balcony to stand together with the King and Queen and wave while the masses on the mall cheered as if he had just saved the world.[12]

Daladier's return to his capital was also a long, slow crawl. French radio had broadcast the route his motorcade would follow into Paris, and throngs swarmed along its whole length. Daladier stood up in the back of the small open car, looking rather red and bewildered according to some observers. Next to him, with a self-satisfied smile on his face, sat Foreign Minister Bonnet. Women detached themselves from the crowd and ran toward Daladier, holding out their babies. His car was bombarded with flowers.[13] All the way into Paris there were surging crowds, shouting cries of relief, and the steady chant:

Vive Daladier! Vive la paix! Vive la France!

Five weeks later, on November 9, 1938, the illusion of the Munich peace would disappear in the most violent pogrom in history, the orgy of state-sponsored anti-Semitic crime in Germany and Austria that became known as the Kristallnacht. The peace Daladier had accepted, cringing and against his instincts, would disappear, scattered by the shock of a second European riot, one not of joy but of hate, not spontaneous but organized, the night of broken glass, when Hitler ripped off the mask of normality and revealed the essentially criminal nature of his regime, lit by fire and pillage. It was a forty-eight-hour assault on the idea of civilization itself, all of it staged on the pretext of one crime committed in Paris by one insignificant teenaged boy.

But after Munich, Daladier waved. He tried to smile. The chants of public euphoria swirled around him and did not stop. As his car crawled through the throngs, he would sit from time to time and then stand again for more acclamation. At some point, his aide, Alexis Leger, heard the premier mutter under his breath, *"Ah! Les cons."*[14]

The Child

Everyone called him "the child."

Whether speaking in Yiddish or German, Herschel Grynszpan's mother and father naturally spoke of their youngest as *das Kind*. When *das Kind* was fifteen, Sendel and Rivka Grynszpan (pronounced "Greenspan") got their son out of Hitler's reach by sending him to live in Paris, where his Uncle Abraham and Aunt Chawa called their rescued nephew *l'enfant*. Two years after that, as the French police hustled this diminutive threat to European peace through a gauntlet of blazing flashbulbs and swarming press, reporters noted that the boy assassin looked closer to thirteen than seventeen. Later, Herschel's French lawyers—antifascists vaunted as the best legal minds in France—always referred to their young client as *le petit*. When she formed a legal defense fund to advocate for "the little one's" essential (albeit not literal) innocence, Dorothy Thompson, then the foremost anti-Nazi journalist in the English language, called him "this boy." Even Adolf Eichmann himself—after interrogating Herschel in Berlin with a view to the propaganda surrounding the Holocaust—referred to him as *der Knabe*: the lad.[1]

—

He *was* small, like many a pawn, and cursed with a baby face. He became famous on the cusp of maturity: In some photographs he looks like a frightened child; in others he is quite handsome, almost sultry, albeit in a boyish way. He had large, expressive, dark eyes and wore his black hair slicked back in the style of 1930s adolescence. He was frail. When he turned seventeen, he weighed just under a hundred pounds and stood a fraction of an inch taller than five feet one. His health was never good; as a child he may have had rickets. In early adolescence, there had been an appendectomy. Worst of all, he suffered from some sort of lifelong gastric problem—perhaps an ulcer—that was intermittently agonizing. Even in prison, he was a regular visitor to the infirmary.

He was clever with his hands and had a yen for sports; his main passion was for soccer, followed by Ping-Pong, which he played with the speed of an ace. According to most adults around him, he was "a gentle, self-effacing, obliging, and affectionate young man," albeit moody. He may have been on the bipolar spectrum.[2] He was subject to recurring depressions and sudden hot-blooded rages, even fistfights, on and off the soccer field.

But views of Herschel's temperament vary. Among his contemporaries on the soccer field and at school, he was known as "the Hun king" because he was "dark-complected and very hot-tempered." "Some who knew him in childhood remembered the boy as a quarreler."[3] Meanwhile, his brother, Mordecai, recalled his kid brother as a wit and a skilled and devastating mimic, whose imitations of pomposity could crack up a roomful of adults. There was something else: Both Mordecai and the lawyer who knew him best, Serge Weill-Goudchaux, used the same word to describe the boy. He was, they thought, fearless.[4]

Herschel had grown up with Hitler's consolidation of the Nazi tyranny. In 1933, when Hitler became chancellor, Herschel was eleven. In 1935, when the anti-Semitic Nuremberg Laws were passed, he was fourteen and a student learning Hebrew in a Zionist yeshiva in Frankfurt, hoping to emigrate to Israel. When he was fifteen, his family sent Herschel to Paris to escape an increasingly dangerous Reich. When Herschel was sixteen, Adolf Eichmann sent Hitler a memorandum arguing that mere legal persecution would never force Germany's Jews to leave the country and surrender everything they possessed to the kleptocracy. Eichmann recommended more persuasive measures such as lawless mass terror: a nationwide pogrom. This proposal foreshadowed the Kristallnacht.[5] When Herschel was seventeen, Hitler summarily deported more than eighteen thousand Polish Jews living in Germany—among them Herschel's mother, father, sister, and brother— stole all their money and worldly goods, and dumped them, penniless, on the Polish border.[6]

It was when Herschel heard about his family's deportation that he decided what he had to do and acquired what he had never so much as touched before: a gun.

Not long before he bought that gun, Herschel had stopped at a booth in a Parisian street fair, where a photographer was making portraits of people for a pittance, printing the images in the form of picture postcards. In his portrait, Herschel stands in front of a crudely painted backdrop, addressing the camera with an unsmiling, don't-mess-with-me stare. His stance is one of casual command. He is well dressed. Herschel's father and his uncle were both tailors, and poor though they were, Herschel presented well. He is wearing a three-piece suit that looks right for autumn, suggesting the picture was taken some time during the six weeks between late September when the Munich Pact was signed and that morning of November 7, 1938. Herschel has crooked his left hand behind his back, soldier-style; in his right hand, an elegantly pinched cigarette tries to proclaim adulthood. His eyebrows arch; his gaze does indeed seem fearless. The person pictured here is not the distraught child one sees in the press photographs taken during the hours and days after he became an assassin. On the postcard, Herschel looks almost like a man.

The idea of sending Herschel to the safety of Paris did not originate with his mother and father. When Herschel was fifteen, as Hitler's anti-Semitic persecution mounted, "Old Katz, the watchmaker," an elder at his synagogue, planted the idea of flight.

> He said to me, "A boy like you can't stay here under such conditions. In Germany a Jew is not a man but is treated like a dog." I told him that all the governments were closed to me.[7] He advised me to go to France. He spoke of this to my father, who accepted on the condition that Uncle Abraham, who had been living in Paris since 1923, agreed to receive me. My father wrote to my uncle who not only agreed to receive me but wanted to adopt me.[8]

And so, on a lazy summer day in August 1936, clutching one small valise, Herschel waved good-bye to his weeping family on the platform of the Hanover *Bahnhof* and boarded a train headed toward France. The frail fifteen-year-old traveled entirely alone. In 1936, Nazi law was shattering families through a quirk in the statutes that the Nazis still punctiliously observed. Jewish children could leave the Third Reich without penalty, while adults leaving Germany would see everything they owned confiscated by the state. Children could leave without having their property confiscated, since legally, they had no property to confiscate. All they had to leave behind was their world.

But many did wish to leave. Herschel's true desire was to emigrate—preferably with his family—not to France but to Israel. In truth, Israel was the dream destination of the entire Grynszpan family, and when Herschel was fourteen, the local Jewish community paid for him to go to Hamburg and study Hebrew in a yeshiva run by the Mizrachi Youth Organization, a branch of Zionism that "allied Zionism with strict religious observance."[9] Herschel later claimed that one day while he was at the Mizrachi yeshiva, he found himself standing with the heiling crowd on the sidewalk as Hitler passed through Hamburg in one of his triumphal motorcades. From the curb, Herschel watched the huge Mercedes sweep by. He had one thought. He wished he had a gun.[10]

At every stage of his odyssey, from his early teens and throughout his time in Paris, up until he became a prisoner of the Nazis and lost all hope, Israel was the place he was seeking to enter.

It was not to be. Herschel Grynszpan never saw the Promised Land.

The boy who in September 1936 dropped his wretched little valise on the threshold of Abraham and Chawa's two-room walk-up on the rue Richard Lenoir was a picture of almost Dickensian distress. He had left Germany frail but brave. He arrived emaciated and in despair.

The trip had been longer and more difficult than anyone expected it to be. It seems to have taken something like two weeks—until the end of August. After leaving Hanover, Herschel's first stop had been Essen—still in Germany—where he spent several days as the guest of a hospitable uncle. Brussels was the second stop, where yet another uncle, Wolf Grynszpan, gave him a greeting that was inhospitable and cold. By the time he reached Belgium, Herschel had no money left at all. He didn't have the visa needed to enter France legally, and nobody in Brussels was ready to advance him the money it would cost to acquire one. He felt hopeless, and his gut was in agony. It was decided that—like many others—he would have to enter France illegally. The expedient was simple; he would sneak across the border.[11] At the Belgian frontier, every day, all day, an overcrowded trolley carried loads of workers back and forth the few miles between their homes in Belgium and their jobs in France. For the police to monitor this traffic would have been a waste of time.[12] The trolley's last stop was in front of the train station in the French town of Valenciennes—a couple of hours' commute from Paris. When Herschel stepped off the trolley, his uncle Abraham was probably waiting for him, ready to love his wandering nephew on sight.[13]

But the nephew he saw gave Abraham a shock. Herschel was emaciated, in agonizing and doubtless humiliating pain. He was also numb with depression, an affliction that, like his abdominal pain, would stay with him for life.[14] He had been torn from the world of his boyhood—which was above all the world of his family—and forced onto alien ground. "Everything fell to pieces around him. He found himself alone and banished."[15] As Abraham later told the French court, "When Herschel came to our home, he was in such a state of depression that it was pitiful. He was ill and suffering from stomach trouble. Could we have thrown him out? It would have been inhuman. Moreover, we had been given the legal and moral responsibility for the child."[16]

Yet Herschel was not a complete stranger in the strange land of Paris. When he ventured downstairs from his aunt and uncle's apartment and onto the sidewalks of the rue Richard Lenoir, the languages he heard most often were his mother tongue of Yiddish, with the German of his second nature swirling in the mix. Of course, there was also the alien sound of French, but in his neighborhood, he could make his way.

There was a class ravine between the German Jewish refugees: Educated German Jews colonized the Left Bank, where they mingled easily with the community of largely left-wing Gentiles in flight from the tyranny. In the fluttering cafés of the boulevard Saint-Germain, everything that was cosmopolitan about France was on display. On the other hand, the Right Bank of the Seine was for the *Ostjuden*, and it was very different turf. Like the adjacent ghetto around the rue des Rosiers, the Tenth Arrondissement overflowed with thousands of Polish and other Eastern European Jews like the Grynszpans, who, when they fled from Hitler, were also running from poverty and third-class citizenship, leaving behind everything including

the ghetto itself. Americans wanting to visualize the Tenth Arrondissement in 1936 could recall images of New York's Lower East Side of 1905
to 1915: pushcart land. The streets were raucous with life. Food was kosher
and signs were in Hebrew. Nobody had much formal education. Business
was conducted not in corner offices but on street corners. Everyone was (at
least in name) religiously observant, just as on the Left Bank everyone was
(at least in name) agnostic. The Right Bank's cultural tone was as provincial
as the Left was cosmopolitan. The percentage of tailors in the population
was almost comically high. Step onto the sidewalk, and rue Richard Lenoir
was almost like the neighborhood in Hanover where Herschel had been
raised. Walk ten blocks away in any direction, and you were back in France.
French France.

Abraham and Chawa Grynszpan embraced their nephew as the child
they had never had. They had lived in Paris since the end of the First World
War. Abraham's income derived from tailoring work outsourced to him
by various large Parisian department stores. In all that time, Abraham
had never failed to support himself and his wife in the decent poverty that
seems to have been the fate of the whole Grynszpan clan.[17] He was forty-
three when Herschel came to live in Paris; in photographs of Chawa at the
time, she looks about the same age. Like Herschel, his aunt and uncle were
physically compact. Abraham's eyes were expressive and soulful. His features were fine-boned. He was known in the neighborhood for the steady
serenity of his manner: Abraham the imperturbable. In every photograph
he looks pensive. He called his tailoring business the Maison Albert. Herschel slept on a cot in the tiny living room, surrounded by sewing machines
and bolts of cloth. Abraham and Chawa dressed with propriety edging toward elegance for people of such modest means.

Abraham and Chawa's first priority was to get the boy well. After weeks
of careful diet and a loving welcome, both Herchel's mental and physical
suffering improved.

But he was a brooder, and as Europe was making being Jewish into a crime, he naturally brooded about what he invariably and reverently called "my people." His mood could easily turn to one of melancholy, and when he discussed "his people," the big brown eyes would often well with tears.

Several of Herschel's chroniclers describe him as "lazy." Perhaps. It is quite true that as a student he was very bright but a classic under-achiever. Yet once he was out of school, German anti-Semitism conspired with French bureaucracy to make it impossible for him to find a job in either country. It is hard to say how willing he would have been to work if he'd had the opportunity. Some biographers hint that a more enterprising type of refugee would have defied the French bureaucracy and found some sort of quasi-legal work in Paris, though the penalty for discovery would have been the deportation he feared above all other things. Yet one might even think that Herschel was law-abiding to a fault. Paris was filled with refugees doing petty jobs off the books, and more significantly, there was an active underground railway successfully spiriting teenagers—young Poles especially—into Palestine in defiance of the British mandate. But illegality meant risk; risk meant a return to Germany.

He was also a bit of a dreamer, given to long solitary walks through Paris, his mind awash in fantasy. Even for a protected teenager, his social life was modest. He had a couple of pals—Nathan Kaufmann and Sal Schenkier—and he belonged to a social club for refugees called Le Sports-club Aurore, where he was a regular at dances and events. His uncle gave him an allowance of 40 francs a week, and via Poland his mother was able—at great risk to herself and others—to send him monthly a small amount of cash.[18] From this money Herschel paid for the three weekly packs of cigarettes he smoked, the movies, his tickets on the Paris Métro, the cost of entry to swimming pools and dances where his very modest social life was conducted, and whatever was needed to buy some coffee on the terrace of the café on the boulevard Saint-Denis called Tout Va Bien ("All Is Well"), where, like all Parisians, he and his pals loved to go, sit, and watch the world go by.

Tout Va Bien featured a terrace, where the coffee was cheap, and a bar inside, where it was not so cheap. The boys spent a lot of time on the terrace. Though far from elegant, the café was the real Parisian thing, complete with fluttering awnings, rattan chairs, and crisp service dished out from classically sullen waiters in slightly spattered black vests and long white aprons.

Herschel was loving and loyal, and by age seventeen, his values gave every sign of being decent and in place. In religion, he was observant, thoughtful, and unquestionably sincere. He certainly told more than one lie in his life, especially when the political pressure began to drill down on him, but he was generally truthful. The clichés of teenaged rebellion and defiance are not relevant to him. He adored his family. By twenty-first-century standards, his manners were rather proper in an old-fashioned Germanic way.

Herschel thrived on outings to the country. A cheap movie theater in the neighborhood was almost a home away from home. He told the examining magistrate that he did not know how to dance, yet he never missed a dance at the Sportsclub Aurore, and a friend from Hanover, another teenaged Jewish refugee in Paris, later testified that he'd seen Hershel at least ten times at dances in the town hall of the Third Arrondissement.

Sexually, he was completely inexperienced.[19]

He was morally immature but acute. He was particularly aware of his own insignificance in the large scheme of things—insignificance as a child, insignificance as a Jew, insignificance as a refugee—and it gnawed at him. He felt his powerlessness. Most adolescents dream of great things, but as a child who was almost but not quite yet a man, he was completely unprepared to find himself suddenly famous, a pawn being played in large events.

Hunted

Herschel saw asylum in France as a matter of life and death.[1]

When he anticipated what would happen if the French Ministry of the Interior rejected his application for a residence permit, he spoke of suicide with enough vehemence to frighten his aunt and uncle. Suicides were not uncommon among the Jewish refugees in Paris—there were hundreds of them—and it was not easy to shrug off the ferocity of Herschel's intermittent despair. It alarmed Abraham and Chawa. What if this frantic talk about killing himself were more serious than mere adolescent hysteria? The threat of suicide could not be brushed aside. If the French ruled against Herschel, he might—just might—really end his life. He *had* to be permitted to stay in France.[2]

And the French were about to rule against him.

All through 1937 and 1938, the undercurrents of French domestic politics were moving against Herschel and the other refugees from Hitler's Germany. Where could Herschel go if France ceased to be a land of asylum? Israel may have remained his dream refuge, but Palestine under the mandate was not open to him. Returning to Germany would have been madness, and in any case, by late 1937 it was impossible: When he left Germany, he had been given a reentry visa, which the regime refused to renew once it expired.

Then there was his Polish passport. In a move designed to frustrate Hitler's obvious intention to deport all the Polish Jews with legal residence in Germany, in March 1938 the Polish legislature passed a law that would annul the citizenship of any Pole—read: any Polish Jew—who had lived for five years or more outside Poland. This law threatened to make the large population of Polish Jews that was legally resident in Germany, including Herschel and his entire family, stateless at the very moment that Hitler was moving to expel them. But even if Herschel had been able to renew the Polish passport he nominally held, Poland with its infamous anti-Semitism was frightening alien ground. Herschel had never been to Poland; he could not speak the language; it was the unlivable land that his parents had fled. The hard fact was that his refuge was Paris, and his security—his life—seemed to be in the hands of the French government and its bureaucratic whims.

During the spring and summer of 1938, once appeasement was becoming settled policy, the French government made a brutal about-face in its attitude toward its Jewish refugees.[3] This was no whim. The Ministry of the Interior knew perfectly well that the thousands of supplicants knocking on its gate would have nowhere to go if it slammed that gate shut. But slam it shut it did. The policy reversed itself, changing from asylum to exclusion; from the hope of legal residence to twists in the law that overnight made refugee presence either impossible or illegal, punishable with jail. French law transformed Herschel from an innocuous refugee living with his legal aunt and uncle to a criminal hiding from the police. Perhaps that is partly why he said in court, "My people have a right to exist on this earth . . . if you are a Jew, you can obtain nothing, attempt nothing, and hope for nothing. You are hunted like an animal."[4]

If you were running from Hitler between 1933 and 1937, France was the place to run. When Hitler came to power in January 1933, German refugees had fled almost by instinct to the France that prided itself on its incomparable cosmopolitanism and its bond to liberty, equality, and fraternity. This was the Paris where the advanced arts came to thrive, the Paris that was a prime locus of science and medicine, the Paris that had been viewed as the capital of the nineteenth century and the center of twentieth-century European civilization. To be sure, the life of refugees in France was never untroubled. Then as now, a self-aware and self-consciously enlightened sector of French life was locked in perpetual confrontation with another large sector of opinion that was hunkered down in various kinds of xenophobic provincialism and anti-Semitism—and proud of it, too. As a result, the fate of the almost fifty thousand Jewish refugees who fled Hitler to France in the thirties was perpetually yanked back and forth by these two opposed fields of force.

When Herschel came to France in 1936, the legal atmosphere under the anti-Nazi Popular Front government was relatively tolerant. Two years later, when a newly constituted French government preaching "peace at any price" set out to appease rather than confront Hitler—and even move beyond appeasement to entente—the laws of France regarding the Jewish refugees became "extremely harsh." Anxiety about annoying Hitler replaced the mildly confrontational mood of the Popular Front. There was fear at the top that France would offend the Nazi dictator by becoming the "refuge for everyone Germany considers its natural enemy."[5] Senior figures in French government began to fear that the refugees were "seeking to draw France into an undesired war . . ." In the popular mind, the refugees were increasingly seen as "war-mongers." "In the minds of the nation's top officials"—Daladier and Foreign Minister Bonnet among them—"it was no longer clear whether it was Hitler or his victims who constituted the greatest threat to French security."[6]

The instruments of the change in French policy were a set of governmental decrees on immigration—they were known as the "decree laws"—that "sharply curtailed immigration at the border and made it extremely difficult for refugees already in the country to stay."[7] Most of these laws and regulations were established in the spring and summer of 1938. A decree of May 2, 1938, established what were interpreted as draconian rules for excluding new refugees and expelling or imprisoning those already in the country. Later, in August 1938, special police were set up on the borders of France, tasked with rooting out illegal immigrants, while George Bonnet's Foreign Ministry initiated new restrictions on the issuance of visas, making legal immigration into France all but impossible.[8] Inspired by appeasement and all that came with it, the decree laws put a definitive end to France's role as a nation of asylum. Those who had been made criminals in Nazi Germany now found themselves criminalized in their place of refuge. Refugees as innocent as Herschel Grynszpan himself would be "hunted like animals."[9]

The most ominous of all the menaces of the decree laws was their un-enforceability. The laws created a situation in which fifty thousand people had nowhere to go. Deportation was out of the question: Simply sending all those refugees back to Germany would have been a preposterous solution, desired by nobody on the spectrum, from fascist to communist, and least of all by Hitler. Meanwhile, the entire point of the decrees was to make the refugees' assimilation into French society, however gradual and grudging, impossible. The laws explicitly named as "undesirables" some large percentage of refugees deemed to be "clandestine foreigners, irregular guests . . . unworthy of living on our soil." Examples were communists and other leftists who failed to "maintain an absolutely correct attitude vis-à-vis the republic and its institutions."[10]

But what about the tens of thousands of others, those with no particular ideology to push, those whom the laws' sweeping terms left placeless and stateless? They had nowhere to go. They couldn't leave, and they couldn't stay. It was not as though they had done anything to deserve their hopeless status. One wave of the law's magic wand had simply transformed them into outlaws. It was as though they were being denied, as Herschel put it to the examining magistrate, their simple right to "exist in this world."

In truth, the only application of the decree laws was the one of jailing people whose only crime was to exist as Jews. And since jailing fifty thousand people was impracticable as well as prohibitively expensive, some easier and cheaper form of incarceration needed to be found. This was the invention of the French internment camp.[11]

This governmental attack on the refugees was only the domestic face of the Daladier government's policy of appeasement, and the decree laws might have been passed as much to please the Nazi dictator as to please the various chauvinist wings of French opinion. The domestic policies were hard to distinguish from the international détente. One of those most involved in passing the decree laws was Daladier's foreign minister, the man most responsible for the appeasement policy itself, Georges Bonnet.[12]

In 1938, Georges-Étienne Bonnet was one of the most important figures in French power politics, and he looked it. He was thin, naturally elegant, and so suave that any more smoothness would have been almost comic. As things were, Bonnet seemed born to wear pinstripes and homburgs, a man at home and at ease negotiating the fate of nations in rooms lustrous with gold leaf and glittering chandeliers. Though Bonnet was no aristocrat, his narrow features, pencil mustache, and hatchet face endowed him with a very *vieille*-France patrician air. Machiavelli argued that the Prince must somehow mingle in one being both lion and fox. Though there was no lion at all in Georges-Étienne Bonnet, there was lots and lots of fox. His demeanor and the sharp slant of his darting, dangerously intelligent eyes made many people make the comparison, and the comparison was not flattering to the fox.

While almost nobody actually liked Bonnet, even his many enemies agreed that he was shrewd to the point of brilliance. It probably asks too much to expect any foreign minister to adhere to the strictest standards of honesty, and the commonly heard quip that Bonnet was "physically incapable of telling the truth" was doubtless overstated. Nonetheless, duplicity was the man's natural modus operandi. While everyone in French politics knew that it was dangerous to underestimate Bonnet, nobody dreamt of trusting him. French politicians masked their fear of Bonnet's dagger by laughing at him behind his back. Bonnet was believed to be under the inflexible domination of his wife, Odette, a right-wing *saloniste* well known to be ambitious, avaricious, and (so it was rumored) corrupt. While most people merely disliked Georges, they despised the buxom Odette. The Bonnets' relationship inspired coarse jokes. Her nickname in the corridors of power was "Madame Soutien-Georges," a raffish play on the French word for "brassiere": *soutien-gorge.*

Bonnet was a survivor, par exellence. Whatever the political bump, Bonnet usually landed on his feet, usually mere inches from the center of power. He was very smart, especially about money, and since he knew more about the finances of the French government than most of his adversaries put together, he regularly outmaneuvered the competition.[13] Even when they were unprincipled, his political assessments were often chillingly accurate, and his achievements were real.

Georges Bonnet was Mr. Peace-at-Any-Price. Nobody in the senior ranks of the democracies was softer on Hitler, and he worked in close collaboration with the Ministry of the Interior in its assault on the Jewish refugees. Churchill despised him: "the quintessence of defeatism." His enemies believed circumstantial and never-proven claims that Madame accepted serious money from the Reich in exchange for influence-peddling among French journalists, using as her intermediary her dear friend the future Nazi viceroy of France, Otto Abetz.[14]

Since the Munich Pact, Bonnet had been in secret negotiations with the Nazi ambassador to France, Count Johannes von Welczeck, seeking ways to move toward an even more intimate bond between the two countries. Pursuing this end in his serpentine way, Bonnet would have been eager to show

Ambassador von Welczeck that France had heard the Führer's complaints about Jewish refugees, and was beginning to act on them.[15]

The impact of the immigration decrees of 1938 on refugees like Herschel Grynszpan was direct and disastrous. All over Paris, frightened supplicants were opening envelopes with their fatal news. In Herschel's own case, his application for a residence permit was summarily rejected, with no reason given and no glimmer of hope for appeal. By an unmysterious irony, Herschel found himself opening his envelope on the very day that France began hosting the infamous Evian Conference, suggested by Franklin Roosevelt, in which nations large and small gathered to debate what to do about the Jewish refugee problem. It was a conference awash in crocodile tears, and the answer it produced was that, with few dubious exceptions, nations large and small would do nothing whatsoever about the Jewish refugee problem. If they were closed, they would remain closed, though they later opened a little more—a *little* more—only after the shock of the Kristallnacht. With French hostility toward its refugees, there was no nation of asylum left.

On July 8, 1938, Herschel received the news that his application for a residence permit had been summarily denied. Herschel stood dumbfounded. It had happened: He held in his hand the instrument of his worst fear. With this rejection, the frail little receipt for that application, which had been all that had conferred his right to remain in France, became worthless. Since paying the fine for his entry into France without a visa, he had played strictly by the Ministry of the Interior's rules. On August 11, 1938, he received a second document: a decree ordering him to leave France within four days.[16] The bureaucratic fiat of the French government had made him a criminal, subject to imprisonment. Countless refugees like Herschel now stood in theoretical danger of deportation, and the real danger of jail.

In the words of Vicki Caron, a prime historian of these events, the effect
of the decree laws was to condemn a large number of people who were manifestly not criminal "to a life of perpetual criminality . . . Refugees seeking
escape from this infernal cycle had only two options: suicide or resorting to
the burgeoning network of false passport and visa operations."[17] Herschel
did indeed react to these edicts with suicidal depression. In this, too, he was
not alone. The decree laws precipitated a new round of suicides among the
refugees.

A month and a half later, Daladier would sign the Munich Pact.

At first Herschel added immaturity and grandiosity to depression: He
wrote one of his personal letters to Franklin Roosevelt begging the president
to grant asylum to him and his family. Another early idea was to put himself on the right side of French law by joining the French Foreign Legion.
Despite his small stature and frail health, this proposal was not so absurd
as it might at first seem. Herschel's wish to enlist in the Foreign Legion was
not an isolated private fantasy. Among the groups exerting practical pressure
against the decree laws were elements of the French military, who thought
the ranks of the army might be made to grow if the government permitted the legal enlistment if thousands of German, including German-Jewish,
refugees, most of whom already had a fierce anti-Nazi ideological commit-
ment. Many refugees did in fact join the Foreign Legion after 1938. Uncle
Abraham even gave Herschel 200 francs to pursue the possibility.[18]

But underneath these strategies, practical and impossible, flowed a long
meditation on suicide. After his arrest, the medical experts who examined
him found that he had contemplated suicide during the depression that
accompanied his arrival in Paris a year and a half before. Now his friend
Nathan Kaufman told the police that Herschel had spoken frequently of
suicide after receiving the expulsion order.[19]

He was being pursued. In mid-October, less than two weeks before the
Nazis hounded his family out of their home in Hamburg, the French police
came looking for Herschel.[20]

A couple of weeks before that, Abraham and Chawa had moved from their small apartment on the rue Mantel, which they had rented after leaving the rue Richard Lenoir, to an equally small apartment on the rue des Petites-Écuries. When Abraham and Chawa left the rue Mantel, Herschel stayed behind, hiding in an abandoned maid's room on the dusty sixth floor of the old building. There was a chair, a mattress on the floor, an alarm clock beside it, with newspapers and magazines strewn amid his paltry belongings. There was also a Hebrew Bible. Herschel had installed a primitive lock on the door. At night, and sometimes during the day, Herschel would emerge from his sixth-floor aerie once again to hang out with his friends Sal and Nat, or go to dances at the Sportsclub Aurore, or take in a double feature. Meanwhile, whatever the neighbors might have noticed about where the Grynszpan boy laid his head at night they kept to themselves. Chatting with the police was not their habit. Even so, Herschel must have kept his eye cocked for the Paris *flics*. If one of them issued the classic command "*Vos papiers?*" the fact that he had no *papiers* to show would mean immediate arrest and almost certainly jail. The great virtue of his hidey-hole on the sixth floor was that it permitted Abraham and Chawa truthfully to tell the police that Herschel no longer lived with them, adding to this fact the lie that they had not seen him since the expulsion order. In fact, Herschel had dinner each day with his aunt and uncle in their new Paris address. The concierge saw him coming and going every evening, and when the storm broke, *she* had no hesitation reporting what she had seen to the police and the press.[21]

Herschel's hideout was a loose and wobbly deception, but for a while it worked. The police searched the old apartment, and then they searched the new one, and, not finding Herschel in either, let the matter drop. For the moment.

Like any hunted animal, Herschel remained in hiding, staying locked in his makeshift refuge at least during the day. Meanwhile his loneliness and desperation did not relent, and his depression deepened. Even when he was a boy, and no less now that he was almost though not quite a man, depression had always alternated with the fire of his impotent rage. But the sudden fury that once flared harmlessly on the soccer field was now burning with fresh and mounting intensity. His thinking matured. Though he had been a victim of anti-Semitism all his life, he now began to develop a new intellectual grasp on it, devouring the Jewish newspapers of Paris with their daily accounts of new persecutions, absorbed especially in a retelling of the Dreyfus affair.[22]

While he seethed, the big world seethed around him. All around, war was coming. He was powerless. He was nobody. Nothing—not money, not influence, not status, not even adulthood—defended him in his desperation. Time itself seemed to have changed. He had led a menaced childhood, but now that menace had become an international phenomenon, looking more and more like the menaced safety of every Jewish child. Then there was his future—the simple lived life of the grown-up that was never to be his—about to be extinguished in a looming Holocaust. Herschel was waiting. With his mattress on the floor, he was alone amid his newspapers, his magazines, and his Tanakh, and his desperation was about to be made complete. Despair mingled with rage, building toward those last resorts: suicide or murder.[23]

Dispossession

Hanover, Germany. On the evening of October 27, 1938, Herschel's twenty-two-year-old older sister, Berta, was heading home, perhaps from a day job-hunting, since she had recently lost her job working as a secretary: Her Jewish boss, under the pressure of Hitler's anti-Semitic laws, had let her go. When she reached the *Altstadt*—the ancient central city of Hamburg—and started down the Burgstrasse, she was buttonholed and told about the rumors racing up and down the street. A wildfire of gossip claimed that only yesterday, in some other town, the Gestapo had rounded up every single Polish Jew in the whole city and, without one word of warning, forced them out of their homes and ordered them to get out of Germany. Then and there, every single one of them was sent back to Poland, without a penny. The Gestapo hadn't even let their victims go for a little food or money or so much as pack a suitcase. They just herded everybody to the *Bahnhof,* pushed them onto trains, locked them in so they were prisoners, and sent the trains rolling east toward Poland.[1]

The street was burning up with the story.

Berta listened, weighed the story in her mind, and decided that it had to be hysteria. She just could not believe such a thing could really happen. Of course every Jew in Germany knew that the Nazi persecutions were getting worse. Every week diminished the hope that somehow the Nazi madness would pass and Germany would come to its senses. She knew that Hitler was determined to drive every foreign Jew out of the Reich. Her own parents had done some planning for the worst. Just this summer, Rivka Grynszpan had gone to Poland twice, looking for possible places of refuge.

But hundreds, maybe thousands of Jews locked into trains headed east? Just like that? Whole populations made prisoner and forced from their homes? No: Despite everything, Germany was still a nation of laws. Berta believed in keeping a level head while the ladies in the bakery and butcher shop worked themselves into frenzies, and when she got home, she was relieved to discover that her brother Mordecai, a nineteen-year-old plumber's apprentice, also thought the rumors were crazy. And so did her mother and father.

The Grynszpan family sat for dinner, comforted one another, and did their best not to think about such things.

At nine o'clock came a rude knock hammering at their front door, and everyone froze in their seats.

The banging was loud, and it did not stop.

Sendel stood up and opened the door to confront everyone's worst fear: the firm, furious eyes of an officer of the *Sicherheitspolizei*, who had orders for them all.[2]

Every member of the Grynszpan family was to collect their Polish passports immediately and accompany the officer to the nearest police outpost, the Eleventh Precinct station. In a lie that was being told at that same moment to thousands of Polish Jews in every city in Germany, the Grynszpans were assured they would not be needing anything more than their passports and coats. This was a mere formality. It would be quickly settled, and then they would be free to come home.

There was certainly nothing to fear.

The Grynszpan family gathered up their passports, put on their coats, and stepped out of the home that had been theirs for the past twenty years. They would never see it again.[3]

—

The air outside was sharp with an autumnal chill; despite the thinnest sliver of moon, the night sky was resplendent with stars. As the Grynszpans walked, the twisting cobbled streets of the *Altstadt* echoed more and more with the footsteps and bewildered voices of their neighbors—the many Polish Jews in the quarter—all walking in the same direction, all with their own police escorts. It was a walk in the dark, but it was short, and they soon reached the precinct station, a four-story pile of Wilhelmine brick, simultaneously pompous and run-down, where every light was blazing.

Inside the building and out, some were milling and pacing, some were sitting on the sidewalks, some were trying to get information or talk sense to the cops. All were trying to keep their balance.

Nothing helped. Nothing was explained or discussed or negotiated. Soon the night sounds were of women crying, of people shouting in German or muttering in Yiddish, and over it all, the drone of engines, as a wide row of police vans flanked the curb, headlights on, motors revving, ready to roll.

At the same hour, scenes very much like this were taking place in cities all over Germany. It was a single nationwide event, an *Aktion*—police action—displaying flawless coordination of the transportation system with the newly nationalized police force under Heinrich Himmler. The *Aktion* was much the same wherever *Ostjuden* were found: the same police at the door, the same vans, and the same waiting trains. In every city, people were being ordered out of homes they would never see again. In every city, the Black Marias and trains were waiting for them.

Hershel believed that the *Aktion* had expelled 12,000 Jews from their homes. The real number was closer to 18,000 people arrested, stripped of their rights, and forced onto trains, all part of a coordinated nationwide network, scheduled so the trains would converge in precisely timed sequence at two points on the Polish border, where all 18,000 people were forced out into the cold and abandoned, without money, food, provisions, or help of any kind whatever.

Of those 18,000 *Ostjuden,* 484 came from Hanover.[4] Vans were con-
verging on a single staging point, where they were to be held until it was
time for their train to pull out.

The staging point was a large, gloomy, ancient building, located centrally on the banks of the Leine and at the heart of the *Altstadt* and its ghetto.
This edifice was known then as the Rusthaus, or Armory. Its distinguishing
feature is a round tower erected from large stone blocks, rising maybe forty
feet above the riverbank: a citadel built for battle in a vanished age; the real
medieval thing, an indestructible fortress from which the Germans could
hurl down rocky hell on any barbarians attacking from the river. This sen-
tinel of stone was once in the dead center of medieval Hanover. It was now
in the dead center of its ghetto. By coincidence, it was across the street from
what had been, until an hour before, the Grynszpan home.

There, all 484 waited. Everything was uncertain. Nobody had been told
what all this was about, but vans from every point in the city were converg-
ing around the Rusthaus. Looming over them was the dark tower that had
been a landmark of Berta's life since early childhood. Suddenly it all turned
perfectly clear. At that moment, as she wrote to Herschel, "we realized that
it was all over for us."

From this point forward, even the pretense of the rule of law was flung
aside. Police inspectors greeted each Jew herded into the Rusthaus by shov-
ing a document at them and shouting, "Sign this! Sign now! You are expelled from Germany!"

"We signed," Sendel later testified, "just like everyone else."

It is perhaps significant that when that first night was over and the
dawn of October 28 rose over the Leine River, all police activity, apart from
guarding against escape, seemed to cease. Likewise for much of the *Aktion*
all across Germany. It was as if the blessing of sunlight reduced the Gestapo
to quiescence the way it is reputed to drive vampires back into their graves.
In any case, as long as it was daylight, the prisoners of Hanover kept milling and mingling in a very big room, forbidden to leave or make contact of
any kind with anyone outside, listless in their captivity, terror merging with

boredom. The hours crawled. People must have lain on the floor and tried to sleep. People must have talked until whatever there was to say had been said once too often. Nobody offered them anything to eat or drink. God knows what the toilet facilities were.

Like everyone else, Berta had left her home at 35 Burgstrasse with nothing but her passport and the clothes on her back. She now understood that she no longer had a home. She was embarking on yet another exile. At the very least, she wanted something to wear.

Berta was bold enough to approach one of the *SiPo* officers. She walked up to him with a smile and explained that her family's apartment just happened to be practically across the street, just a minute or two away. *So* close. So would it perhaps be possible for her to dash across the street and throw a few things into a suitcase? She would be getting nothing but clothes and would come right back. And just to prove she meant it, she suggested the cop walk over to the apartment with her. He could keep watch over every move she made. He could stand guard while she packed. Then he could escort her back. It would be just a few minutes.

So Berta and the *SiPo* crossed the street to 35 Burgstrasse, and while the officer looked on, Herschel's sister raced through, pulling clothes from a closet and stuffing them into one small suitcase. As she packed, she tossed the clothes hangers onto the dining room table.

Then Berta and the cop walked back to the citadel unnoticed.

One wonders: Was he gentleman enough to carry her bag?

Once the Grynszpan family was—for its fifteen minutes—world famous, Berta's hangers became famous, too. Herschel's crime in the Paris Embassy would shock the world in several ways, but until Herschel made his dramatic move, the big world had barely noticed the brutal and lawless deportations from Germany. The shooting did have one positive effect. Suddenly everyone was aware that a serious injustice had taken place in Germany. Goeb-bels hit back with a media campaign attempting to prove how the Polish deportations had been carried out with exemplary courtesy and civilization, and that the Jews' property was being scrupulously respected. To marshal evidence for this lie, he sent a camera crew to the home of the Grynszpans to document how all their belongings were just as they had left them. Then they noticed the hangers. *Proof* that the family had enjoyed ample time to pack and prepare before leaving! Close-ups of those hangers were published around the world.[5]

When that day of waiting was over, the police were once again in action. More than twenty Black Marias, waiting to be filled, circled the Rusthaus. Each of these gloomy vehicles could carry around twenty prisoners, and the *SiPo* began systematically getting all 484 prisoners loaded for transportation to the station and the train that would take them east. Each van stayed put until all had been fully loaded; they then took off together, headed for the *Hauptbahnhof* in a dark twenty-plus van caravan. On its way to the station, the convoy had to roll right past 35 Burgstrasse. As they drove, Sendel peered through the barred windows, watching his life slide away.

On the major avenue, the sidewalks were lined with a "spontaneous demonstration," probably by local party members, jeering as the vans rolled by, shouting in chorus:

Jews to Palestine! Jews to Palestine!

Jews to Palestine! Jews to Palestine!

The prisoners peered out through bars.

Jews to Palestine!

At the *Hauptbahnhof,* their train—special train 4199—was waiting, and they all were ordered to board, which they did, to the sound of shouted orders, mixed with the slamming, and locking, of doors.

The stationmaster recorded everything very precisely. "Special Train SP Han 4199 made up at 19:30—about two hours before departure. Consisting of 14 well-lit carriages each with 55 seats, of which 35 to 40 were occupied. The departure of the Jews, carrying large quantities of hand luggage [sic] proceeded on platform 5, which had been closed to the public before the train was assembled. The Jews were allowed to purchase food and tobacco.

"The special train departed on schedule at 21:40, from track 11, platform 5."[6]

Hanover lies only 285 miles from the Polish border, and special train 4199 reached the frontier on a straight shot due east on a major line, without changes or connections. Even so, 4199 took nine hours to reach its destination, crawling through the night of October 28 at 30 miles an hour. At the same time, from every corner of the Reich, trains very like 4199 were moving toward Poland, their departures and pace timed for systematic arrival. Train 4199's route was uncomplicated, but many of the other trains had to stop and start and stop again for changes and connections, screeching and slamming and lurching all night long. Yet the timing of this unitary nationwide movement was precise. These trains ran on time. Some trains reached Poland at dawn of October 29, others at dusk on October 28. Train 4199, like many others, was heading toward an obscure little border town called Zbaszyn.

When the dawn of October 29 brought light to the windows of 4199, it probably awakened whoever had managed to sleep in their seats. A steady, nasty, icy rain was slashing against the windows of every car, streaking and spattering, freezing on the glass. Movement in the corridors began. Outside the windows, nothing but wet, frozen, brown fields were visible, but everyone knew that after nine hours, the train must be near its destination. Whispered fears; frightened silences. On the Grynszpan's train, the Gestapo moved from seat to seat, completing dispossession, frisking their victims, patting them down, looking for money. The rule was that no Jew could leave Germany with more than 10 Reichsmarks: about USD$4 in 1938. In the Gestapo, it was understood that the officers could often pocket the money they filched in these small-time shakedowns.

—

Twenty-three years later, in Jerusalem at Adolf Eichmann's trial for crimes against humanity, Sendel Grynszpan was called as the first witness and asked to testify about the experience of these deportations.

Hannah Arendt, the celebrated political philosopher, who had been sent by *The New Yorker* to cover the trial, was in the courtroom that day, listening to Sendel's testimony.

In the same report, Arendt recklessly called Herschel a "psychopath," suggesting that he may have been a pawn of the Gestapo.[7] But she saw his father as a saint. Sendel Grynszpan's testimony (Arendt used the alternate spelling *Zindel*) left her as profoundly impressed as she would be by any event in that epochal trial. Sitting in the press box, she listened as Herschel's father, by then an old man, was asked to tell the court about his experience of the deportations.

Here is what he said:

It was a Thursday, October 27, 1938. A policeman knocked on our door and told us to report to the police station with our passports. He said, "Don't bother to take anything else, you'll be right back." When we reached the police station, my wife, my daughter, my son Marcus [Mordecai's German name] and myself, we saw a number of people sitting or standing. Some were weeping. The police inspector was shouting at the top of his voice, "Sign here. You are being deported." I had to sign like everyone else. Only one man by the name of Gershom Silbery, or Gerschl Silber, refused. To punish him they stood him in a corner of the room for twenty-four hours.

We were taken to the concert hall beside the Leine, where about six hundred [sic] people had been assembled from various parts of Hanover. We were kept there for about twenty-four hours, until Friday night, when police vans took us, about twenty at a time, to the station. The streets teemed with people shouting "Send the Jews to Palestine!"

We were taken by train to the German border and Neu Bentschen [Zbaszyn] on the line connecting Frankfurt an der Oder with Posen. We arrived around six o'clock on Saturday morning. There were trains from all over Germany: Leipzig, Berlin, Cologne, Düsseldorf, Bielefeld, Essen, Bremen. We were about twelve thousand in all. That was Saturday, October 29.

When we got to the border we were searched. We were only allowed to take 10 marks; any excess was confiscated. That was German law, we were told: You didn't have more than that when you arrived in Germany, and you can't take any more away with you now. We were kept under guard and not allowed to communicate with anyone. The SS told us we would have to walk the two kilometers to the border. Those who couldn't walk were beaten until the road was wet with their blood. Their baggage was taken away. They were dealt with cruelly and barbarously. It was the first time I realized how barbarous the Germans really are. They made us run, while they shouted, "Run! Run!" I was struck down along the roadside, but my son Marcus took me by the hand and said, "Come on Papa, run. They'll kill you if you don't."

Finally we reached the border. We crossed it. The women went first because they began firing at us. The Poles had no idea why we were there or why there were so many of us. A Polish general and some officers came to examine our papers. They saw that we were all Polish citizens—we had special passports, and they decided to let us into Poland.

We were taken to a tiny village of six thousand inhabitants, although there were twelve thousand of us. It was raining hard. There were a number of old people among us, some of whom fell or fainted; others had heart attacks. Although we hadn't eaten since Thursday evening and were very hungry, we did not want to eat the Germans' bread. We were taken to the stables of a military camp, as there was no room anywhere else. We didn't write immediately because we were too hungry. On Sunday a truck came from Poznan and we all rushed round it. They threw bread, and those who managed to catch any had bread. Then more trucks arrived; it turned out that there was enough bread for all of us.

Then I wrote a letter to my son Herschel in Paris.[8]

Arendt sat transfixed. No testimony in the entire Eichmann trial would touch her more deeply than this.

"The story took perhaps ten minutes to tell," she wrote, "and when it was over . . . one thought foolishly: 'Everyone, everyone should have his day in court.'"

That story was plain, simple, and unadorned. It made her reflect, as so many have, on "how difficult it was to tell the story." Arendt felt that the account required that the truth be told with a purifying plainness: that an almost holy simplicity was the only way to address the unspeakable. Hershel's father seemed to her possessed of that simplicity. She concluded that to tell these truths, "at least outside the transforming realm of poetry—it needed a purity of soul, an unmirrored, unreflected innocence of heart and mind that only the righteous possess.

"No one either before or after was equal to the shining honesty of Zindel Grynszpan."[9]

Sendel's memory betrayed him on only one minor point. The first communication sent to Herschel from Zbaszyn was not a letter from him, but a postcard from his daughter Berta.

That postcard was in Herschel's pocket when he was arrested.

The Assassin's Night

Berta's postcard arrived in the mailbox of Maison Albert three days later, on November 3.

Dear Hermann,

You have undoubtedly heard of our great misfortune. Let me tell you what happened. On Thursday evening rumors circulated that all Polish Jews had been expelled from a city. But we didn't believe it. On Thursday evening at 9 o'clock a "SiPo" came to us and informed us that we had to go to Police Headquarters and bring along our passports. We left dressed just as we were, and went together to Police Headquarters, accompanied by the SiPo. Almost our entire quarter was already there. Right away, a police van brought all of us to the Rusthaus. Everybody was brought there. Nobody let us know what this was all about, but we knew that we were finished. Each of us had an extradition order pressed into his hand, saying we had to leave Germany before the 29th. They wouldn't let us go home again. I asked to be allowed to go home to get at least a few things. I went, accompanied by a SiPo, and packed the essentials in a suitcase. And that is all I saved. We don't have a penny. [The next sentence, though legible, is crossed out: Could you send us something to Lodz?] More next time. Love and kisses from all of us.

Berta.[1]

A month earlier, on October 1, before he went into hiding, Herschel had read a long article in one of the Jewish dailies presenting evidence that some sort of mass *Aktion* against Germany's Polish Jews was imminent. The story scared him; he'd been scouring the papers for developments.

Berta's card stirred up an intense wave of his youthful turbulence, marked by surges of bravado beaten back by riptides of despair.[2] The day he got it, Herschel wrote Berta a distraught response in which he promised that he personally would be sending money to his stranded family soon.[3]

This promise was pure wishful thinking. Herschel had no money to send. His only hope of sending any amount worth sending meant turning to Abraham.

The next day, November 4, the news went public in a Yiddish daily in Paris, *Pariser Haint.*

CRITICAL SITUATION OF POLISH JEWS
DEPORTED FROM GERMANY

More than 8,000 persons have been overnight rendered stateless. They were rounded up and deported, largely to Zbaszyn, in a no-man's land between Germany and Poland. Their living conditions are uncomfortable and distressing. 1,200 of them have fallen ill and several hundreds are without shelter. As there is a risk of epidemic, Red Cross doctors with the help of doctors from the OSE (Oeuvre de Secours aux Enfants) have distributed typhus vaccinations and 10,000 aspirin tablets. A number of instances of insanity and suicide have been recorded."[4]

Herschel's mood grew even more desperate. He clung to his friend Nat, pouring out his worst fears—and his suicidal fantasies. Nat's consolation was simple: Show Herschel the silver lining. Being deported to Poland might not be all bad. At least his family was out of Germany, safely beyond the Nazis' reach. This could even be a good thing. It really could.

Herschel was not consoled.

Berta received her brother's promise of money on November 7, the day Herschel committed his crime. She responded immediately to "your dear letter," explaining that the family's plight was largely unchanged; if anything, it was a little worse. Though Berta made no mention of typhus or suicide, she describes being fed gruel from charity kitchens and snatching at bread tossed into the starving throng from trucks. The family was sleeping on sacks stuffed with straw in the abandoned army barracks. In eleven days nobody had been able to change clothes.

"Believe me, Hermann [Herschel's German name], we won't be able to stand this much longer . . ." And she concludes: "We haven't yet received money from you. What do they say there about what will happen to us? We can't go further. Berta."[5]

Along with this second postcard from Berta, Abraham also received word from Zbaszyn. It was from his brother Sendel, and it was a forthright but dignified appeal for financial help.

> Dear Brother and Sister-in-Law.
>
> We are in a very sad situation. We are poor and in misery. We don't get enough to eat. You, too, were once in need. I beg you, dear Brother, to think of us. We don't have the strength to endure this. You mustn't forget us in this situation.
>
> Sendel[6]

Berta mailed her answer on November 7. By the time it reached Paris, Herschel (who never saw it) was world famous and in prison.

And the Kristallnacht had taken place.

—

Saturday November 5, the second day after receiving Berta's card, was the Sabbath. As soon as the Sabbath sun set on November 5, Herschel and Nat, both ardent movie fans, headed out to a double feature.

They had big plans for the next day, too. At five in the afternoon of Sunday, November 6, the Sportsclub Aurore was holding one of its dances. Nat and Herschel had been counting on it from long before Berta's card arrived, and downcast as he was, they were not going to miss it.

The smash movie in Paris that Saturday night was the Marx Brothers' *A Night at the Opera*, but it was playing only in the expensive first-run theaters outside the neighborhood. Herschel and his buddies stuck to local joints like the Saint Martin's Cinema, a cheap and seedy place that was an easy stroll from the rue des Petites-Écuries. The Saint Martin's was showing a double feature that night. The picture at the top of the bill was something called *Souers d'Armes* ("Sisters in Arms"). The second feature, now lost in *absolute* oblivion, was entitled *Marie Marin* ("Marie the Sailor").

The features got out around eleven thirty, and both youths headed straight back, Nat to his home, Herschel to his hidey-hole, where he went right to sleep. He needed rest, because tomorrow was the day when he would or would not save his family.

That tomorrow was Sunday, the day after the Sabbath, and Chawa laid out a large midday meal at the Maison Albert for her side of the Parisian clan. Chawa's sister Basila came with her husband, joined by her brother's wife, Mina Berenbaum. All were gathered at a table of six, where of course the subject of conversation was the crisis and what to do.

We know only the general gist of what happened around the dinner table that Sunday afternoon, but whatever happened was fiery.[7] After Herschel was arrested, family members were reluctant to reveal details even under heavy interrogation. We have many more details about the tail end of the encounter because of the testimony of Herschel's pal Nat Kaufmann, who happened to drop by the Maison Albert in the middle of the argument and later told what he had heard and seen.

There was an argument between Abraham and Herschel, and the argument was about money. It began as a simple disagreement, but it did not end there. The disagreement became a quarrel, and probably thanks to Herschel's fierce temper, the quarrel turned into a shouting row. This was where Nat Kaufmann showed up and witnessed the end, with Herschel standing at the door hollering that he was leaving and would never, ever, ever come back, and with the usually imperturbable Abraham answering by all means, go, get out.

Herschel came to the dinner intending to get Uncle Abraham to send money to Zbaszyn to relieve his family, and send it immediately. To Herschel, speed was essential, and his plan for getting the money to Poland was sublimely simple. He knew that at some point between September 1936 and autumn 1938, Sendel Grynszpan had smuggled a significant sum of money to Abraham in Paris, earmarked for the expenses of the boy's care.

Herschel may or may not have known exactly how this money had been spirited into France—under the Nazis, such knowledge was a truly dangerous secret—but he did know the exact amount: 3,000 francs, worth $85 in 1938 dollars, the equivalent of $1,200 in the early twenty-first century. It was a sum that could make a serious difference in Zbaszyn. Since Herschel was the only Hanover Grynszpan still at liberty to decide anything, Herschel believed he had the right to use the money as he thought best.

The story of how Sendel had sent these 3,000 francs to his brother for the costs of Herschel's care ought to have been simple and transparent, but the transaction became shrouded in lies and secrecy because of its illegality. German law under the Nazis forbade Jews sending money out of Germany under penalty of prison or death. As a result, everyone connected with the matter tried to cover up the essential facts. They lied. Of course they lied.[8]

But this initiated a tangle of falsehoods that later became the subject of controversy and made the 3,000 francs the fodder of diverse conspiracy theories, complicated by speculation in the press and capped by the most noxious conspiracy theory of all—that of the Nazis. Immediately after Herschel's arrest, Abraham foolishly and falsely claimed that after his nephew's expulsion, he had given Herschel 3,000 francs to make his way back to Germany. When it was clear that Herschel had not gone back to Germany and never intended to, Abraham had to retract his story, and the conspiracy theorists moved in. The Germans meanwhile wanted to float the theory that the money was some sort of payoff from Herschel's coconspirators in "world Jewry."[9]

But on November 6, 1938, all that mattered to Herschel was that his uncle Abraham was—or at least had been—in possession of 3,000 francs, and that those 3,000 francs, which had come from his father in Hanover, should now be sent back to his father in Poland.[10] Abraham agreed that money should be sent, but he was in no rush to send that kind of cash into the Zbaszyn "no-man's-land," an obvious den of Nazi and Polish thieves. He would send help only when the situation became clear enough for him to be sure that the money would reach his brother, and not line Nazi pockets.[11]

A few buildings down, Nat Kaufmann was preparing to head off to the five-o'-clock dance at the Sportsclub Aurore. He was almost finished getting dressed for it. He knotted his tie; inspected his jacket. Remember, we are in 1938: Seventeen-year-old city boys wore jacket and tie for most things except manual labor. Certainly for dances.

At this point, the disagreement between Abraham and Herschel had mutated into an argument. Abraham wanted to wait until the situation was clear. Waiting for a safe moment to send the money to Poland was not acceptable to Herschel. His family needed the money now. He may or may not have mentioned his brave, unfulfillable promise to Berta to send money by return post.

Probably in the calm and measured tones that were typical of him, Abraham explained that the situation in Zbaszyn was dangerous and unclear. So far, they knew only that the family was being held prisoner, trapped between the Nazis and the Poles, neither of whom could be trusted for a single instant. Sending any amount of cash into such a situation would be foolish. Did Herschel imagine that the Gestapo thieves would let a Jew, a Jew whom they held entirely at their mercy, freely walk around with 3,000 francs in his pocket? Sending money into the Zbaszyn no-man's-land was as good as throwing it away. The situation had to become clearer before they acted. They would have to wait.

But no. Herschel's refusal to wait turned the argument into a quarrel, with voices raised around the table. Herschel was accused of being reckless. Abraham was accused of being ungenerous or worse. It appears that Abraham pointed out that Herschel was a child, and that as the man in the family, Abraham's decision was final.

Whatever he said made Herschel's anger flare out of control.

Herschel rose to his feet. Abraham was now also on his feet. He would not be shouted at. His voice was loud and clipped.

Nat Kaufmann had left his apartment building and reached the sidewalk outside 6 rue des Petites-Écuries. He pulled open the big main door and started climbing to the Maison Albert. He reached the fifth-floor landing and was ready with a prepared smile as he gave a short warning knock, opened the unlocked apartment door as usual, and peered in.

He found Herschel standing near the apartment door, yelling unrestrained. By now Chawa was also on her feet, also shouting, but trying to get both Abraham and Herschel to quiet down. Abraham, the neighborhood's picture of calm, now reached a point where whatever remnant there was of his shredded temper was blown away. He, too, was shouting. Chawa was weeping, still trying to make them stop.

But Herschel did not stop. Herschel would rather live *anywhere* else than here.

Live somewhere else? Did Abraham hear the child say something about living *somewhere else?*

Chawa's effort to return them both to sanity was wasted. All the masculine shouting drowned out her weeping voice.

Yes! Herschel would rather *die* than stay in this house.

Oh, *really?* Did the child *really* want to live somewhere *else?* So be it!

Herschel hollered back that he'd be *delighted* to leave right now. In fact, he would rather commit *suicide* than stay even one more minute. Nothing could keep him here. If he had to stay, he would kill himself. He would rather die like a dog in the street than stay under this roof. He was leaving, and he was never, ever, ever, *ever* coming back. He *swore* it!

Herschel snatched up his coat—it was a voluminous beige raincoat—and was struggling to pull it on as Chawa plunged toward him, begging him not to go. And at the moment she began to grapple with Herschel, Abraham seems to have regained his senses. The cyclone of his anger turned into churning anxiety. The child *meant* it. Herschel kept struggling with his coat while Chawa struggled to pull it off, imploring him to stay.

At last hearing his wife, Abraham immediately saw that she was right, but only as Chawa lost the tussle with the sleeves. The boy was shaking.

"I AM *LEAVING!*" he shouted. "GOOD-BYE!"

As Herschel turned toward the door, Abraham pulled out all the money he happened to have in his pocket and on pure impulse stuffed it into Herschel's coat. Then he stood back, hands down, silent.

Then, at four fifteen on the afternoon of November 6, 1938, blind with righteous fury, Herschel spun past the thunderstruck Nat and was out the door, slamming it behind him and clattering down all five flights as fast as he could go.

The moment Herschel slammed the door behind him, Chawa and Abraham turned in supplication to Herschel's dumbfounded friend. Please, he had to go catch up to Herschel now and talk sense to him. Do what it takes to make him calm down. Distract him, take him to the dance. Stay with him. Don't let him do anything crazy. Make him remember how much we love him. Above all, *bring him back*. Please.

Nat was out the door in an instant, swinging down the stairs as teenagers do. Below, he bolted into the slanting midafternoon sunlight, knowing exactly how to catch up. Herschel had to have turned left, heading toward Tout Va Bien and familiar corners of their life.

When Nat burst out of the entryway to 6 rue des Petites-Écuries, he turned left and raced to the corner, crossing the rue du Faubourg Saint-Denis, dodging traffic until he spotted his small friend's angry back. This was likely near the boulevard du Strasbourg, the main drag of their lives.

Herschel was still on fire, fists shoved into the pockets of his overcoat, perhaps fingering the still-uncounted sum Abraham had stuffed into one of them. Meanwhile, Nat was back in his assigned role: getting Herschel Grynszpan to calm down.

He had no idea what the fight had been about; all he'd heard was Herschel yelling that he would commit suicide and Abraham yelling back, telling him to clear out. Still, as they walked, Nat invoked sweet reason. He condoled. He explained that Abraham regretted everything and was begging to get his nephew back. He insisted that whatever he had said, Abraham didn't *mean* it. He was just angry. They're good people. Don't walk out on them. Go back.[12]

"*Never!* I'm *never* going back there! Not *ever*. I've sworn it. Never, *never* . . ." He would rather *die like a dog* than spend another *minute* under their roof.

Well, was Herschel at least coming to the dance?

The dance? Herschel pondered the idea. Well, why not? Where else *could* he go? He wouldn't have any fun, but he needed to think. So, sure, why not? Let's go.

They were soon heading toward Le Sportsclub Aurore, a quarter mile away that they covered at a good teenaged clip. They arrived in time.

Herschel spent the entire occasion sulking among the wallflowers. The music began at the innocent hour of five and the party broke up somewhere around seven thirty. Herschel's anger may have subsided or changed a little, but not enough to make him reconsider his determination never, ever, *ever* to return to the Maison Albert.

But where would, where could, he go? Sitting out the dances, Herschel had a chance to look at the money Abraham had stuffed in his pocket: two 100-franc bills. In addition, he had a little more than 100 francs of his own (for a total of about $7.50 in 1938 or $115 in the early twenty-first century). He didn't *have* to go home. That was enough. He could make his first decision. He would spend the night in a hotel.

When the hall thinned out around seven fifteen, Herschel's agitation had subsided into an inert blanket of depressive gloom. His eyes were no longer wild; he no longer seemed frantic. When they left the club, Herschel was docile and silent, walking quietly alongside his friend. They headed straight back toward the old neighborhood. As they walked, Nat decided to give reason one more try. *We're almost home, so do me a favor and go back. Try to make up. They want you back; they told me so. Maybe by now things will look different.*

Wasted breath. It only triggered another tirade about never, ever, *ever* going back. He would sleep in a hotel.

More arguing was pointless. It was seven thirty, and Herschel would have to come to his senses on his own. They split up on the rue du Château-d'Eau, under the looming presence of the Tenth Arrondissement's wonderfully ornate Mairie. One version claims they agreed to meet at Tout Va Bien after supper, around nine o'clock. The other version is that they just parted ways. Nat said good night, turned, and headed toward his place.

And Herschel was left alone on that dark corner, adamant, watching his best friend disappear. He was homeless—like his family. He was an outcast—like his people.

Less than fifty yards away, across the street from where Nat left him, there was a tiny shop that Herschel had walked by and ignored a thousand times. It sold cutlery, but it was also a doll store and doll hospital. Amid the knives and forks, its windows were filled with baby dolls that would make a girl's heart leap, along with doll dresses and doll hats and doll cradles. The shop was called A la Fine Lame ("The Cutting Edge"). Sometime in the next hour, and probably within the next five minutes, Herschel walked past it again, but this time noticed that among all the frilly things in the window lay an array of pistols. Small, easily concealed pistols that worked.

In the darkness of the increasingly deserted boulevard, Herschel now stood with his fists in his pockets, looking and thinking.[13]

They were for sale, and if he included the money Uncle Abraham had given him, he had enough to pay for a hotel *and* buy a gun. A la Fine Lame was shuttered and closed tight, but its hours were posted on the door. The shop would open at 8:30 a.m. sharp, Monday.

Monday was the next day.

Either before or after that long meditation, Herschel began to meander through the dark Paris streets. The walk took an hour, but Herschel did not stray very far away from home. He had vowed never to speak to his aunt and uncle again, but he didn't put any great distance between them. Rather than leave his neighborhood, he circled it, as if trying to tie a long piece of string around it and bind it tight. As long walkers often do, he was trying to lose and find himself at the same time. The radius he circled as the night deepened cannot have been more than a half mile, and when he decided on a hotel, he did not go to the other end of the city or the terminus of some night ride to elsewhere. His hotel was three blocks from the apartment where his aunt and uncle were pacing the floor, their agitation deepening by the minute. Herschel was running away and staying behind at the same time.

By eight o'clock that night, well after the time Herschel should have been back from the dance, Abraham and his brother-in-law decided they could no longer just sit and wait. They had to begin a search, and they left the apartment.

Their natural first stop was Nathan's place next door. When they arrived, Nathan, who was with his parents finishing supper, told them what he knew. They had gone to the dance. Herschel was still steaming mad. After the dance, he still refused to come home. He told Nathan that he would eat at Tout Va Bien and spend the night in a hotel. Which hotel? Nathan hadn't a clue.

Uncle Abraham was now becoming agitated in a new way. More than one suicidal soul had chosen a dreary little room on the fifth floor of an anonymous hotel for their final stop.

The Hôtel de Suez on the boulevard de Strasbourg was a minute's walk from A la Fine Lame, and even closer to the Maison Albert on the rue des Petites-Écuries. It was very much what you would expect for the neighborhood, especially once you grasp that the Tenth Arrondissement is what the traveler sees stepping out of the Gare de l'Est, the main terminus in

Paris for trains arriving from the east—that is, from Germany and points beyond. The neighborhood hotels were used to dealing with people just arriving from Germany and Austria, especially the less fortunate ones. Rich, confident visitors went to other neighborhoods, leaving places like the Suez for those who didn't have much money, or valid papers, or were scared; people obviously lying about their names and their background, people who had left Germany because they had no choice, and people who could barely ask for a room for the night in French.

The Hôtel de Suez was not squalid, but it was plain and poorish, a respectable small-change operation. It lay directly on the path between his uncle's apartment and Tout Va Bien, so we can be certain that Nathan and Abraham walked past it, probably more than once, as they searched the neighborhood for the runaway. But Herschel had checked in half an hour before their search began, and he had used an assumed name.

Herschel had walked into the lobby of the Suez around eight thirty, carrying neither papers nor luggage. At that moment Nathan was still eating his agitated supper at home; Abraham was just admitting to himself that Herschel really might not be coming back.

The man at the desk of the Hôtel de Suez that night was the proprietor, and he had the impression that this young customer could not speak French at all. Luckily, the proprietor's daughter spoke excellent German, and so he summoned her. Assuming he was totally ignorant of the language, she was mildly surprised when he asked for a room in competent but heavily accented French. The girl listened pleasantly as Herschel told various lies. His name, he muttered, was Heinrich Halter (a Gentile name), and he had just arrived on the train from Germany . . .

The girl at the desk smiled and gently informed young Herr Halter that if he wished to speak German, that would be fine with her. Everything became much easier.

Welcome, Herr Halter. And where are you from in Germany?

Hamburg, he lied. His train had just come in, and he had left his luggage in the baggage check at the Gare de l'Est because he didn't want to lug it through the streets while he searched for a place to stay.

The girl understood.

She was delighted to tell Herr Halter that she happened to have a room that might suit him. The cost was 22.50 francs. She did not ask to be paid in advance.

Herschel signed; she gave him the keys. Herschel paused, and then, very shyly, asked if it would be all right if he went out for a while.

The hotelier's daughter assured Herr Halter that he should feel free to go out and come back whenever he liked. Even if he came back so late that the front desk was closed, the porter would be on duty to let him in.

Herschel thanked her, and then went back into the streets of his own familiar neighborhood. He did not return until after midnight.[14]

Where Herschel went and what he did during the next two and a half hours is unknown. Conspiracy theorists have spent decades trying to fill this murky hole in the narrative with sinister secret meetings and master spies. Or sometimes love trysts. Or contacts with the masterminds of "world Jewry," or perhaps a final meeting with his Gestapo controllers.

The likely truth is that Herschel walked through familiar streets alone and in the darkness, living with what he had decided to do. Dreading it; planning it; making himself believe in it. He played and replayed it in his mind. He choreographed every move, mixing perfect precision with perfect naïveté. For once there was nobody he could turn to. He was alone in a new way. He was sealed inside the close confines of his secret.

Since it was after midnight when Herschel returned to the Hôtel de Suez, he had to ring the outside buzzer to be let in. The boss and his daughter had gone to bed, but the porter had not yet left, and a night clerk had just arrived. The porter greeted Herr Halter and, noticing that he still had no luggage, said nothing. With a simple good night, he gave Herr Halter his key and told him where he would find his room.

It is hard to gauge how much real sleep takes place in what people describe as a sleepless night. The night porter saw a light under the door of Herschel's room until all hours, and Herschel later claimed he had hardly slept. Yet as we know from an exhaustive psychological report made after his arrest, he had many dreams.

Something was moving around his neck. Hands; somebody's hands. The hands of a man, and the man was a Nazi, and they were tightening and squeezing and tightening, *and . . .*

He snapped awake, bouncing in the bed.

There were no hands. He was alone. He was in a hotel in Paris. He was still alive. Tomorrow was coming.

He had trouble getting back to more sleep, and thought he never would.

But he was in Hanover again. He was with his parents. He stood with them outside the tailor shop, and there were crowds all around it. There were Nazis in the crowd, Nazis in their brown uniforms, and they seized his father and began to beat him while the crowd watched. Then they grabbed his mother. They were beating her, too. Then they spotted Herschel, and lunged after him as well.

But Herschel was too fast for them. He dodged, or ducked, and was back in the crowd, forgotten by the Nazis.

The crowd was made up of regular people from Hanover. They were not Jews, but they were not Nazis, either. They were his father's Gentile customers. And now the Nazis turned on the customers, slapping them, spitting at them, kicking them, shouting, "You are damned! You are damned! You are selling the German people to the Jews!"

DAMNED!

And he bounced awake again, his heart slamming so violently that he clasped his hands to his chest and struggled to catch his breath.[15]

But this was not Hanover. He was still in a strange hotel room in Paris. Tomorrow was still coming, and now it was closer to morning than night.

He had to sleep. He had to be ready.

Getting back to sleep was slow, but it did come back.

It was morning now and it was eight thirty. Herschel was standing in the rue du Faubourg Saint-Martin, outside A la Fine Lame. The shutters were up. The store was open. The sun was shining. Herschel had money in his pocket, and he could see the shopkeeper inside. He went into the store. He saw an array of guns. They were waiting for him. One of them could be his.[16]

He snapped awake again, with his heart pounding in his chest. Another dream. This was still his dim little hotel room in Paris, though there was fresh light in the window.

It was morning—the real morning of November 7, 1938. It was 7:30 a.m.

And it was time.

The Assassin's Day

Modest though it was, the Hôtel de Suez staff brought a morning cup of coffee and a fresh roll up to guests in their rooms, so they could have *le petit déjeuner* in bed. After taking advantage of this luxury, Herschel washed. He was always scrupulously clean, but of course on this morning of mornings, he didn't have any fresh clothes, and he put on the same suit and tie that he'd worn for yesterday's catastrophic family dinner. He did not shave. The many press close-ups taken of him later that day, when he had not been near a razor for thirty-six hours, show no trace of a five-o'clock shadow. He had the skin of a boy.

In the lobby Herschel asked the porter for the use of a pen, and at a little lobby desk reached into his inside pocket and extracted the street photographer's portrait-postcard of himself that he so prized, the one in which he looked so much like a man, addressing the camera with fearless eyes. It was a genuine postcard, and the reverse side was still blank. In the address section he wrote:

Maison Albert
Paris, X
Rue des Petites-Écuries, 6

In the message box he wrote:

My dear parents, I could not do otherwise, may God forgive me. My heart bleeds when I hear of your tragedy and that of the 12,000 Jews. I must protest so the whole world hears my protest and that I will do.

Forgive me. Hermann

Then, in a small white margin above this message, he inscribed a phrase in Hebrew:

WITH GOD'S HELP[1]

It was somewhere between 8:20 and 8:30.[2] Since he didn't have a stamp, he slipped the card, with its vow and its prayer, back into his pocket. He stood up, returned the pen, and paid his bill, which in its entirety came to 25 francs; the 1938 equivalent of 75 cents, or in twenty-first-century dollars, about $10.65. He then left the hotel and walked back to A la Fine Lame, at most a few minutes' stroll along familiar sidewalks.

He reached the shop at 8:38 a.m. It seems to have been *exactly* 8:38. The French police can be very thorough, and in their meticulous investigations they learned that the owners had arrived that morning eight minutes late, a slip-up they remembered because they were punctual people and it bothered them.

So Herschel was the day's first customer. The owners were M. and Mme. Carpe. Mme. Carpe was just rolling up the steel gratings that protected all the guns and dolls in the show window. As she dusted the grating's grime from her hands, Herschel approached her and told her in relaxed foreigner's French that he had come to buy a gun.[3]

Mme. Carpe was a little taken aback. A gun? But this new customer was a child.

Still, Mme. Carpe ushered Herschel into the shop. As she did, the little bell rigged to announce a customer's arrival jingled. Just once.

M. Carpe was behind the counter. When madame explained why Herschel was there, M. Carpe, like his wife, was perplexed, even disturbed.

Well now, he wondered aloud, what would a fine young fellow like Herschel be wanting with a gun?

Herschel's answer was well prepared.

Pulling out his wallet, he flashed both the hundred franc notes in it and explained that his father was a businessman who did a brisk cash business. As his dad's messenger, his job was to carry this cash to the bank, sometimes twice or three times a day. It was risky, carrying all those loose bills through a tough neighborhood. He needed protection.

Thinking this over, M. Carpe decided the statement was at least believable. It might even be true.

M. Carpe opened the showcase and began to produce various possibilities, keeping alert, as was his custom, to how the customer handled the weapons he put into his hands. Within seconds, it was clear to M. Carpe that Herschel Grynszpan had never touched a firearm in his entire life and knew nothing at all about how to handle or shoot one.

Herschel needed what he could afford and what he could conceal, which soon narrowed his choice to a stubby 6.35 mm pistol, designed for use at very short range, with a barrel barely longer than its grip. The shell magazine clipped neatly into its handgrip. Like Herschel himself, the gun was small. It didn't look like much. But it could kill.

The price of 210 francs dangled from a tag tied to the trigger guard (a price of about $6 in 1938, or $90 in the early twenty-first century United States). A box of the bullets cost another 35 francs. So the whole price came to 245 francs.

Herschel held the gun, weighed it in his hand. It was tiny. Very light.

M. Carpe did explain that there were some rules and regulations about buying a gun. First of all, M. Carpe would need to see Herschel's papers. Herschel produced his Polish passport, bearing his real name and the Maison Albert's recently outdated address on the rue Mantel.

After collecting 245 francs, M. Carpe offered this obvious amateur some basic lessons in firearms. First, he showed Herschel how to extract the ammunition clip from the handgrip, how to load it with five cartridges, and then how, when he slid the magazine back into place, the first cartridge popped into the firing chamber, ready to go. He showed Herschel the safety and how to click it on and off. Then, after emptying the magazine, he demonstrated how to extend his arm and squeeze off a round. Then he repacked the box of shells, and wrapped it and the pistol in brown paper, tied with string.

Next, M. Carpe handed Herschel an official police form: a declaration of ownership of a firearm, which he helped Herschel fill out.

The very next thing Herschel was to do after leaving the shop was to file this document with the police. M. Carpe then led Herschel to the door and pointed to the precinct station and Mairie, at a diagonal across the large intersection. Herschel nodded in what seemed uncomplicated agreement and dutifully set out in that direction. But the moment he knew he was out of view, he took a sharp left and then another, turning onto the boulevard de Strasbourg, heading in the opposite direction, toward Tout Va Bien.

November 7, 1938, was a mild, even warm Indian summer day; there were probably breakfasters on the terrace, while the inside of the café was doubtless crowded with people having their morning coffee before boarding the nearby Métro for work.

Herschel headed straight for the men's room in the basement and bolted the door tight behind him.[4]

It was 8:50. In that smelly little space, he fumbled his package from his overcoat pocket and tore off the string and brown paper. He was nervous, but even if his fingers were trembling, he easily extracted the ammunition clip, and setting the box of shells on the sink, filled the magazine with five bullets, feeling the spring in the magazine snap each one into place. When it was full, he slid the magazine back into its sheathe in the handgrip. Its next click was followed by an immediate second click, which was the sound of the first bullet slipping into the firing chamber. The pistol was ready to fire.

He checked the safety. He'd been shown all about it: "On" meant the gun would not fire. "Off" meant it would. It was easy to switch the safety from On to Off, just by feel. He dropped the ammunition back into his raincoat pocket and slipped the now fully prepared weapon into the inside left pocket of his suit jacket.

He was ready.

He unbolted the bathroom door and walked out of Tout Va Bien.

He was soon in the Métro, and at the ticket window, where he did something rather strange.

He asked the clerk for a round-trip ticket.

This is a small mystery. It seems likely that Herschel had already resolved to turn himself in to the police immediately after committing his crime. He was clear that public visibility was the whole point of his protest. If he was not on the scene to explain his protest to the world, he might as well not shoot anyone. Herschel seems to have left the Tenth Arrondissement assuming that he was never coming back. So, why a round-trip ticket?

The punctilious clerk in the ticket booth told him that round-trip tickets became available only before nine o'clock, and it was now 9:05. Too late. He bought a one-way ticket, and five minutes later was on the Line 8 train, headed south toward the Madeleine station, where he made the transfer that took him to all the official buildings on the Seine.[5]

What was then the German embassy to the French Republic, on the rue de Lille in Paris, is a very impressive piece of Napoleonic architecture. It had been a palatial private residence until the early nineteenth century, when Napoleon acquired it for his two stepchildren, Hortense and Eugène de

Beauharnais, the grown offspring of Joséphine de Beauharnais, whom he had made empress of the French.

Eugène was delighted to have a palace of his very own, but he occupied the place only briefly. At some point, Napoleon married him off to a daughter of the king of Bavaria, and when Eugène died in 1824, Napoleonic power was defunct. Through a series of bewildering twists and turns in the *Almanac of Gotha*, the Hôtel Beauharnais ended up the property of the German imperial family. Richard Wagner was a frequent guest. Otto von Bismarck stayed in the Hôtel Beauharnais when he was in Paris. Kaiser Wilhelm II relished his many visits there, holding court in France until the First World War put a stop to his Paris sojourns.

Centrally located, the Hôtel Beauharnais stands about a hundred meters from the French National Assembly. The French ministry of foreign affairs is just a little beyond that. The building is in the heart of the beast.

Herschel's ride to it took less than half an hour. The building was instantly recognizable by the large flag with its swastika rippling before it in a gentle breeze.

Even one month after the Munich crisis, when the world was still on tenterhooks between peace and war, the German embassy to France had no security of any kind, apart from a little cadre of French cops, who stood guard outside on the sidewalk. We even know the name of one of the cops: François Autret.

Stepping up to Officer Autret, Herschel very quietly asked in French marked by a strong German accent how to get into the building. There was nothing confrontational in either the question or the cop's answer, but Autret did ask what brought the boy to the embassy. Herschel fumbled his response, blurting something about a visa. Well, Autret said, in that case he was in the wrong place. The visa office is in the consulate on the boulevard Huysmans. But Herschel knew that; he'd been there with a visa problem of his own. He quickly recovered his fumble by adding that he also had some important business in the embassy itself. The cop produced a Gallic shrug and pointed to the main entrance.

Then, Herschel simply walked in.

He stepped into a foyer at the foot of a grand staircase. At the bottom of the stairs there was a plain French woman, bent over pails and mops, cleaning the marble. At the top of the stairs, an important-looking gentleman had just begun his descent. The lady was the building's concierge, a Mme. Mathis. As for the grandee descending the stairs, it was the ambassador himself, Johannes Graf von Welczeck, a fiercely committed and conscienceless Nazi, whom Hitler had made ambassador after tearing up the Treaty of Versailles and ordering his army to occupy the Rhineland. Baron von Welczeck had replaced a leftover Weimar appointee who had the pre-Hitlerian notion that relations between France and Germany ought to be peaceful and mutually beneficial.

At that moment on November 7, Ambassador von Welczeck was on his way out for his morning constitutional.

The boy approached Mme. Mathis, and in a breathless, slightly too-loud voice told her in French that he had come to the Embassy to deliver some very important documents and needed to speak to "an official." Note that he did not ask to see the ambassador.

At that same moment, the ambassador himself swept out onto the rue de Lille, passing them both without one word or glance.

Mme. Mathis smiled at the small young man who was so obviously intimidated by the moment and place. Trying to put him at his ease, she pointed upward and explained that at the top of the grand staircase he would find a reception desk manned by a clerk who was there to assist anybody who had come to make a delivery.

So Herschel climbed the grand staircase.

—

The clerk at the head of the stairs was a classical German civil servant named Wilhelm Nagorka. He had worked in the German Foreign Office before Hitler, he worked there while Hitler ruled, and he continued to work there long after Hitler was gone, his career a triumph of bureaucratic durability.

It is on Wilhelm Nagorka's testimony about the next two minutes that, without exception, every conspiracy theory about Herschel Grynszpan rests. Herr Nagorka's testimony was undoubtedly truthful. Formally and informally, before tribunals and in relaxed conversation off the scene, on the day of the event, in preparation for his trial, during the war, and after the war, everywhere and always, Nagorka invariably repeated exactly the same thing about what happened next.

It was simple. Herschel approached the front desk and asked Herr Nagorka in German to see "one of the embassy secretaries"—again, not the ambassador—because he had come to deliver some "important documents."

He said that, and that only.

With German propriety, Wilhelm Nagorka replied that if the young man would be so good as to leave the documents in question with him, he could rest assured that they would be promptly delivered to an appropriate official.

Herschel stood his ground. These papers were far too important to let out of his hands. He had to deliver them, directly and personally, to an official of the embassy.

Herr Nagorka was not one to argue with visitors. In that case, if the young man would kindly follow him to the reception room, he would speak to the proper person.

Herschel was led to a small waiting area to the side, where he was left alone. In all likelihood, that is when he reached into his left inside suit pocket and by feel found the safety of the 6.35 and gently switched it to Off.

—

There were supposed to be only two embassy secretaries at their desks that morning, and it turned out that one of them, a man named Achenbach, had overslept and was late. So Nagorka turned to his only choice, a twenty-nine-year-old lawyer named Ernst vom Rath.

Ernst Eduard Adolf Max Graf vom Rath came from an upper-class Willhemine family of successful businessmen and public officials. His father, Gustav vom Rath, had served occasionally as a senior public official when not acting as an equally senior executive in the large sugar factory that was one of the family businesses. Ernst was the oldest of his three sons, and at twenty-nine, he, too, was a lawyer.

Everything about Ernst vom Rath proclaimed him to be a somewhat standard-issue, thoroughly proper scion of his class and kind. Vom Rath was tallish without being exactly tall, very much as he was quick-witted and bright without being exactly brilliant. He was nice-looking, slender, with light brown hair and a pleasant, competent manner. He was unmarried and lived very quietly in an immaculate apartment near the embassy. Even though his French was not really all that might be desired in a diplomat (though he did work hard at lessons), his landlady was impressed and grateful for his perfectly regular early hours, his thoughtfulness, and his unfailing good manners. Later claims that he led some sort of riotous nightlife are the reverse of fact. At work, he wore a business suit of excellent quality, on the sleeve of which he never sported the swastika armband that certain other members of the service tied to their clothes as they tried to kiss their way upward.

After study at Königsberg (where he was rumored to have had a love affair with a Jewish woman and fellow student), Ernst sat for the German bar in 1932, the year before Hitler took power. His ambition was to be a diplomat, following in the footsteps of his mother's brother, Roland Köster, who was none other than the leftover Weimar ambassador to France whom von Welczeck, a fanatical Nazi, replaced in 1935. In what was surely a function of nepotism, young Ernst was suddenly removed from the ordinary sequence of promotion for young diplomats and given a plum job as private secretary to his uncle the ambassador—even though at that time he did not know French.

As a Weimar appointee and a senior figure in the old-line German establishment, Köster was an internal opponent of the regime until his death in 1935. Hitler regarded him as a nuisance or worse but did not immediately replace him with a Nazi for fear of alienating the French. The Dutch lawyer and historian Sidney Smeets writes: "In his own way, Köster resisted well. He refused to fly the swastika flag, which was now the second national flag, at the embassy; he invited Jews to embassy receptions; did not mention the regime in speeches; and even received German political refugees at the embassy." In 1934, he declined to take the obligatory national oath to Hitler personally. By 1935, when his nephew was assigned to the Paris embassy, Köster's position was becoming downright dangerous. He was convinced that his living quarters and office were bugged and began to confer with "like-minded" embassy employees during long walks in the Bois de Boulogne. It is thought that he made his nephew his personal secretary so that he could have at his side at least one person he could trust in an embassy increasingly packed with Nazis who were ideologically hostile to him. He died in office of pneumonia, shortly before Hitler's reoccupation of the Rhineland.[6]

And the rest of the family? Though Nazi propaganda claimed that Ernst's father was sympathetic to the regime,[7] there is good but inconclusive reason to believe that Gustav vom Rath was also privately an opponent of the regime. In their book *Crystal Night*, Rita Thalmann and Emmanuel Feinermann report that after Ernst's death and the Kristallnacht, "Magnus Davidsohn, a reader at the principal synagogue in Berlin, paid a visit with his wife to Councellor vom Rath's parents, who happened to be neighbors and acquaintances of many years' standing. When he expressed his condo-

lences and the sympathy of the Jewish community, Herr vom Rath, distraught with grief, responded, 'My dear Reverend, neither you nor any other
Jew is responsible for this. I think my son was assassinated on orders. He
spoke too much, and a hired assassin killed him.'"[8]

In 1940, the Nazis appointed Gustav to work in the Gestapo office
in Berlin, where he knew Heinrich Gruber, a Protestant pastor later imprisoned for helping Jews. Testifying at the Eichmann trial of 1961, Pastor
Gruber reported that his organization's relation to Gustav vom Rath "was
rather friendly, and I must say that this man helped us clandestinely on
many occasions."[9]

But was Ernst also an internal resistor to the regime? It seems likely.
When he was a student, before Hitler took power, he joined the Sturmabteilung, the Nazi paramilitary wing, in a burst of youthful nationalist enthusiasm. After Ernst's death Goebbels made the most of this fact, mendaciously
touting vom Rath as a heroically committed National Socialist and martyr
for the cause. In fact, following the Night of Long Knives in June 1934,
vom Rath recoiled from the regime. His anti-Nazi uncle obviously trusted
him, and Ernst very likely followed Köster's lead. After his first Paris post-
ing ended and he was dispatched to Calcutta, Ernst inveighed against the
regime, albeit in private, with friends.[10] Senior Nazis in Paris viewed him as
being, like his uncle, ideologically unreliable, and it seems the Gestapo were
observing him. After the war, Otto Abetz, the most senior Nazi in France,
both before and after France fell, wrote that vom Rath "was an adversary of
National Socialism, and he tended toward mystical ideas, even seeing Hitler
as the Antichrist."[11] Schwab claims that vom Rath was a nonobservant but
devout Christian; Abetz speaks only of his "mystical tendencies." The elaborate investigations of his life and opinions that followed his death found no
evidence that he was an anti-Semite. After his uncle's death in 1935, Ernst
grew steadily more hostile to Hitler. Certainly, by 1938, he was more and
more seriously disturbed by the government he served.

Yet serve it he did, at his desk every day in a building over whose entrance the swastika rippled in the breeze. It is one of the many ironies of

Herschel Grynszpan's story that he very likely shot the one man in the embassy who—secretly—agreed with him.

When Roland Köster died, young Ernst's fast-track career came to a screeching halt, and he was shunted to the embassy in Calcutta. There he contracted severe dysentery and what was at least advertised as a mild case of tuberculosis and was sent back to Germany for treatment. He suffered from precarious health for the rest of his life. Yet by 1938, Ernst had made his way back to the Paris embassy and a promotion, though doubtless without the perks he'd enjoyed when his uncle was in charge.

When Wilhelm Nagorka appeared at his office door, Ernst vom Rath was just settling into his desk chair and enjoying the morning sunshine. Vom Rath's office was small, and considering that it was in the Hôtel Beauharnais, quite plain. Its great feature was windows flooded with sunlight, which vom Rath found so luscious that he pushed his desk flush with the sill so he could face it all day. For that reason he usually sat with his back turned to his office door.

Nagorka's knock was official and correct.

The young lawyer answered and was told that there was a young man outside claiming to have some documents that must be personally delivered to an officer. And with the shrug of a man whose very routine day had just begun, vom Rath smiled and agreed to see the visitor.

Nagorka found Herschel sitting in the waiting room exactly as he had been left, hushed, a little hunched, still in his raincoat. Nagorka informed Herschel that a secretary to the legation—he did not mention vom Rath's name—could see him now, and Herschel stood up and followed Nagorka into the corridor where the more modest offices like vom Rath's were located. After another official rap, Nagorka opened the door and ushered the visitor in. Vom Rath swiveled a quarter turn in his chair to take in the trembling little fellow with the huge, doe-like eyes, draped in his raincoat.

Nagorka quietly closed the office door and began walking back to the receptionist's desk.

Though vom Rath did not rise, he greeted Herschel politely, suggesting he sit in one of the comfortable leather easy chairs near his desk. Herschel duly walked over to it and sat.

Now then, Herr vom Rath understood that his visitor had come to deliver some sort of document?

As if reaching for papers, Herschel slid his hand into his left suit coat jacket, got a firm grip on the pistol, and just before pulling it out, shouted at the top of his voice: "You're a filthy Kraut, and in the name of twelve thousand persecuted Jews, *here* is your document!"[12]

On the stroke of *here*, he flashed the gun and fired his first shot.

At the second shot, vom Rath leapt to his feet. Herschel also jumped up and kept pumping out slugs as fast as he could pull the trigger.

Herschel's aim was atrocious. He fired the first two shots from a sitting position, pointing the 6.35 straight at vom Rath's torso. Since the target was only a few feet away, he could hardly have missed, but all three of the remaining shots missed their mark totally.

Neither of the two bullets that hit him was enough to knock vom Rath down. Though he cried out—*Hilfe!*—nobody heard that. They heard only the shots.

The door to his office was still closed; to reach it, vom Rath had to push past his assailant who blocked his path. This he did with one solid punch to Herschel's jaw.

Though he did not hear vom Rath's cry for help, Nagorka heard all five shots, and after an instant frozen in disbelief, the clerk turned to run back to the office. This took only seconds. When he got there, vom Rath was standing in the open office door clutching his abdomen with both hands.

"I am wounded here," vom Rath breathed as two more embassy employees rushed to the spot. The first to arrive was a clerk named Krueger; the second was Ernst Achenbach, the attaché who had overslept that morning and was just opening his adjacent office for work. Achenbach occupied himself with helping vom Rath, while Nagorka and Krueger, stupefied and alarmed, peered into the smoke-filled office.

Herschel stood alone in the middle of the room. The radiant sun that vom Rath so prized was still brilliant at his back, piercing the lingering clouds of gun smoke that were slowly spreading around the room.

Seeing the two clerks in the door, Herschel began to tremble.[13] Soon he was visibly shaking; then it became uncontrollable, an almost violent quaking. His empty hands flopped at his sides: the empty 6.35 lay at his feet, its price tag still tied to the trigger guard by a piece of red string.

Yet the shaking child made no other move at all.

Herschel Grynszpan was waiting.

Nagorka and Krueger inched through the open office door. Watching them, Herschel stood still. Apart from the gun on the floor, there was no hint of menace about him. He did not step back or away as they came close. When they flanked him on both sides, each taking an arm, he did not recoil or resist.

His body had stopped shaking.

"I don't intend to escape. I won't do anything more."[14]

These were his first words.

Outside the office Achenbach offered first aid while the embassy *chargé* placed calls for medical help.

Quite soon after walking out of his office, vom Rath collapsed. The nearest hospital was the excellent Clinique de l'Alma. Vom Rath was rushed to it, where it was immediately obvious to the ER doctors that he was far more seriously wounded than the first few minutes had made it seem.

As Herschel was being led out of the embassy, he quietly asked to be turned over to French rather than German police. And that is what happened. The street was filling up with the morning rush as people hurried past the fluttering swastika.

The moment he was in public, Herschel began to holler.

"*SALES BOCHES!*" ("Filthy Krauts!") he hollered in French as loud as he could. They were almost beside Officer Autret when he hollered it again: "*SALES BOCHES!*"

Ignoring this ruckus, the clerks explained to the cop that this boy had just shot an official of the embassy in his office.

"*SALES BOCHES! SALES BOCHES! SALES BOCHES!*"

They also told Officer Autret that though the official was wounded, he was not dead.

In later testimony, Herr Krueger claimed that at this point Herschel said loudly, "It's a shame that he isn't dead." This may or may not be true. Krueger was a sycophant, while Nagorka's testimony remained steady, level-headed, and in all other matters more reliable than that of his colleague. Nagorka consistently said he had no recollection of Herschel saying anything of the sort to anyone.[15]

In any case Herschel then hollered at the gathering crowd a final ear-splitting "*SALES BOCHES!*"

Then it was over. He was once again quiet and calm.

As Officer Autret quickly patted him down, looking for another weapon, Herschel said to him in a normal voice, and in polite French, "Don't worry. I'll come with you."

Whereupon Officer Autret put Herschel Grynszpan under arrest for a crime that, if Herr vom Rath were to die, might carry Europe into horror and the boy to the guillotine.

7

Hitler's Luck

Exactly when and how Hitler learned about the assassination attempt is not known, but he clearly learned about it quickly.[1] And it perfectly suited his plans.

The assassination in Paris was exactly what the dictator had been waiting for, and very soon after Herschel shot vom Rath, Hitler and Joseph Goebbels were planning the propaganda for the mass anti-Semitic campaign that two nights later would turn into the Kristallnacht.[2] The crime of Herschel Grynszpan—his protest—would be used as the pretext for what was to be, to date, the largest and most vicious attack on the Jews and Jewish life in modern history, a prelude to the Holocaust. Soon enough, the boy who had dreamt of being God's pawn would be weeping bitter tears.

Herschel shot vom Rath at 9:35. He was led out of the building around 9:40, escorted through the lobby past the ambassador's deputy, a man named Curt Bräuer, who at that moment was the most senior official in the building. While Herschel was led out the grand entrance to the entryway, where the Swastika floated unashamed, Bräuer had called the embassy physician, a certain Dr. Claas, who came immediately: When he arrived, Herschel was still standing in a sidewalk cluster with cops and officials shouting *"Sales boches! Sales boches!"* And by the time Officer Autret took the tiny assassin by the arm and led him in his billowing brown raincoat toward the precinct station, Dr. Claas was in an ambulance with his patient, on the way to the nearest emergency room. As these events flashed by, Embassy Counselor Bräuer ducked into the embassy communications room, and in minutes telephoned the Foreign Ministry in Berlin, dictating a five-hundred-word report in which he described with succinct precision exactly what had happened in the preceding fifteen minutes.

Counselor Bräuer's transcribed telephone call is a key document for a couple of reasons. It is the first eyewitness report of the crime ever made, and its Teutonic exactitude demolishes in advance virtually every conspiracy theory later spun around Herschel. The master conspiracy theory was of course the lie that Hitler and Goebbels immediately began to spin around the boy: that Herschel was a pawn of "world Jewry" seeking to foment a second world war by assassinating the German ambassador to France. But there were many other conspiracy theories. For example, that Herschel was a pawn of the Gestapo, seeking to incite a pogrom by making the German people believe that "world Jewry" was trying to instigate another world war. Or that he was a pawn of the British, seeking to subvert the Franco-German rapprochement that the Nazis claimed would avert a second world war. Or, not least, that the killing had been part of a homosexual lovers' quarrel.

Here is what was transcribed from Bräuer's telephone call:

Today, at 9:35 WEZ [Western European Time], Secretary of Legation vom Rath was shot in his office by a German-speaking individual. The shot has passed through the left side of the body. The investigation so far has established the following: at 9:30 WEZ, a very young man approached a clerk of the embassy and insisted upon speaking to one of the secretaries, since he had an important document to deliver. He was led to Legation Secretary vom Rath's office. After the clerk left the room, there was an explosion. When the clerk hurried back to the spot, he saw Secretary of Legation vom Rath lying on the floor, bleeding.

The clerk alerted the policeman stationed in front of the embassy, who arrested the perpetrator and led him to the police station for questioning.

He was carrying a Polish passport, and gave his name as Grynszpan.

I have arranged for medical assistance for the Legation Secretary and his transfer to a hospital, and have logged the protocol accordingly.

After the entry had been properly logged, the investigation is quickly going forward, with consultation at an appropriate time with a representative of the embassy.

An additional message will follow. When the investigation has yielded new results, press coverage of the case should properly be handled in Berlin. Further information from the State Department on the way to handle the case is requested.[3]

Bräuer's call was made and recorded at ten o'clock, Paris time. The full text seems to have been promptly forwarded to the Führer and to the propaganda minister, Joseph Goebbels.[4]

Thus, vom Rath had barely been rolled into the ER and Herschel barely booked when Hitler grasped that it was an opportunity for rabble-rousing and some sort of anti-Semitic coup. Goebbels immediately ordered a massive anti-Semitic propaganda campaign based on the shooting, a campaign that Hitler himself must have ordered, probably in direct communication, by telephone. It was all very quick.[5]

As it happened, Hitler was traveling on the morning of November 7. He had spent the night in Weimar—that cradle of German democracy—where the day before he had delivered a major address attacking democracy as a decadent form of government. The speech was delivered in a stadium before an audience of one hundred thousand people. November 7 was to be a light day, devoted to two or three minor appearances and a train ride to his favorite city, Munich, on his private train, a fortress on rails called the Atlas, or sometimes, oddly, the Amerika, or, more formally, the Führerzonderzug.

Hitler's denunciation of democracy the day before had been specifically aimed at British democracy. With negotiations for rapprochement secretly proceeding between Count von Welczeck and Bonnet, Hitler was careful to leave the French government out of his attack. The speech was really an anti-British tirade, but in 1938 attacks on democracy in general were welcome because for large numbers of Germans, the democracy of the Weimar Republic was responsible for two decades of humiliation, poverty, and the spectacle of their nation—which ought to have been the greatest power in Central Europe—reduced to impotence. They believed Hitler when he insisted that only a "disciplined" government like his dictatorship could restore German power and truly defend the peace. Only a "disciplined" government could silence the critics who wanted to subvert the strong, proud, resurgent nation he had led out of the doldrums of defeat.[6]

A hundred thousand people rose to their feet, hailing their savior. Hitler stood in the back of his magnificent open Mercedes, giving adoring crowds his salute—*the* salute—as his motorcade crawled through the streets of the old town, taking him from the stadium to his favorite Weimar stopping place, the Haus Elephant.

The hotel's façade rippled with massed Nazi banners. Elite squadrons, often in goose step, patrolled its every doorway and path. Security measures that dwarfed any then in use by any other head of state locked down the entire vicinity. In front of the hotel lay a large plaza called Markt Square where Führer worshippers congregated by the thousands, rapt, gazing upward at Hitler on his hotel balcony and greeting him with upraised hands and shouts of *Heil! Heil! Heil!*

It was in the Elephant, over what could easily have been a late breakfast, that Hitler was handed the telegram.

The likelihood is that Hitler immediately telephoned his propaganda minister, Joseph Goebbels, in Berlin.

Unlike Hitler, Joseph Goebbels was an early riser.

On the morning of November 7, 1938, Goebbels was in his splendid office, presiding over a dull meeting on music in the New Germany. Early on, an aide silently slid the Paris telegram onto his desk, murmuring that the identical telegram had been simultaneously delivered to the Führer. Pausing to read Bräuer's report, Goebbels instantly grasped its import. The office was cleared of its visitors; soon Goebbels was doubtless on the line with Hitler. It is probable that as he spoke he felt blessed relief surging up from the core of his black heart. In recent weeks, a complex sexual scandal had left Goebbels's favored position in Hitler's circle teetering on the edge of a catastrophic fall.

This call just might be his salvation. Hitler needed him again.

Goebbels was well aware that Hitler was waiting for some pretext to embark on a wave of terror against German Jews. Hitler had never intended to honor one syllable of the Munich Pact, and within a month of signing it, he had decided to shatter its terms by invading what was left of Czechoslovakia.[7] The invasion was going to be expensive, and Hermann Göring, who was in charge of Hitler's five-year financial plan, had informed Hitler that the German government's currency reserves urgently required a large new infusion of funds. Without more money—much more money—the Nazis could not continue to rearm at the rate necessary to make Germany the hegemonic European power. And just as expansion called for more money, the need for more money in turn called for expansion.[8] Full transformation of German power required seizing the resources of Eastern Europe, notably Eastern European oil, steel, and wheat.[9]

That meant war. And war called for a lot of new cash, quickly. It was a vicious circle.

But since the key to much more money meant confiscation of Jewish resources, the vicious circle meant the great pogrom. The financial motive of the Kristallnacht was to terrorize the Jews of Germany into flight, the better to confiscate the property their exodus forced them to abandon.

Hitler conceived of his anti-Semitic policies—such as the Nuremberg Laws—as a way of raising revenues by so harassing German Jews that they would leave and abandon their property to the Reich. But by 1937, it had become clear that this method of raising money was not working well. First, nothing like the anticipated revenues were being realized, and nowhere near enough Jews were leaving Germany. Second, those who did flee were not rich enough to leave behind as much money and property as Hitler in his paranoid fantasy had imagined they had. For obvious reasons, the larger the net worth of a given Jew, the more reluctant he or she would be to abandon it.

As the planned invasion of Czechoslovakia approached, something had to be done. The order went out for proposals on ways to speed up the flight of Germany's Jews, especially the more affluent ones.

In January 1937, an ambitious young bureaucrat named Adolf Eichmann had produced a memo on this subject that was received with high favor at the top. Eichmann pointed out that legal measures such as the Nuremberg Laws of 1935 had thus far failed to do what they were designed to do. The Jews were not leaving Germany en masse merely because of legal persecution.

Eichmann argued that the missing element was terror.[10]

To produce this terror, Eichmann suggested a vast nationwide pogrom, a state-sponsored crime wave that would sweep aside even the pretense of legality. What was needed was unrestrained mayhem: a vast, nationwide criminal riot, a brief but brutal reign of lawless violence directed against every Jew in the Reich. During some clearly defined period of two or three

days, the entire Jewish population should confront unrestrained and ubiquitous murder, arson, larceny, kidnapping, extortion, and assault. Every
school and social institution should be broken into, trashed, and if possible
destroyed. Every home should be forcefully entered and every person in
it should be terrorized. Every synagogue should be burned to the ground.
The entire rabbinate should be rounded up and publicly humiliated, beaten,
and if the occasion arose, murdered, while Jewish sacred objects should be
desecrated in as obscene and blasphemous a fashion as could be conceived.
Jewish businesses, from the most modest to the most successful, should
be looted and demolished. Finally, every Jewish man who looked as if he
might have a little money in the bank should be summarily arrested, sent
to a concentration camp, and subjected to a few months of systematic penal
brutality that would make him understand that any hope of getting out
of the concentration camp at Dachau meant getting out of Germany. Not
later. Now.

Hitler was impressed.

Referring to Eichmann's memorandum suggesting a nationwide pogrom, Hitler's biographer Ian Kershaw writes, "From the perspective of the
regime's leadership, how to get the Jews out of the economy and force them
to leave Germany still appeared to be questions without answers . . . Like
an answer to a prayer, the shooting of the German Third Legation Secretary Ernst vom Rath in Paris by a seventeen-year-old Polish Jew, Herschel
Grynszpan, on the morning of November 7, 1938, was an opportunity not
to be missed." Kershaw adds, "It was an opportunity eagerly seized upon by
Goebbels. He had no difficulty in winning Hitler's full backing."[11]

On the morning of November 7, Hitler and Goebbels seem to have agreed
on a general propaganda line: This Jew assassin, though a child, was a pawn
that world Jewry was using to sabotage the growing friendliness between
France and the Reich.[12] And what was world Jewry's ultimate aim? To pro-

voke a second world war. The German people must be made to understand the sinister intentions of this conspiracy and cry out for revenge.

Especially if Herr vom Rath were to die.

With no written record, the content of Hitler's conversation with Goebbels that morning can only be inferred from Goebbels's actions after hanging up.

Goebbels immediately formulated the concept of the campaign by inventing a kind of propaganda syllogism:

The Jew Grynszpan represents world Jewry.
The German vom Rath represents the German people.
That means that the shooting in Paris was world Jewry's attempt to shoot down the German people.

Goebbels's remaining time in Berlin was very short. He was scheduled to board his private train to Munich to be present for the elaborate pageantry of Movement Day, a yearly mass gathering of the Nazi party faithful.

Movement Day was the most solemn of the secular holidays the Nazi party had invented to honor itself, and it was held every November 9.[13] At first, November 9 was emblazoned in the minds of most Germans as a day of shame. Germany effectively surrendered in the First World War on November 9, 1918, when Kaiser Wilhelm II abdicated and a republic was proclaimed. Hitler had used the fifth anniversary of this day to stage his first attempt to seize political power, the so-called Beer Hall Putsch of November 9, 1923. This effort to seize control of the municipal government of Munich was an ignominious failure and would be remembered primarily for its clownish incompetence except for its sinister consequence. It was the Beer Hall Putsch that lifted Hitler out of the lunatic fringe and put him near the top of the Weimar Republic's most important adversaries, second only to

the German communists, and therefore a major player in German politics.
And in a shrewd effort to exploit that transformation of his stature, Hitler
had used the nine-month prison term imposed on him for causing the riot
to compose *Mein Kampf*, the book that put his program for a resurgent Germany on the main table of the national debate.

Once he achieved power, Hitler turned the date of Germany's defeat
and his own emergence into a huge national holiday, celebrated with a swirling mix of high ceremonial solemnity and gut-busting vulgarity. The throng
about to assemble in Munich would be immense; the one hundred thousand
people Hitler had addressed the day before in Weimar had been little more
than the overflow of the celebrating crowds. Every major Nazi would be in
Munich, as would every district leader, every capo from every Nazi club,
every bullyboy left over from the Sturmabteilung—the soon-to-be bypassed
private army of street thugs that had been key to Hitler's rise—would be
streaming into Munich for two days of celebrating themselves and knocking
back maximum amounts of beer and bratwurst.

So November 9 was an important Nazi day. Since 1938, the world has
remembered it only as something quite different: the anniversary of the
Kristallnacht.

Goebbels was scheduled to leave for the eight-hour train trip to Munich
soon. Hitler would leave Weimar on his private train around noon. They
would meet together in Munich shortly after eight o'clock that night. The
first edicts coming explicitly from the highest level were released at 8:20 on
the evening of November 7.[14]

With only a short time left before leaving the city, Goebbels still had
major decisions to make. He knew that the story of the Paris shooting would
break worldwide within an hour or two at most, and that every reporter in
Paris, including the anti-Nazi democratic press, would be all over it. Goebbels would be effectively out of touch with propaganda headquarters until
evening and he needed to give preliminary orders for handling the breaking
story. The first was very likely to appoint some official of the propaganda

office to be the executive officer in charge of the new campaign. He probably summoned from his office somewhere in the building a specialist in anti-Semitic propaganda named Wolfgang Diewerge.

Diewerge was the perfect man: a promising propaganda tactician who had already provided first-rate service over a similar, though much less important scandal, the assassination of a higher-up in the Swiss branch of the Nazi party by a young Jew named David Frankfurter. Diewerge would be in charge of the immediate response to the Paris shooting and the regime's handling of Herschel Grynszpan and instrumental in the Grynszpan affair in all the tumultuous years to come.[15]

Goebbels rapidly outlined Diewerge's assignment, and before he left the building for his train, he dictated to Diewerge the kind of headlines he expected to see in every German newspaper, beginning with whichever afternoon editions could still clear their front pages. The banner headlines should speak about "Jewish Murder Bandits," he instructed. Herr vom Rath was to be depicted as a shining devote of the Nazi Party. Herschel Grynszpan was to be portrayed as a sociopath, a pawn the puppeteers of the world Jewish conspiracy were using in their frantic effort to sabotage not only the Munich peace, but also just as important (and Goebbels emphasized the point) the movement of the French Foreign Ministry toward friendly accommodation and understanding with the Reich.

Finally, and most important of all, by that evening, Diewerge was to see to it that coverage in every German newspaper and radio broadcast would emphasize that if vom Rath were to die, it was thought that this crime would stir up among the German people "the most serious consequences" for the Jews of Germany.[16] The latter phrase served as a signal to the party faithful that if vom Rath were to die, riots would—or more precisely should—follow.

And so a redeemed Joseph Goebbels began his trip to Munich, stumping along with the limp that the little man managed to make look almost commanding. He went to the Mercedes that would sweep him to his train. On Hitler's orders, in less than an hour he had organized, initiated, and made the appointment necessary to create the largest and most violent anti-Semitic campaign in modern memory.

Given the dominant role that Joseph Goebbels will play in the rest of Herschel's story, this may be the moment to pause and reflect on Goebbels the man, and where Hitler's great propagandist stood politically when the shooting in Paris took place.[17]

Paul Joseph Goebbels was quite possibly the most intelligent of all the senior Nazis. He was certainly the best educated. He was an undeniably brilliant individual who, as the historian Andrew Roberts writes, "is fully deserving of the cliché, 'evil genius.'"

Yet as a youth, Goebbels never aspired to great political power. He hoped for the life of an artist and intellectual. As a young man, Goebbels had a genuine talent for scholarship, and in the days when an advanced degree from Heidelberg was no minor matter, Goebbels proved his talents by earning a doctorate from Heidelberg on eighteenth-century romantic fiction. It was on the basis of this degree that Goebbels was invariably referred to as "Doctor Goebbels" in the halls of Nazi power.[18] But Goebbels could never have been satisfied with the comparative anonymity of scholarship; like Hitler himself, Goebbels felt called to be an artist: a novelist, a playwright, and poet in the grand tradition. He was much less talented for these pursuits than for scholarship, and much of Goebbels's youth was thrown away fruitlessly chasing them.[19] As an imaginative writer, his lack of success was absolute—at least until he became a power in the Nazi party, when he could command "success." Early defeat left him without even the small consolations of obscure publication and amateur productions.[20] For the rest of his life, some part of Goebbels's being was blackened by the bitterness of the failed writer. By the time he met Hitler, that cynicism defined him.

He had grown up a brainy little boy whose schooldays were marked by the tangle of shame and pride, self-contempt and arrogance that is so common among brainy little boys. The mixed blessing of his exceptional IQ was complicated by his physique. Goebbels grew up frail and very short—disadvantages that were clinched by an inoperable clubfoot, giving him a pronounced limp until the end of his days. His limp, his stature, and his brain isolated him. People found them comic and mocked him, and he knew it. In fact, the jokes and insults didn't stop even after Goebbels rose to something not far from omnipotence. Within the Nazi establishment, his nicknames included "the Poison Dwarf" and "Wotan's Mickey Mouse."[21]

Yet if the first phase of his career foundered, the second phase was marked by demonic success, most of it driven by a trait most would find counterintuitive in a man obsessed with exercising great power.

Goebbels was driven by an insatiable need for subservience.

Subservience empowered him. On his own, he threw his energies away, but when he could find a stronger, more self-confident personality and submit to his dominance, Goebbels became not merely functional but unstoppably ingenious and commanding.

And of course the empowering personality Goebbels found was Adolf Hitler.

Goebbels was probably more intelligent than Hitler, and at first, he easily saw through the juvenile incompetence of Hitler's theories about life and history. He also entered politics well to Hitler's left, highly sympathetic to the Soviet Union and appalled when Hitler denounced Bolshevism as a Jewish conspiracy. As for anti-Semitism, Goebbels was certainly anti-Semitic from early youth, but at first he mocked the "primitive" anti-Semitism of such Nazi hate meisters as Julius Streicher. Two of his prime professors and mentors at Heidelberg had been Jewish, and as a student, Goebbels had liked and admired them both.[22] Before Hitler, he was a bigot, but a garden-variety bigot. He was not yet a fanatic.

All this changed under the impact of Hitler's energized charisma. The force of Hitler's personality left Goebbels awestruck. He considered it epochal.[23] He concluded that he could fulfill himself only by subordinating his undisciplined intellect to the pre-intellectual, post-intellectual force of Hitlerian self-assurance. The embittered onetime intellectual became besotted with contempt for the intellect. He was certain that intellect's opposite, Hitler's "genius," was the path for the will to power.

Goebbels found himself in fanaticism. By 1938, his anti-Semitism was second to none. Even his fellow Nazis found it a little nutty. He out-Hitlered Hitler on the Jews. If he had once been bright enough to see through Hitler's theories, now he was bright enough to talk himself into them. In the process, the once aspiring young artist became an implacable enemy of artistic freedom in any form. The sickening truth is that the hyper-philistinism of the regime was not the invention of the crude vulgarians who filled the Nazi ranks. They didn't know or care enough about *Kultur* to hate it. It was the sometime artist and intellectual, the Heidelberg scholar, who organized exhibitions of "decadent" art, ordered book burnings, and virtually murdered Germany's once-famous intellectual culture.[24]

For Goebbels, Nazism was not a political agenda but a faith, an exalted, empowering path to self-confidence and power for both himself and Germany. Goebbels did not just believe in Hitler. He worshipped Hitler.

Goebbels is known as the proponent of the "Big Lie." This deserves some comment: Like many propagandists, Goebbels felt fully justified, morally justified, embracing lies. But ordinary propagandists rationalize that they are lying for the common good, or some transient benefit. For Goebbels, the Lie was exalted. He was lying not just for the truth, but *the* Truth, the transformation of humanity into a new order. That transformed the Lie into the Truth's nearly sacred enabler. As he worshipped Hitler, he worshipped falsehood. An all but mystical faith in the Lie helped Goebbels become one of the great propagandists of the twentieth century. He had quite consciously embraced Satan's prayer: "Evil, be thou my good!"

Not surprisingly, Goebbels's place in Hitler's good graces mattered more to him than anything else. He was faithful beyond the bitter end. He and his wife genuinely believed that life after the defeat of National Socialism would not be worth living. They were also aware that the crimes of Nazism would be revealed. In the bunker, when the inevitable end became obvious to all, Goebbels made no move to save his own skin, and wept bitter tears when Hitler ordered him to leave his side. Goebbels refused that order—"This is the first time I have ever disobeyed the Führer." Hitler relented, and Goebbels stayed in the bunker until Hitler had shot himself. He then left only to die. Before Hitler's suicide, Goebbels requested and got permission for his entire family to join him in there. There, to spare their children life without the Führer, the couple administered drugs that rendered their six children unconscious and then murdered them all with cyanide. This done, Magda and her husband committed suicide together, a few yards from the still-burning corpse of their master.

Goebbels was compulsively lecherous. There could never be too many women, and once the failed dramatist became absolute czar of the German film industry, his casting couch was rarely vacant.

So long as his little flings remained shallow and transient, Magda Goebbels and Hitler just barely tolerated the vagaries of Goebbels's sex life. But in 1937, Goebbels became involved with a Czech actress, Lída Baarová, a rising star in the German film industry.[25] Many women who reached Goebbels's casting couch were ambitious, but Baarová was more than ambitious. She had the will, talent, and looks to sustain a great career, and Goebbels's relationship with her was neither transient nor shallow. Unlike the maternal, dignified Magda, Lída was beautiful and glamorous and had star quality. Everyone said she could be "the new Dietrich," except that unlike the passionately anti-Nazi Marlene, Lída seemed loyal to the Reich. The affair was no secret. Goebbels saw to it that the affair was conspicuous, and he repeatedly appeared at important public appearances with her at his side. Seeing and being seen with the new Dietrich was clearly part of Goebbels's intoxication. Goebbels wanted the world to know that he loved Baarová as he had never loved any woman before. Life was not life without her.

But like many of the unfaithful, Goebbels wanted his wife and his mistress, too. For one thing, he knew that separation would be politically worse than unwise. Goebbels's marriage to Magda had been promoted in the media as the family idyll of the New Germany. For another, he wanted the security of Magda and the thrill of Lída. And so he implored Magda to accept a ménage à trois. After months of enduring the routine rationalizations of infidelity, Magda agreed to try it for a few humiliating days.

They were intolerable. At this point, Magda shrewdly turned for protection to Hitler himself. Hitler's views on sexual morality were political and flexible—consider how long he overlooked the blatant homosexuality of Ernst Röhm. Yet when prudery suited his purposes, he could also show a strict, even priggish side. The purity of the Aryan family was one of National Socialism's most sacrosanct fantasies. Hitler was not ready to see it sullied by Goebbels's infantilism. Magda in turn was at least as besotted with Hitler worship as her husband, maybe even more so. Hitler felt special protective affection for Magda Goebbels, whom he saw as an ideal National Socialist mother and matron.

Magda's humiliation left Hitler enraged. In his eyes the affair was a squalid betrayal of the regime and therefore of himself. Goebbels was summoned and ordered to terminate the relationship, immediately. Goebbels groveled. He begged for compassion. He pleaded for the tender purity of his love for Baarová. Hitler dismissed all these sentiments with curt contempt.

Even after this confrontation, Goebbels tried to finagle some way to keep both his goddess and his god. No go. On October 21, just two weeks before Herschel shot vom Rath in Paris, the exasperated Hitler told Goebbels that enough was enough: Baarová had to leave Goebbels's life immediately and forever, or Goebbels's career would be over immediately and forever.

That did it. Baarová left Goebbels's life immediately and forever.

November 7 fell two weeks after this confrontation. Hitler's decision to give Goebbels a central role in the new anti-Semitic campaign came as redemption, even salvation.

The Führer needed him again. Ordered to demonize Herschel Grynszpan and prepare for the emergence of Germany as a criminal state, Goebbels's season in the hell of Hitler's displeasure was at an end.

Arrest and Fame

Everything was happening at once.

While Hitler and Goebbels were plotting their new anti-Semitic strategy, Herschel was being booked at the precinct station; Ambassador von Welczeck was returning from his morning constitutional; Ernst vom Rath was being admitted to the nearby Clinique de l'Alma; and Georges Bonnet, the foreign minister of France, was reacting with alarm.

It took only a few minutes for officer François Autret to lead Herschel to the dreary stronghold of time-begrimed stone that was the precinct station for the quartier des Invalides et de l'École Militaires. The boy was booked and searched. The police emptied Herschel's pockets and found loose change: 38 francs (about $1 in 1938). It was all that remained of the 200 francs Uncle Abraham had so frantically shoved into his coat pocket when the boy stormed out the night before. There were also three invitations to the dance at the Sportsclub Aurore.[1]

The money and the invitations were innocent enough, but everything else on the kid was incriminating. There was a box of shells for the revolver that Herschel had dropped on the floor of vom Rath's office, the never-filed "purchase declaration" that M. Carpe had warned Herschel must be submitted to the police, and most important, two postcards: the one that Berta had sent from Zbaszyn, "You have undoubtedly heard of our great misfortune," and the still-unstamped picture postcard, the portrait of the assassin as a young man, "To my dear parents . . . I could not do otherwise . . . may God forgive me . . . I must protest so that the whole world hears my protest . . ." From a legal point of view, those two postcards were proof of premeditation and political motivation: legal issues that would be in play during the weeks to come. Yet to Herschel, premeditation and political motivation were everything. They were what made his protest what he wanted it to be.

Somewhere around 10:20, having peacefully completed his morning exercise, Ambassador von Welczeck must have returned to his embassy, only to discover that he had missed all the excitement. The shooting left him very agitated. Thinking back, the ambassador recalled his non-encounter that morning on the embassy stairs: how as he had descended toward the street, he had swept past a diminutive young person, an obvious nobody, and granted him scarcely a glance. The killer! Was it possible that anything—or anyone—so insignificant as this diminutive visitor could deflect the new understanding that was brewing between Germany and France?

Suddenly, the Führer himself was on the line.

Some of what the Führer said to the ambassador must be inferred from von Welczeck's actions when the call was complete. Either immediately before or immediately after speaking to Hitler, von Welczeck sent an agent—a counselor named Lorz—from the embassy to the precinct station with a dual mission: first, to determine whether the crime had indeed been premeditated and politically motivated, and second, whether its perpetrator was indeed a Jew.[2]

This insertion of a German agent into French police work was illegal. When the press got wind of Lorz's visit, a cover story was issued, claiming that while Ambassador von Welczeck had *wanted* to send such an agent to participate in Grynszpan's interrogation, he graciously withdrew his request when he was told that the move would be illegal. His informant, he said, was Foreign Minister Bonnet himself.[3] In short, the reverse of what really happened.

—

The man in charge of the station was a commissioner named Monneret. When Monneret greeted Lorz, it had been a little more than an hour since the shooting. "I saw," Lorz reported to his superiors, "that the perpetrator had not yet been questioned."

Herschel was brought into the room. He was pale. And he was small. Lorz reported that though Herschel had gone through puberty, he looked like a child.

Speaking in French, Lorz posed his first question: Why had he committed his crime?

Herschel answered that he was seeking revenge for "the whole world" on the "*sales boches.*"

And why did he want revenge?

Because of what the Nazis were doing to his people.

And was Herschel a Jew?

He was a Jew. And he had done the shooting because he was seeking justice for his people—especially for his family.

The Nazis needed nothing more.[4]

After speaking with Hitler, von Welczeck also set out to exaggerate and maximize the significance and scale of the crime. It could not be left as a matter of a distraught child shooting a minor official. "The Jew Grynszpan's" action must be presented to the world as much more important and dangerous than that.

Therefore someone made the decision to claim that Herschel's target had been the ambassador himself, a lie contradicted by Bräuer's report to Berlin from twenty-five minutes before: "At 9:30 a very young man approached an embassy staff member and *asked to speak to one of the secretaries...*" [my emphasis].

Von Welczeck promptly set out to disseminate this fraudulent claim.

Here is Georges Bonnet's summary of a meeting between himself and Ambassador von Welczeck at noon that day:

> Count von Welczeck asked to see me on a matter of extreme urgency. I received him immediately. The ambassador was in a highly emotional state. He told me that at the moment he was leaving the embassy early that morning, he heard at the door a young man asking to see the ambassador. Looking back and seeing a very young man, the ambassador had supposed he could be seen by one of his secretaries.[5]

Von Welczeck was clearly lying: Neither Bräuer nor Lorz nor the ambassador himself had heard about any threat made to him personally.

Yet von Welczeck's claim to have been Herschel's prime target was plausible. Many modern histories claim that Herschel came intending to kill the ambassador, and it seems that killing the ambassador did play a part in Herschel's musings before committing the crime.[6] Later, in an interview with *The New York Times*, von Welczeck or one of his subordinates let his imagination run wild. Either the ambassador or a spokesman told the *Times* reporter that not only had von Welczeck been the prime target, but that Herschel had come to the embassy determined to kill everyone in the building. The *Times* published a statement, fabricated by someone at the embassy, that Herschel had purportedly made on the scene. Even though he'd managed to kill only one German, the story claimed, "he was satisfied and 'lucky to get even one German, though a bit removed from the top.'"[7]

Von Welczeck and Bonnet were determined to keep this incident from damaging the secretly burgeoning new understanding between France and Germany, a Franco-German rapprochement that would be even more cordial than the Munich Pact. Hitler's recent speeches had been very easy on France, insisting that there was no basis for hostility or suspicion between France and the Reich. Yet Hitler did keep referring to that thorn in the side of the Reich, fifty thousand mainly Jewish refugees living in Paris, all of them poisoning public opinion with their Jewish lies about National Socialism.[8]

The two countries were dancing around an understanding implicit in all their negotiations, and yet unsayable by either. The underlying idea was somehow to secure French immunity from German invasion in return for France giving Germany what was called "a free hand in the East"—the same free hand that had been given to Hitler at Munich. France was already bound by treaty obligations to defend Poland if the Nazis attacked. The unstated idea of a "free hand in the east" was to find a way for France to ignore this obligation and permit Germany to take military possession of Poland. Germany could not admit (though everyone knew) that it intended to invade and conquer Poland. And France could not admit (though everyone knew) that it intended to buy its safety by letting them do it.[9]

Hitler had ended his call to Paris by informing von Welczeck that he had decided to dispatch his own physician, a smooth young doctor named Karl Brandt, who would travel to Paris by the "fastest means possible," designated as the dictator's personal representative at vom Rath's bedside. Karl Brandt had been traveling with Hitler in Weimar—whenever Hitler was in public, as his personal physician, Brandt was always in the background, a few watchful steps behind—and he would have the privilege of riding in Hitler's private train car when the Atlas left Weimar for its late-afternoon stop: Nuremberg. From Nuremberg, Brandt would separate from the entourage and depart that evening for Paris, flying all night in one of Hitler's private Junkers, accompanied by a professor of surgery from Munich, and arriving at Le Bourget airport at dawn.[10]

Such were the "fastest means possible" in 1938.

Hitler's motives for sending Brandt were surely multiple. For public consumption in the world press, he wanted to dramatize the high importance he attached to the life of the young diplomat. Brandt was also commissioned to inform the wounded man that Hitler had promoted him from being third secretary of the legation to first. But of course Hitler had a darker purpose. He wanted to know with certainty whether and when vom Rath would die. The propaganda blitz he had set in motion with Goebbels depended on it, and it is clear that Goebbels's plan to exploit vom Rath's death for a massive anti-Semitic campaign was explained to Brandt during his ride to Nuremberg with Hitler. Brandt arrived in Paris knowing more than he could say—and his mission in Paris would also be marked by an unexpected medical discovery.

As Herschel was being booked, Ernst vom Rath was conveyed by ambulance to the Clinique de l'Alma on the nearby rue de l'Université, with which Dr. Amédée Baumgartner, one of the most distinguished surgeons in Europe, happened to be affiliated. Georges Bonnet, intensely alarmed and eager to show French solicitude, immediately intervened, asking Baumgartner to take charge of the case.

While vom Rath still lay collapsed on the corridor floor at the embassy, a colleague in an adjacent office had given him first aid. He was awake for the first aid, and was even able to breathe a few sentences about the attack, but by the time the wounded man was in the ambulance, vom Rath's grip on consciousness was feeble, and it was clear to Dr. Claas that his wounds might be life threatening. By the time he was admitted to the Clinique de l'Alma, Ernst vom Rath was unconscious.

Herschel had emptied the magazine of his pistol, firing five shots point-blank at vom Rath. The kick of his small pistol made Herschel's shooting hand flail so wildly that only two of the five shots aimed at vom Rath's torso actually connected with the man himself. One of the bullets turned out to be relatively innocuous. At the sight of the gun and the sound of the first shot, vom Rath had leapt from his chair while Herschel, in his naïveté, had kept firing while he was still seated. Thus, both bullets penetrated the lawyer's torso on an upward path. One pierced his lower left side and went streaking through the thoracic cavity, miraculously missing everything im-

portant until it buried itself in the muscle of his right shoulder. If this had
been the only bullet, vom Rath might well have lived.

The other bullet made up for it. It, too, entered by penetrating vom
Rath's left side, but a little lower down. Then it ripped through a direct hit of
vom Rath's spleen, smashed past his pancreas, perforated his stomach, and
stopped only by burying itself in his upper back. Spleen, pancreas, stomach:
That trajectory was so dangerous that discussion of moving vom Rath to
a better-equipped hospital was cut short when Baumgartner said the patient would certainly die en route. So the surgery was performed in the Clinique de l'Alma. The operation began at twelve thirty. It lasted three hours.
Baumgartner removed vom Rath's shattered spleen, sutured the perforated
stomach, and removed blood clots. Physicians later assessing Baumgartner's
performance were impressed: It was "complex and daring."[11]

But there is a mystery buried inside the admirable medical long shot of
Baumgartner's operation. During the surgery, while inside vom Rath's thoracic cavity, it seems that Baumgartner may have discovered a preexisting
case of advanced stomach and intestinal tuberculosis. This meant that even
if vom Rath had otherwise had some remote chance of surviving the pistol
wounds, he was a very sick man—in fact, a dying man—*before* Herschel
shot him.

The source of this claim was none other than Dr. Karl Brandt himself,
who confessed as much to a friend in Paris during the war. Here is what he
is quoted as having said:

> Despite the injury, vom Rath probably could have been saved if he had
> not been suffering from severe tuberculosis of the stomach and intestines.
> I immediately discovered this during the examination of the patient, and
> looked at my two French colleagues in a questioning manner. When they
> remained silent, I whispered only one word, "Phthisis?" [Consumption?]
> They both of them nodded briefly and in earnest. It was not in our interest
> that this should become public knowledge, because it would otherwise
> have disturbed the causal link between the shots of the Jew Grunspan

[sic] and the death of the young diplomat. We felt it was very proper in the period thereafter, when Dr. Goebbels set in motion his action against the Jews [*Judenaktion in Szene setzte*], that the French doctors continued to remain silent.[12]

The key sentence here is worth repeating: "It was not in our interest that this should become public knowledge, because it would otherwise have disturbed the causal link between the shots of the Jew Grunspan [sic] and the death of the young diplomat."

Brandt's claim may or may not be believed. An autopsy was performed on vom Rath's body on November 9; death was attributed to the second bullet. Intestinal tuberculosis may or may not have been discovered.[13] But if Brandt truly believed vom Rath could have been saved, the truth about vom Rath's tuberculosis was suppressed for a political reason: It did not suit Nazi propaganda's need to attribute his death exclusively to "the shots of the Jew Grunspan." And the French doctors were somehow complicit in this medical cover-up. Most importantly Brandt confessed that Hitler had told Brandt about Goebbels's plan to use vom Rath's death as the pretext for a staged action against the Jews *before* the doctor left Nuremberg on November 7.

After Lorz left the precinct station, Commissioner Monneret began to question Herschel in earnest, and Herschel responded to Monneret's questions with a combination of exactly detailed truth and a large number of foggy, easily exposed lies. He told the truth about every aspect of the crime and every step of the way after he left Abraham and Chawa's apartment until he was turned over to Officer Monneret. His lies and evasions, on the other hand, had to do with every aspect of his newly illegal residency in France. He admitted that he had received an expulsion order from the prefect of police, but claimed to have obeyed it: leaving France to spend time with his uncle in Essen, Germany. A simple glance into his Polish passport—there were no stamps indicating entry into Germany or any other country—proved this false. He claimed that in the months since August, his aunt and uncle had been unaware of his whereabouts. Since it was evident that he had not left Paris since August, this lie was immediately highly questionable, even though in some versions of his story, Herschel was portrayed as a homeless drifter. Abraham and Chawa tried to tell the same lie in a statement to the press, but the press was not fooled. One reporter merely approached the concierge at the rue des Petites-Écuries and asked if she had seen a small seventeen-year-old coming and going.

She had.[14]

The press mirrored Inspector Monneret's interest in Herschel's status as an illegal resident. The day after the shooting, Herschel's status as an undocumented alien dominates the headline of *Le Figaro* and is just as prominent as the sinking condition of Herr vom Rath. Ever since the Anschluss, the chauvinist side of the French national personality had been ascendant. On every side, from the fascist-leaning right to the communist-leaning unions on the left, fear and resentment had mounted to a degree that made Daladier's condemnation of aliens filling Paris one of his most important commitments as premier of a new government. From 1933 to 1937, enlightened France had opened its doors to refugees from Germany. Even Herschel's slippery entry without a visa had been forgiven with a small fine and a talking-to. But once the public glimpsed how many Jews would be fleeing Austria, that enlightenment guttered out and was replaced with punitive chauvinism—the same chauvinism that was responsible for the Ministry of the Interior's rejection of Herschel's completely unobjectionable application for residency. Now, by decrees passed under Daladier, it was a crime punishable with a prison sentence to harbor an illegal alien—a law under which Abraham and Chawa were promptly arrested.[15]

But when it came to his interrogation over the crime, Herschel answered with lucidity and honesty: about the Hôtel de Suez where he had spent the previous night, about the purchase of the pistol at A la Fine Lame, about the dance at Sportsclub Aurore, even the exact timing of his ride on the Paris Métro to the stop nearest the embassy. He was interrogated before a lawyer represented him, so a number of his answers were, from a lawyer's point of view, naïve. But they were the truth.

I said to him: "You are a filthy Kraut ['*un sale boche*'] and now I will give you the document in the name of twelve thousand persecuted Jews." I pulled the revolver, which I had hidden in the inside pocket of my jacket, and fired: At the moment when I pulled the weapon, the attaché rose from his seat. However, I fired all the bullets. I aimed at the middle of the body. My victim hit me with his fist and left the room, calling for help. I remained in the office, where I was arrested a few moments later . . . I received the postcard which was in my wallet on Thursday [the postcard from Berta, which Herschel had received on November 3, four days before], and at that moment I decided to kill a member of the embassy in protest. I knew of the subjugation of my fellow Jews from the press. That was the only reason which caused me to take the step I took.[16]

By the end of the morning, Commissioner Monneret had heard enough to make his next move: revisiting the scene. Surrounded by detectives, he would walk Herschel through everywhere he had been over the last eighteen hours: the rue des Petites-Écuries, the dance, the place where he parted from Nat, A la Fine Lame, the Hotel, Tout Va Bien, the embassy. The idea was that while this trail was still fresh, Monneret could put Herschel's story in the context of real information, real witnesses. But first they had to get the boy into a police car. The cops would have to form a flying wedge to get him past the photographers outside. A police convoy pulled up in front of the building, and suddenly the assassin was there in the doorway, surrounded by detectives, a diminutive kid in a raincoat, crossing perhaps thirty feet to a waiting car through the blaze of a hundred flashbulbs.

The press was all over the story. Within twenty minutes of the first anonymous tip, swarms of reporters and photographers were piling into the embassy press room; others were staking out a press deathwatch in the lobby of the Clinique de l'Alma, while another gaggle was blocking the sidewalk outside the dreary portal to the precinct house of Invalides et de l'École Militaires.

Herschel was always uncannily photogenic, and he was never more so than on that twenty-foot walk through that gauntlet of the Star Graphics. Every picture from that perp walk is eloquent with pure adolescent agony.

At that moment, Herschel did not see the world he used to know and would never see again. Instead he saw *light*, a world-whitening assault of blinding flashes from bulbs on a hundred news cameras aimed and fired in unison when he appeared in the doorway. By reflex Herschel pulled up his cuffed hands—perhaps to protect his eyes, perhaps to conceal his face. The child who had wanted to make the whole world hear had been looking for fame. But he was not ready for fame like this. The cops pushed through to the big revving patrol car, and by the time they got him through that corridor of electronic fire, Herschel had been transformed. A new life had begun. He was no longer a teenaged nobody living in a walk-up with his aunt and uncle. The corridor of fire was about to make him, briefly, a world celebrity, a pawn to be played in the high politics of war and terror and in the Holocaust that was coming.

Two Speeches

Herschel would never again see the light of freedom. For the rest of his short life, he would remain a high-profile inmate in one or another prison or concentration camp. The French held him at Fresnes prison outside Paris, a huge penitentiary with an "advanced" juvenile facility, complete with group cabins and a soccer field. But the boy was never tried in France, and when that nation fell in 1940, the conquering Germans pursued him in a wild chase through the collapsing countryside until at last they took him prisoner and flew him to Berlin, where he was held in Gestapo headquarters or various Nazi concentration camps until his mysterious death. Wherever they imprisoned him, the Nazis kept him alive and well—the safest Jew in Germany—the better to pillory him as the designated defendant in the great show trial that Hitler and Goebbels wanted to stage, proving to the world that "world Jewry" had used him as its pawn to provoke a second world war. Yet wherever he was kept incarcerated, Herschel remained, child and man, someone whom the zeitgeist had transformed into a human symbol in the greatest moral struggle of his era, moved from prison to prison and used for both good and evil in the struggle over the fate of civilization.

Herschel passed the first night of his incarceration in Paris locked in the legendary gloom of La Santé prison, where he had been taken at midnight after having gone through a last high-level round of interrogation at the headquarters of the French Sûreté on the Île de la Cité. Late that night, he was photographed in the hallways, still in his three-piece suit and his beige raincoat, with his soft brown eyes furrowed into hard focus as he was once again led through the throng of the press with its flaring flashbulbs. At the Sûreté a high official questioned him. His statement was recorded and the record shows he had begun to slightly embellish the more precise account of the crime he had given to Commissioner Monneret:

> After I received [Berta's postcard] I planned an act of vengeance and pro-test against a representative of the Third Reich. I wanted to create a stir great enough so that the world would not ignore it, because Germany's conduct provoked me beyond measure. The person himself was of slight importance . . . [Note that Herschel did not claim he had come to the embassy intending to kill the ambassador, but "a representative of the Third Reich."] I . . . took out my revolver from my suit coat pocket and before firing, I said, "Isn't it enough that Jews have to suffer so severely from German persecution, and that they are thrown into concentration camps? Now they are being expelled as if they were nothing but stray dogs." [Herschel's shout at vom Rath—"you're a *sale boche*, and in the name of twelve thousand Jews, *here* is your document"—has been trans-formed into a little speech.] Wounded by the bullets, the official [Herschel probably did not yet know his victim's name] put both his hands on his abdomen, and he still had the strength to give me a punch in the jaw, calling me, at the same time, "dirty Jew." He made a rush for the door of his office, crying out "Help!" I wanted to avenge myself further for the epithet he had just bestowed on me, and I tried to hurl the weapon at his face, but I missed him.[1]

Herschel was already tweaking his story for public consumption.

As well he might. On the morning of November 8, he woke up famous.

His anguished young face was on the front page of every newspaper in the world. He had wanted to seize the world's attention, and as the day dawned at La Santé—while Ernst vom Rath lay dying in the Clinique de l'Alma and the Nazi party gathered for its obscene festival in Munich—Herschel did have the world's attention. He was scheduled to appear before an examining magistrate that afternoon. The hearing would be public; the press would be there in force. His moment had come. He had become an assassin in order to make this speech.

He was brought before the examining magistrate at three o'clock. The judge, Jean Tesnière, was a jurist known for his expertise in juvenile cases.[2] The proceeding was not unlike an arraignment under the common law. Judge Tesnière's task was to determine whether a crime had been committed and whether there was reasonable cause to hold Herschel as its alleged perpetrator. Since the answers to those two questions were self-evident, the occasion was in effect the moment for Herschel to transform his confession into a statement. Making that statement, the boy managed to summon up some unexpected eloquence.

Judge Tesnière's chambers were crowded with lawyers, the press, and the police. No less than three detectives escorted Herschel into the room. The day before, his frantic Uncle Salomon had hired two undistinguished Yiddish-speaking lawyers to represent Herschel as well as Abraham and Chawa, who by then were both under arrest for harboring an illegal alien. When questioned about his motives, Herschel himself addressed the judge directly. All reports indicate that he spoke in fumbling albeit moving French. The German-speaking judge several times had to help him find his words. He was drained from the day before; he was manifestly severely depressed.[3] Yet he spoke with some power. At no point did Herschel attempt to sidestep responsibility for the crime or its essential nature. Yes, it was premeditated, and yes, its motive was political. The question he addressed before the judge was *why* he had premeditated this political act.

Here is what two newspapers recorded of his speech to the judge:

The Jewish people have a right to live, and I do not understand all the sufferings that the Germans are inflicting on them. I don't understand this long martyrdom. If you are a Jew, you can obtain nothing, attempt nothing, and hope for nothing. You are hunted like an animal. Why this martyrdom?[4]

Another newspaper, *Le Temps*, quoted him as follows:

It was not for hatred or for vengeance against any particular person that I acted, but because of my love for my parents and for my people who were unjustly subjected to outrageous treatment. Nevertheless, this act was distasteful to me, and I deeply regret it. However, I had no other means of demonstrating my feelings. It was the constantly gnawing idea of the suffering of my race that obsessed me. For twenty-eight years, my parents resided in Hanover. They had set up a modest business, which was destroyed overnight. They were stripped of everything and expelled. It is not, after all, a crime to be Jewish. I am not a dog. I have the right to live. My people have a right to exist on this earth. And yet everywhere they are hunted down like animals.

Later:

I did not wish to kill. I could not consent to live like a dog in the German Reich. When I committed this act, I was obeying a superior and inexplicable force. What's more, vom Rath, the secretary at the embassy, called me a dirty Jew.[5]

Judge Tesnière was apparently a little perplexed by Herschel's claim that vom Rath had called him a "dirty Jew." "Was that before or after the shooting?" the judge asked. "I couldn't tell you exactly. My mind was in great emotional turmoil."[6]

More significant is the claim that Herschel was "obeying a superior and inexplicable force" when he shot vom Rath. Many years later, Herschel's German-speaking attorney, Serge Weill-Goudchaux, would recollect his conviction that Herschel understood himself to be a vehicle—a pawn—animated by that "superior and inexplicable force." "Grynszpan was a mystic—God having chosen him to save his people," Weill-Goudchaux wrote in 1960, "a very intelligent and very appealing autodidact."[7] It is of course possible to see Herschel's mysticism as some sort of manic delusion, yet whether he was or was not motivated by "a mysterious and inexplicable force," Herschel's speech before the examining magistrate was, in its way, inspired. He spoke in a state of exhaustion, and in an alien tongue, but he rose above his situation and really did say what in his adolescent grandiosity he wanted the world to hear. And the world did hear. One day later it would *see* what he was saying—"this long martyrdom . . . stripped of everything . . . hunted like an animal"—in the horrific scenes of the Kristallnacht itself, which would make Herschel's statement read like prophecy.

Because the Kristallnacht was waiting to happen.

On November 8, as Herschel was making his tremulous speech before the examining magistrate, two programs of terror were being prepared in Munich. The first was to be short-term terror of the coming great pogrom, focusing on the Sturmabteilung (SA) and its leading role. But long-term terror was also being prepared, using the more lethal and sophisticated SS to draw into early focus what loomed in the distance as the coming Holocaust. On the nights of November 9 and 10, all across Germany and Austria, the SA would burst into what Hitler himself called its "spree" of brute violence. Yet at the very same time that the SA was careening into the most violent moments of its own night of nights, a candlelit midnight ceremony would take place before the Führer in the vast plaza known as the Fernheldenhalle. There the SS was to have its power enhanced by the solemn swearing in of more than a thousand new recruits to its officer corps. The spectacle of these officers taking their oath would be a characteristically impressive example of the fascist aesthetic of the crowd—that choreography of mass man, in which the Nazi sense of massed power as beauty was carried to symphonic excesses. And it would take place at precisely the time that the synagogues of Germany were being torched, Jewish shops and homes were being trashed, Jewish women were being raped, and Jewish children were being terrorized in yet another piece of mass man at work, though the theme was not fascist ceremony but fascist violence.

Movement Day itself would fall on November 9, and in Munich the entire leadership of the Nazi Party was assembled around its Führer, along with the grassroots leadership—the local leaders of the homegrown gangs of thugs who comprised most of the SA. On November 9, these leaders and their bands would spearhead (though it was soon joined by others, including some of the SS) the nationwide wave of arson, murder, larceny, and mayhem that would transform the relation of German and Austrian Jews to the criminal government that ruled them. In Europe and America, the night would dash the delusive dreams about peace and sanity in Central Europe that had marked the Munich Pact before its betrayal. The dream of peace that whole populations had so ecstatically embraced with Munich's sacrifice of Czechoslovakia would be dispelled through one night of lawless terror.

At virtually the same time that Herschel was explaining his motives to the examining magistrate, Heinrich Himmler was also delivering a speech. It was delivered to the crème of these SS recruits—a group of the most promising new officers in the corps. In it Himmler outlined in broad strokes the thinking that would undergird the Holocaust—except in this insane harangue, he outlined it in reverse, warning his men about the Jewish plot to exterminate the German *Volk*, a genocide of the Gentiles.

Himmler's speech did not even mention the shooting in Paris. His focus was on the big picture and what he informed those present would be the world-transforming events of the coming decade.[8]

According to Himmler, the coming event of the next decade would be the apocalypse. As a Nazi apocalypse, it naturally had to be a *racial* apocalypse, a cataclysmic racial war, a final battle between the Aryan races and all their enemies—namely Freemasons, Marxists, Catholics, and above all others, international Jewry. The Jews were the key enemy, because with its sinister cleverness, the demonic force of the Semitic mind lay behind all the other threats. The Jews covertly controlled all the others. "I consider the Jews as the driving force," Himmler told his men, "the essence of everything that is negative."[9] International Jewry was also the force behind all the democratic governments. Its covert control extended to the governments of Britain and the United States; it controlled all the decadent democracies. In fact, international Jewry was, in its covert way, omnipotent and ubiquitous.

But thanks to the Führer, international Jewry was running scared. In the form of the Third Reich it confronted the resurgence of the nation it believed it had conquered with the defeat of Germany at the end of the First World War in 1918. Supine Germany had awakened from its dogmatic slumbers; National Socialism had made it what every self-respecting state should be: formally and implacably anti-Semitic. Under the direction of the Führer, the covert Jewish grip on Germany after its defeat in 1918 was being smashed. "The Jews cannot remain in Germany," Himmler made plain; "it is only a matter of years and we shall increasingly drive them out with unparalleled and ruthless brutality."[10]

But driving the Jews out of the Reich—since in 1938 exile rather than extermination was still the official policy of the Third Reich—was only a *temporary* solution to the Jewish problem. Driven out, the Jews would settle in every democratic country from Belgium to Sweden to Britain, the United States, and France. When the devious power of the Jews over "everything negative" began to be felt, the countries flooded with these Jewish refugees would wake up to how they were being manipulated and become as anti-Semitic as the Reich.[11] This was already happening, Himmler confidently claimed, in Italy, Czechoslovakia, and Poland. He explained the secret logic behind Hitler's policy of expelling all Jews in the Reich. It was to create a flood of refugees that would dangerously infiltrate Sweden, Norway, Holland, and Belgium, at which point those countries overrun by their scheming covert Jewish enemies would wake up to the danger and themselves become violently anti-Semitic. In fact, with time, the policy of expulsion would engender worldwide anti-Semitism. "They would have no more place for the Jews."

Such, Himmler argued, was the course of events that world Jewry feared above any other. Evidence of its fear was the stream of propaganda hostile to the New Germany flowing from the democracies. The Führer wanted only peace, but the New Order—the reassertion of the Aryan race—was a lethal threat to Jewish hegemony in Central Europe. To conquer that threat, international Jewry planned to provoke a war between the Reich, on the one hand, and an alliance of the Jewish-dominated Soviet Union and the democracies on the other.

This war would be apocalyptic. It would be something more than one political entity gaining dominance over another. It would be a battle to the death. It would be a war between extermination of the Gentiles or—such was the implication—the extermination of the Jews.

Here Himmler's paranoiac fantasy entered nightmare territory. The key political fact of the era, he claimed, was that the Jews planned a genocide to exterminate Gentile Germany. This genocide would be the consequence if the Reich were to be defeated in the coming war. Himmler's biographer explains:

> The Jews thought they could eliminate the danger to themselves by destroying the fountainhead of anti-Semitism: Germany. If Germany lost this apocalyptic struggle, there would be nothing left for the Germans but to he herded into "Indian-style reservations"—i.e. concentration camps—where they would be starved and butchered whether or not they had supported the Nazis. Having conjured up a powerful Jewish race, fearful for its own survival, he found it easy to suspect a planned Jewish offensive against Germany. Then he used the Jewish threat to Germany as justification for future measures against the Jews.[12]

Himmler went on. The threat to this Jewish hegemony and its control of the Western world was National Socialist Germany. Hitler threatened the secret omnipotence of the Jews. Above all, they were responsible for Germany's loss in 1918, and now the Jews were alarmed by the spectacle of a new Germany and the threat it posed to their otherwise ubiquitous power. The Führer wanted only peace, but peace would be impossible as long as the Jews remained devoted to destroying the German threat. They would stop at nothing to repress and destroy the New Germany. More—they were determined not merely to defeat Germany. They wanted to annihilate it. They looked at Aryan Germany with one ultimate goal in mind: genocide.[13] They understood that only the destruction of Germany itself would save their power and protect their cosmopolitan diaspora across all nationalities. They were therefore doing all they could to lead their puppets into a cataclysmic war with Germany in which the outcome was either to annihilate or be annihilated.[14]

The SS was the prime weapon the Führer had created for this struggle. The men in this room were the leading edge against the coming war against the Jews. This, Himmler pointed out, was likely to precipitate a moral crisis in the minds of many, including many in that very room. Himmler was at pains to warn his recruits about the moral crisis they would confront as leaders in this war against the Jews. As they protected civilization against the murderous battle to come, they would have to pursue the struggle ruthlessly and without pity. They might well feel a natural moral inhibition against the killing and violence that the job would force them to face. They must remember that they were defending their own people—their families, their children, and their comrades—against the even more terrible violence that the Jews were planning to perpetrate against the German *Volk*. He told the SS Gruppenführer that they might be perplexed when he himself—acting against his own conscience and personal feelings—ordered them to punish and eliminate the enemy at a level of ruthless action they had never before imagined was possible or even conceivable.

Merely to summarize this little-known speech, with its anticipation and rationalization of the Holocaust and with its insane reversal of the role of victim and victimizer, leaves one breathless. "I have the right to live," Herschel had told Judge Tesnière. "My people have the right to exist on this earth." Standing before his judge in the darkness of prophecy, he spoke more truly than he could possibly have known.

10

The Whole World Hears

Ernst vom Rath clung to what was left of his life for two and half anguished days. During that time he drifted back and forth between unconsciousness, semi-consciousness, and being alert enough to recognize the people in his room and say a few words to them. His family—his father, mother, and brother Günter—was at his side, arriving from Cologne on the morning of November 8, by which time Doctors Brandt and Magnus from Germany were also present. Dr. Baumgartner and the German doctors released regular bulletins to the gaggle of the press crowded into the Clinique de l'Alma's lobby on the deathwatch, hungry for scraps to feed to the world's front pages. Ernst's condition after the surgery of November 7 was a slow, steady, and irreversible decline. During the morning of November 9, his family arrived early, followed by Dr. Baumgartner and later by Brandt and Magnus. The approaching end was obvious. Around 3 p.m. that afternoon, vom Rath slipped into a coma. At 4:25 p.m., he died. Present in the room were the family and Karl Brandt. Brandt immediately left the room to inform Hitler.[1]

Herschel could not have known that vom Rath's death would be so very convenient for Hitler, nor could he have known that his action would be the pretext for the most destructive pogrom in history. Least of all could he have known that by a savage irony that pogrom would indeed shock the world into recognition of Nazi anti-Semitism as nothing previous had managed to do.

I must protest so that the whole world hears my protest.

Well, the whole world *did* hear Herschel's protest. Hitler *made* the whole world hear it. Five weeks after Munich, the horrors of the Kristallnacht would be the blunt instrument that shattered democratic illusions about Nazism. For many of the Munich Pact's true believers, that night brought the hideous dropping away of the veil. Appeasement, once almost universally acclaimed, stood revealed as the intoxicating delusion it was, and only people most committed to that delusion—often dubiously committed people, like Georges Bonnet—clung to it. Increasingly in Britain, in America, in all the democracies, the truth became obvious. Hitler was fanatic to the point of madness. War was inevitable.[2]

Remorse was one of the many passions that swept through Herschel in the aftermath. "God, oh my God! I did not want that. Listen to me, I'll explain to you, how it happened and tell it to others who might call down on me God's curse."[3]

A week after the Kristallnacht, Goebbels's propaganda machine transformed the funeral of Ernst vom Rath into a massively choreographed national event, the purpose of which was to proclaim vom Rath—he who had called Hitler "the antichrist"—a passionate Nazi believer and one of the first stalwarts to fall in the Jews' war against the Reich.[4]

On November 9—Movement Day—Munich swarmed with Nazis the way an infection swarms in a festering wound. The toxic threads gathered together in that city ran deep into the whole body politic. The SA, the Nazi Party's paramilitary organization, its very own army, was entrenched in every city and hamlet of the Reich. On November 9, all the

leaders of that evil network had assembled in Munich. The countless ca-
pos of the Nazi Party filled every hotel, every rooming house, and every
bed where a Nazi could be billeted. Of course, the entire senior echelon of
the ruling party was likewise on hand: Goebbels, Göring, Himmler, and
Hitler himself.

The city was red and black with fluttering swastika banners hanging from every edifice. The social atmosphere was an uneasy mixture of
gut-busting vulgarity in the streets and beer halls merging with pompous
pagan ceremony sleek with a fascistic sense of scale coupled with an equally
fascistic worship of mass man.

To the Nazi propagandists, Germany's ashen downfall had led to a
gleaming rebirth; the humiliation of defeat had empowered the phoenix of
the New Germany. Nazi planners did everything in their power to sanctify
that resurgence. For the Nazis, on November 9, 1923, the salvation of the
nation had begun in earnest. Above all, that salvation entailed a rescue of
Germany from the defeat that, in Hitler's paranoid world view, was the work
of what he called the "November criminals": the assortment of parliamen-
tarians and revolutionaries involved in the abdication and overthrow of the
Kaiser.

In other words, the Jews.

On the night of November 8, Hitler had made an appearance at the Bürgerbräukeller—where the 1923 putsch had begun—delivering a tirade against
anti-German sentiment latent in France and Germany, which he claimed lay
located just beneath the deceptive surface of appeasement. Hitler admitted
that as of November 9, the democracies under Chamberlain and Bonnet
were genuinely seeking peace with the Reich. But what about those enemies
of the Munich peace, Winston Churchill, Anthony Eden, and Duff Cooper? Who knew when some capricious turn in British politics would put one
of these demons into power?

Alan Steinweis summarizes Hitler's thinking on that date:

Privately, Hitler had already decided that a German war against Britain and France was probably inevitable. The goal of his foreign policy was not to prevent such a war but rather to throw anti-German hard-liners in both countries off balance, and to make sure that the German people understood that the war had been forced upon them by international Jewry and its lackeys.[5]

For Hitler, appeasement was a transient tactic, smoke and mirrors. His thinking was exactly in line with the lurid apocalyptic prophecies about a murderous showdown between Aryans and Jews—the vision that Himmler had presented to a roomful of generals from the SS a few hours before Herschel stood before the examining magistrate in Paris, stammering in his maimed French: "My people have a right to exist on this earth."

Hitler greatly enjoyed his evening in the Bürgerbräukeller. It was all very convivial. From the beer hall, he went (with Goebbels among others) to the Führerbau in Munich's Nazi Party headquarters, and from there adjourned to the nearby Café Heck, which, creature of the night that he was, he did not leave until 3 a.m.

While this went on, the great pogrom that was to follow seethed like an abscess about to burst. That night and the day before, scattered riots with acts of violence and arson had begun seeping into sundry German towns and provinces. These first flashes were scattered and probably not coordinated, but neither were they "spontaneous." They were incited from above. As of November 7, Goebbels and Hitler had quite deliberately invited this sort of "spontaneous" wildfire. All the media coverage spoke of reprisals.[6] THE SHOTS IN PARIS WILL NOT GO UNPUNISHED! So read a banner headline in *Völkischer Beobachter* while vom Rath was still alive. Meanwhile, all around the world, some sort of retribution was anticipated. On the front pages of November 8, many Western newspapers openly speculated on the possibility of organized vengeance.

Most of those first riots were the work of local gangs from the SA.[7] Since Hitler's accession to power, the brown shirts in the Nazi Party's private army of thugs had been impatiently waiting for the order to bust loose. Their motives were financial and emotional. The men of the SA anticipated fine payoffs from the confiscation of Jewish property, but they also anticipated the thrill of organized violence driven by hate. Greed mingled with savagery. They had been seriously frustrated when the command from on high was slow to come. The unleashing of SA brutality, which had been essential to Hitler's rise as a revolutionary, had to be restrained by Hitler's need for the appearance of legitimacy as the chancellor. At least, that is how it was until November 9.

Yet the Kristallnacht did not come as a surprise.[8] The days of restraint were over. Steinweis cites one Jewish witness after Herschel shot vom Rath: "No Jew in Germany could doubt that the most negative developments were to be expected." Yet "no Jew could yet comprehend that the consequences would be so horrifyingly destructive."[9] Everyone knew that something would happen. They did not know that something would be universal terror.

So November 9 was a busy day for Adolf Hitler. His schedule listed three major events. The first occasion came at noon; the second was planned for the dinner hour; and a third was slated for midnight. From noon until 2 p.m., Hitler led a solemn march of the Nazi minions through the streets of Munich, starting at the Bürgerbräukeller itself and proceeding to the huge memorial monument on the Odeonsplatz called the Feldherrnhalle. From there, the march proceeded to the Königsplatz, where the remains of the sixteen Nazis who had died in the original putsch were entombed in two fascist temples. There the roll of these "fallen" heroes was called with the assembled crowd crying out *present!* as each name was intoned.

Five hours later, in Munich's Old Town Hall, there was a banquet for a mob of high-ranking Nazis, especially "old fighters" from the SA, noted in

Goebbels's diary as "a gigantic event." It was at this banquet that the full-scale Kristallnacht was instigated.[10]

Vom Rath's death was perfectly timed. Brandt had informed the Reich Chancellery by telegram fifteen minutes after vom Rath died; we may be sure that he informed Hitler by telephone at least as quickly. Thus, the news of it reached Hitler during the few hours of spare time that fell between Movement Day's noon march from the Bürgerbräukeller and the evening banquet. During these hours, Goebbels, failed writer that he was, retired to his hotel to work on a book. Hitler spent it in his apartment with Göring, fulminating against Western criticisms of his anti-Semitism. If Nazi treatment of the Jews left the democracies so horrified, he wanted to know, why didn't they open their gates for tens of thousands of Jewish refugees? Hypocrites!

So Hitler went to the banquet fully aware that vom Rath was dead. He may even have been in a position to give the news to Goebbels, rather than the other way around. As the banquet began, Goebbels informed Hitler about the scattered pogroms going on around the country. "I describe the situation to the Führer," he wrote in his diary.[11] At the head table, where Hitler was seated beside Goebbels, an aide put before him a piece of paper with some sort of message on it. This may have been a staged gesture. In any case, Hitler immediately plunged into intense conversation with Goebbels, though what was said is knowable only from Goebbels's diary: "He decides: Let the demonstrations continue. Withdraw the police. For once the Jews should feel the rage of the people."[12] Some witnesses claimed to have heard Hitler say, "The SA should be allowed to have its fling."

Hitler then left the building, seeking to distance himself from the violence to come. Knowing that letting the demonstrations continue meant plunging the entire country—Austria, too—into an orgy of Nazi-sponsored criminality, Hitler maneuvered to distance himself symbolically from what would follow, leaving Goebbels behind to stir up the crowd. Hitler was, after all, the head of a nominally legitimate state. The prime duty of sovereignty is to *protect* the public from anarchy rather than inflict it. He wanted in some measure to dissociate himself from the crimes that were coming—and it is an astonishing fact that he almost succeeded. Many contemporary witnesses to the Kristallnacht believed Goebbels had instigated the pogrom with mere passive assent by Hitler. Even in some twenty-first-century histories, Goebbels is still seen as the prime instigator. This is almost certainly illusion. Goebbels could not have instigated such an event without the Führer's consent and leadership. Hitler was always in charge.[13]

Hitler's departure left the propaganda minister at the head table. Goebbels rose to make a hysterical speech about vom Rath's death; it would turn the banquet into pandemonium, and from that nerve center spread the violence throughout Germany and Austria. The national pogrom had already begun by midnight, when Hitler was presiding over the solemn induction of a thousand new SS recruits—the men whose generals Himmler had instructed the day before on the racial Armageddon to come. As they took their oath of personal allegiance to Hitler himself, people were being beaten—sometimes to death—homes were being ransacked, stores were being smashed, and synagogues were burning all across Germany.

The oratory of Joseph Goebbels, like his master's, was marked by almost hysterical histrionics. His speeches typically built toward incendiary climaxes delivered at an electronically amplified shout. He was all too adept at rousing large crowds—the bigger the better—into ecstasies of adulation or rage.

His speech on the night of November 9 began in an excited way, seizing the attention of the packed room. The urgency of Goebbels's opening tone meant something major was about to happen, and Hitler's absence lit up the importance of the moment. The audience sat rapt.

Goebbels came to the point quickly. He began by waving the piece of paper that an aide had handed to Hitler shortly before.[14] "I have news here for you tonight, to demonstrate what happens to a good German when he relaxes his vigil for one moment." Presumably everyone in the room was aware of the Paris shooting; presumably like the rest of the world they had been waiting and wondering whether vom Rath would die. "Ernst vom Rath was a good German, a loyal servant of the Reich, working for the good of our people in our embassy in Paris. Shall I tell you what happened to him? He was shot down! In the course of his duty, he went, unarmed and unsuspecting, to speak to a visitor at the embassy, and had two bullets pumped into him. He is now dead."

The news was out. Rumbles of outrage filled the hall.

Goebbels slammed his fist on the lectern: "Do I need to tell you the race of the dirty swine who perpetrated this foul deed? A Jew! Tonight he lies in jail in Paris, claiming that he acted on his own, that he had no instigators of this awful deed behind him. But we know better, don't we?"

The crowd began crowing for vengeance; Goebbels had to quiet them. "Comrades, we cannot allow this attack by international Jewry to go unchallenged. It must be repudiated. Our people must be told, and their answer must be ruthless, forthright, salutary! I ask you to listen to me, and together we must plan what is to be our answer to Jewish murder and the threat of international Jewry to our glorious German Reich!"

Goebbels then imparted "the plan" to his angry audience.

The plan was the pogrom. When he finished speaking, there was a rush to the telephones and telexes, ordering more "spontaneous" anti-Jewish riots. He surely told his audience that more—hundreds more—of these "spontaneous" demonstrations were expected. He surely told them that the Führer had decided that demonstrations of the people's outrage were not to be interfered with by the police or fire brigades. They should not be carried out in uniform but in civilian clothes. The party should not seem to be responsible. But the riots should begin.

By ten thirty that night, the fires of arson were burning synagogues and unleashed chaos was shattering places of business across all of Germany and Austria. Goebbels's speech had instigated them by crying havoc and letting slip the dogs of war—the dogs of war being, in this case, the SA, which had been impatiently waiting for its hour of vengeance since Hitler assumed power. Herschel's hated name and demonized face were plastered like graffiti onto the walls of nationwide vandalism: smashed stores, ransacked houses, ubiquitous street violence, looting, extortion, rape, and murder on every side, all of it passively watched and not prevented by the police and fire departments that had been ordered not to interfere with the "spontaneous vengeance of the people." If a synagogue was burning, let it burn to the ground. Fire departments stood by doing nothing, or hosing streams of water not onto the flaming Jewish pyres, but onto any "Aryan" property that happened to be adjacent, protecting it against the conflagration. If a Jew was being beaten in the streets—or at home—let the violence run to the bottom of the night: A spree was a spree, and the forces of order had been told to stand aside and let the brown-shirt forces of disorder do their worst. There was much more to the criminality than mayhem and murder. On November 10, as a result of orders received directly from Hitler himself, some thirty thousand Jewish men—especially middle-aged men who were thought to be affluent—were summarily arrested and in the end dispatched to concentration camps: Dachau, Buchenwald, and Sachsenhausen. Despite the regime's claims to the contrary, they were systematically abused and terrorized in the camps, eventually to be released only on the condition that they leave the country and hand over all their property to be "Aryanized" by the state.

Despite much scholarship, the number of people murdered and the amount of damage done have never been fully assessed.[15] Read and Fisher put the number of murder victims at "at least 236 . . . with more than 600 permanently maimed. Hundreds more died in concentration camps during the next few weeks."[16] Some 7,500 stores were ransacked, looted, and destroyed. In addition arson or other wreckage destroyed 267 synagogues. Jewish community centers, cemetery chapels, and the like were burned to the ground.[17]

Four days after the pogrom, the regime announced a collective "fine" of 1 billion Reich marks, a state confiscation of any insurance benefits that would be paid to the victims, and closing down all wholesale and retail businesses. On December 3, all Jewish-owned businesses were dissolved, in order to be transferred to Aryan ownership. Jews were required to surrender any stocks they owned, and "jewelry, precious stones, and metals, as well as art objects had to be sold to state purchasing offices."[18] Indeed, the purpose of the Kristallnacht brought a second agenda to the transformation of bigotry into savagery. This was to raise money—lots of money—for the kleptocracy. Special taxes were to be levied on Jews. "The shooting of vom Rath was utilized to provide much needed support of an economy burdened by the heavy demands of the rearmament program."[19] Jews were prohibited from attending theaters, concert halls, and movie houses, while Jewish newspapers and Jewish schools were closed down. Any Jewish child in an "Aryan" school was to be expelled.[20] In addition, when Goebbels made a public announcement calling for the riots to end, he made it clear that they would begin again if there were to be any significant protest against them in foreign countries. In other words, every Jew in Germany was being held hostage.

All in the name of Herschel Grynszpan and the death of Ernst vom Rath.

The German regime had revealed itself as a criminal regime, a sponsor of mass incarceration, the purpose of which was theft and exile. It was the sovereign sponsor of murder, larceny, arson, assault, rape, vandalism, religious persecution, and blasphemy. It had embarked on the course of state-sponsored criminality that would become the Holocaust.

11

Grief and Grandiosity

After the Kristallnacht, Herschel was whipsawed between grief and grandiosity. Shame and horror were one part of what he felt. On November 12, the Paris police told the Associated Press that he had "alternately wept and prayed" when he learned about the pogrom, and quoted him: "Is this the price for the act of one desperate, foolish man like me?" He vowed—so police told reporters—that he "would pray every Monday for forgiveness for what I have done to my people."[1] He was assailed by remorse. From prison, he sent his friend Sal Schenkier a letter that was a lament: "The thought that I caused this catastrophe brings me close to madness. My God, do you really think I am the reason for this disaster? At night, I dream about the ghetto, about Jewish women and children running away from the mounted SA, who have whips in their hands. God, oh my God! I didn't want that. Listen to me. I'll explain how it happened so you can explain it to people who might call down God's curse on me."[2] In his way, he even grieved for vom Rath. "Unfortunately the man I shot is dead. I did not wish to kill him but only to wound him. I only wished by doing so to protest. May God pardon me for having killed a man who was perhaps not guilty."[3]

But repentance was only one aspect of Herschel's response. Mingled with his grief and remorse was a kind of boyish grandiosity, just as there was a certain grandiosity in the gestures of his grief. Here was a powerless waif, a politically invisible being, who suddenly found himself at the center of major events. He had shot vom Rath in order to make his protest heard, and indeed his shots had been heard around the world. Suddenly visible—his face was on front pages worldwide—he began to imagine that he was important on the grand scale. His protest had been heard; perhaps he himself would be heard, and heard at the highest level. Not long after the shooting, he addressed a letter to Franklin Roosevelt, with a plea for his family to come to America. It is a measure of his self-intoxication that he wrote another letter, this time to Hitler himself, making a plea for an end to persecution of the German Jews, and offering his "forgiveness," and that of the Jewish people, if the oppression stopped. And not every anti-Nazi treated him as a hero. There was a common view among senior Jewish leaders that the crime had been reckless and disastrous, the bravado of a narcissistic, self-righteous child—a view that at its most severe became a theory even at quite senior levels of the Jewish leadership, that Herschel had been the sociopathic pawn of the Gestapo itself, used by the Nazis precisely to provide a provocation for the pogrom. Yet after a visit from his uncles, he wrote in his prison diary: "They told me not to worry as the whole world was behind me."[4] He believed it. In his mind, he had merged the role of foolish meddler with that of tragic hero. The "whole world" surely would not hold him responsible. He was heroic in his tragic foolishness. As he saw it, he had been moved to act by a power greater than himself. And when he acted, history had trembled.

It is true that as he matured, the ironic but ugly reality of his situation wrapped itself more tightly around his mind. For the rest of his life, he would fear being once again used as a pawn in the Nazi persecution of his people, and his many maneuvers and plans, both while he was in his cheerful cabin for youthful offenders at Fresnes prison or in the dank cellars of the Gestapo in Berlin, were increasingly shadowed by this fear. Understanding that he had been used in the Kristallnacht, he vowed never to be used again. Once he became a prisoner of the Nazis, the threat that he would be used, perhaps in some even worse crime, became more vivid and dangerous than ever. Once in German hands, he knew he had to act, and his adolescent vanity died. The once callow, rash, driven boy who had so foolishly assassinated Ernst vom Rath would need every resource he could summon up, and he brought all his intelligence, cunning, and developing maturity to the battle of wits that faced him.

Meanwhile, the fact remained that he was a criminal. To be sure, just as the Nazis saw him as a demon, some antifascists saw him as a hero, and many more saw him as at least a wretched innocent overwhelmed by evils beyond his comprehension. Yet he had murdered Ernst vom Rath, and freely admitted—freely *insisted*—that he had done it for political reasons. If duly convicted of having committed the political murder of an accredited diplomat on French soil, he perhaps faced the guillotine. His life could be saved only if his obvious guilt could somehow be mitigated. The only question was how? The first and most obvious answer would be a demonstration in court that the crime was dwarfed and made comprehensible by the vastly greater criminality of the regime that motivated it. But would such an appeal work in a France on the verge of war?

Herschel needed a lawyer, and a good one.

Whoever represented Herschel had a dual mission: to save the boy's life and do as much damage to the Nazis as possible in the process. Herschel's trial would be part of the era's larger propaganda war, a battle fought not only in the courts but also in the press and in public opinion. For that reason, Herschel's lawyer needed to be a celebrity. His anti-fascism had to be not only profound but also famous. Moreover, he would have to be Gentile; a Jewish lawyer would be too obvious a target for Nazi propaganda about Jewish conspiracies. He had to save the boy and humiliate the Nazis *without further jeopardizing the Jews who were still in Germany*, all of whom were quite explicitly hostages to the regime. Goebbels had been very clear:

Further protests would result in further persecutions. That threat had to be taken seriously. So the obvious answer was not so obvious after all. It was not that easy to outmaneuver Joseph Goebbels.

One lawyer above all others seemed capable of outmaneuvering Goebbels. His name was Vincent de Moro-Giafferi, and he was perhaps the most famous lawyer in France. Moro-Giafferi was best known for his spectacular defenses; it was said he had only once lost a client, however guilty, to the guillotine: Henri Landru—also known as Bluebeard. Moro-Giafferi had spent his entire career in the spotlight. In 1902 he had been admitted to the French bar at the age of twenty-four, its youngest member. He later served in the Chamber of Deputies; he had been in the cabinet of Premier Édouard Herriot as undersecretary of state for education. His implacable hostility to Nazism was famous: In 1933, Moro-Giafferi had played a flamboyant role in a mock trial ridiculing the Nazi show trial over the Reichstag fire. And always, an eager claque of fascinated young lawyers followed his every move, crowding the courtrooms. He was Catholic, and not French by birth: Like Napoleon, Moro-Giafferi was a Corsican; his lavish office was decorated with Napoleonic antiques. He was memorably corpulent; as Gerald Schwab noted when they met, Moro-Giafferi was almost as wide as he was high. With his bulk and his look of amused eminence, he was born for the newspaper cartoonists. He was perfect.

The Grynszpan family knew it. On November 10, the day after the Kristallnacht, Salomon Grynszpan wrote to Moro-Giafferi:

> I have the honor to request that you assume the defense of my nephew Herschel Grynszpan.
>
> I have decided to dispense with the services of the two lawyers, MM. Szwarc and Vésine Larue, whom I had engaged originally. At the same time I request that MM Fraenkel and Erlich, who speak Yiddish, work with you.[5]

The next day—November 11—Herschel himself wrote to Moro-Giafferi:

Please excuse that I write in German. The reason is that I am not able to
write in French. I would like to request that you assume the defense at
my trial. I close the letter with the hope that you will accept my entreaty.[6]

These requests seem straightforward, but various pettifogging squab-
bles postponed Moro-Giafferi's final appointment as Herschel's lawyer.
For example, MM. Szwarc and Vésine-Larue chose not to leave the case
quietly, and Herschel resented their dismissal, even though he had himself
requested representation by Moro-Giafferi. The two local lawyers spoke Yiddish; they were culturally comfortable with the boy and were skilled at holding his hand. It was only when Moro-Giafferi found a more sophisticated
Jewish lawyer, Maître Serge Weill-Goudchaux, to serve as his liaison with
his diminutive but strong-willed client that the arrangement was solidified.
Herschel himself—who was beginning to learn something about leverage—
refused to appoint Moro-Giafferi unless and until his parents had been rescued from Zbaszyn and brought to his side in Paris. Sadly, that reunion
never took place—the combined malevolence of the German and Polish
foreign offices saw to that—but the press followed every twist and turn.[7]

Moro-Giafferi officially became Herschel's lawyer only through the intervention of an American, Dorothy Thompson.

In 1938, Dorothy Thompson was the foremost anti-Nazi journalist in the
English-speaking world, and it was through her fervor over Herschel's fate
that his case became, and remained, as famous as it did. Thompson wrote a
widely syndicated biweekly column for the *New York Herald Tribune*: "On
the Record." She was also a political commentator on *The General Electric
Hour*, a radio program broadcast weekly to some five million radio sets in
the United States. Dorothy Thompson's voice was *heard*.[8]

Thompson saw Herschel as a sacrificial victim whose protest had made him a tragic but radiant icon for all Hitler's other victims. Speaking on November 14, she told her radio audience:

> A week ago today, an anemic-looking boy with brooding black eyes walked quietly into the German embassy in the rue de Lille in Paris, asked to see the ambassador [sic], was shown into the office of the third secretary, Herr vom Rath, and shot him. Herr vom Rath died on Wednesday.
>
> I want to talk about that boy. I feel as though I knew him, for in the past five years I have met so many whose story is the same—the same except for this unique, desperate act. Herschel Grynszpan was one of the hundreds of thousands of refugees whom the terror east of the Rhine has turned loose on the world . . .

After recounting the horrors of the pogrom, Thompson turned to Herschel's forthcoming trial. "I am speaking of this boy. Soon he will go on trial. The news is that on top of all this terror, this horror, one more must pay. They say he will go to the guillotine . . ." Confronting that threat, she called for what she called a "higher justice."

> Is there not a higher justice in the case of Herschel Grynszpan, seventeen years old? Is there not a higher justice that says that this deed has been expiated with four hundred million dollars and half a million existences, with beatings, and burnings, and deaths, and suicides? Must the nation whose Zola defended Dreyfus until the world rang with it, cut off the head of one more Jew without giving him an open trial? . . .
>
> Who is on trial in this case? I say the Christian world is on trial. I say the men of Munich are on trial, who signed a pact without one word of protection for helpless minorities. Whether Herschel Grynszpan lives or dies won't matter much to Herschel. He was prepared to die when he fired those shots. His young life was already ruined . . . [But] the Nazi government has announced that if any Jews, anywhere in the world, protest

at anything that is happening, further oppressive measures will be taken. They are holding every Jew in Germany as a hostage.

It was powerful stuff—yet Thompson seems to have been quite genuinely surprised when her November 14 broadcast produced a huge listener response. Two days later, she reported in her newspaper column: "The response . . . was flabbergasting. I am in receipt of 3000 telegrams, still uncounted letters, and several hundred dollars in checks, although I did not ask for money and was speaking solely for myself. The telegrams come from forty-six states. Almost all of them gave their addresses and asked what they could do."

What could be done? Thompson organized a committee to defend Herschel Grynszpan, stressing that the committee would appeal only to non-Jews for contributions, "so that the Nazis can't say this is another Jewish plot."[9]

The committee was to be called the Journalists' Defense Fund (F. Scott Fitzgerald was a member), and the appeal raised more than $40,000—the equivalent of more than $675,000 in early twenty-first century dollars. Its European chairs were an American, Edgar Ansel Mowrer, head of the *Chicago Tribune*'s Paris bureau, and a Frenchman, André Géraud, a fierce anti-Nazi polemicist who went by the pen name Pertinax. And the committee's choice of the attorney to defend Herschel was Vincent de Moro-Giafferi. One of its first expenditures settled the fees of MM. Szwarc and Vésine-Larue.[10]

Meanwhile, the Nazis had their own ideas on how to exploit the forthcoming trial. Their grand strategy was to spread among the French populace—which was still intoxicated with Munich appeasement—the notion that international Jewry had used Herschel as its pawn to thwart some sort of friendly understanding between France and Nazi Germany. At first, the Germans assumed that Herschel would not only be convicted—he was, after all, obviously guilty—but that the trial might be used to convince the French that he really was part of a Jewish conspiracy to sabotage the peace.

By special order of Hitler himself, the propagandist assigned to manage the Grynszpan affair was a jurist and committed anti-Semite named Friedrich Grimm.[11] He was joined in this long effort by Wolfgang Diewerge, the man Goebbels had put in charge of managing the press at the time of the murder. Both were productive writers. Both had worked together before. Both had the personal confidence and admiration of Goebbels himself. Together, they made a team.

Grimm was a jurist with what were then viewed as impressive credentials. During the Weimar Republic, he had been a *Privatdozent* at the University of Münster; later, he became a professor of international law. He had gone to law school in Geneva, and was bilingual in German and French, a key factor in his career when he became a kind of Nazi answer-man on the subject of French affairs, both before and after France's fall.[12]

Yet Grimm's academic qualifications as a jurist mask his true political destiny. His photographs show a man with keen, intelligent eyes and an affluent face. He could be someone's rich uncle. In fact, Friedrich Grimm was a high-toned hack, expert at manipulating the courts and using the language of the law to advance the agenda of a regime intent upon destroying the rule of law. He was a bureaucrat, skilled at maneuvering at the highest levels. He was also deeply dishonest and, like so many anti-Semites, just as deeply self-deceived. He *believed* in his lie. It was his truth, and it was a truth that justified any falsehood. He personally met Hitler in 1932 and was converted to the almost mystical belief in Hitler's genius that was typical of many people with intellectual pretentions—Goebbels himself being the prime example—who ought to have known better. Grimm belonged to an urbane group that, like Goebbels, could bring the trappings of a genuine intelligence to bear on Nazi fanaticism. He was expert in the liar's game of twisting fantasy into belief, even for himself. After he moved out of the prestigious but dreary confines of academia, he was Goebbels's man.[13]

Grimm's stamping ground was Paris. Diewerge worked in Berlin. His office was in the same building where Goebbels sat in splendor. In addition to being an unswerving propagandist, he was, like Grimm, a skilled bureaucrat, as used to writing obsequious memoranda as racist tirades. He was a prolific writer, churning out anti-Semitic screeds pitched at a somewhat lower level than the more high-toned prose of his partner. The only photograph of Diewerge I have seen shows a very different man than his Francophile collaborator. Grimm has the serene look and slight corpulence of a self-satisfied bourgeois, a man used to "honors," a man for whom testimonial dinners might be given. Diewerge on the other hand has about him a lean and hungry look. He has a clean-shaven virile face, with thin, almost feminine lips that look cruel in a way that somehow accentuates that virility. His eyes are deep-set, even hollow. Like his master Goebbels, Diewerge *looked* like a fanatic.

The first propaganda extravaganza following the Kristallnacht was necessarily vom Rath's funeral.[14] Vom Rath had to be glorified in death because his demise had to justify the pogrom. He could not be treated as the polite, intelligent, not-very-important young man he seems to have been. Least of all could he be portrayed as the embryonic dissident whom the Gestapo suspected of treachery. He had to be a hero, and a Nazi hero at that. A fictitious vom Rath had to be invented: a martyr fallen for the New Germany, someone whose death *warranted* burning synagogues, smashing homes, trashing stores, and murdering rabbis.

Vom Rath therefore was given a state funeral that was elaborate even by the gaudy standards of Nazi theatrics. Two special trains, one French, one German, bore his remains first from Paris to Aachen on the Franco-German border, thence from Aachen to Düsseldorf, where he was to be interred among his ancestors. In Germany, the funeral train crawled toward the grave at a mournful twelve miles an hour while from village to city to town, all flags flew at half-mast; all stations were draped in bunting; and along the fifty-five miles from Aachen to Düsseldorf the tracks were lined, under a suitably gloomy fog, with men from Nazi organizations—many of whom had so recently been busy destroying Jewish shops and torching synagogues—standing at attention, evenly spaced somber sentinels honoring the lugubrious cortege. The living passengers on the funeral train included the vom Rath family and Friedrich Grimm as propaganda meister, along with reporters, lesser propagandists, and various state notabilities led by Ernst von Wiesäcker, an exalted official of the German Foreign Office, who had delivered the funeral oration in Paris, proclaiming vom Rath to be "the Foreign Ministry's first martyr to fall for the Third Reich."[15] Once it reached Düsseldorf, the body was transferred to a bier in a large indoor sports arena, the Rheinhalle, the lofty heights of which were draped in swastika banners while spotlights beamed down on the coffin à la Twentieth Century Fox. A double row of mourners filed past, paying their respects. The next day, Hitler arrived for the funeral service itself, seating himself beside the vom Rath family, to whom—as was widely noted—he spoke not one word. The entire ceremony was broadcast live on German national radio. The funeral march from Beethoven's *Eroica* symphony was played. Chief among the orators was the foreign minister of Germany, Joachim von Ribbentrop, who recalled that the day of vom Rath's death was also the anniversary of the 1923 putsch, and ended by quoting Hitler's rallying cry: "We understand the challenge, and we accept it."[16]

Friedrich Grimm may have ridden to Düsseldorf on the vom Rath funeral train, but for most of the remainder of 1938 he was busy in Paris, trying to concoct evidence of the Jewish conspiracy he was so certain *had* to have taken place. But while conspiracy theories of every kind and political coloration sprouted on the case like mushrooms on a rotting log, his efforts were futile. After their own elaborate investigations, the French police concluded that Herschel had really and truly acted entirely on his own. And Otto Abetz, Grimm's superior among the Nazis in Paris, confessed after the war that the massive effort to prove the existence of a conspiracy produced no evidence of any kind. Grimm at one point was reduced to claiming that the absence of any evidence about the Jewish plots emanating from the Sports-club Aurore in itself proved the club's guilt: Those clever Jews were so good at covering their tracks!

Meanwhile, Grimm attempted to bend Judge Tesnière in a pro-German direction. This effort had considerably more success. Grimm needed to be close to the legal proceedings, but as a German lawyer, he was not admitted to the French bar. He circumvented this difficulty by manipulating the vom Rath family. Under French law, one active party in a criminal proceeding can be the one known as the *partie civile*, who is usually the victim of the crime. Grimm arranged to name Gustav vom Rath, as the father of Ernst, as the *partie civile* in the trial of Herschel Grynszpan and arranged to have a French lawyer, in fact under his instructions, represent Gustav in court. The actual vom Rath family had next to nothing to do with the proceedings.[17]

Grimm, however, was a busy man. He had two fully staffed offices: one in the German embassy in Paris, and another in Berlin. Gerald Schwab defines Grimm's mission: "Grimm's task was twofold: first, to prevent the French inquiry from highlighting the evident causes of the crime, that is, a detailed examination of anti-Semitic excesses in Germany; and second, to eliminate to the extent possible any element which might reflect negatively on Germany and thus influence French attitudes toward the Third Reich."[18]

At first success seemed likely. At an early stage, Judge Tesnière ruled that since the events of the Kristallnacht had followed the shooting, they were not relevant to the prosecution of the crime and could not be introduced as evidence. This was of course a setback for those like Dorothy Thompson who wanted to find "higher justice" by making the trial a showcase of Nazi crimes. To be able to prove that Herschel had been driven to despair by a German government that was thoroughly and lawlessly anti-Semitic would have been a propaganda coup for Moro-Giafferi. Yet at least in the early stages of the planned prosecution, the path to that strategy seemed closed: the pogrom—the most damning evidence of all—was held to be inadmissible. Instead, Moro-Giafferi had to gather information about the Polish deportations. That surely would be admissible—but there was yet another even more serious obstacle. What if using even that evidence provoked further persecution? If so, the best way to save the boy's life could not be used because the best way to humiliate the Germans could not be used.

The obvious strategy was blocked on every front. Moreover, the political deck in France was stacked. Large swaths of French public opinion still sought some sort of special relationship with Germany. Even when German anti-Semitism was deplored—and it was not always deplored—a people inspired to ecstasies by "the men of Munich" were prepared to overlook Germany's racial "excesses" to get "peace at any price." One of the most objectionable aspects of the Munich agreement had been that document's complete indifference to the fate of minorities in the Sudetenland. But it was an easy price to pay for the imaginary peace it bought.

Yet as time went on, Herschel's prospects for leniency in his French trial grew stronger almost to the exact degree that France's prospects for peace grew weaker. In 1938, when the intoxication of appeasement was still in the air, the boy seemed certain to be convicted with little or no clemency. The shadow of the guillotine lay heavy on his head. But in March 1938, Hitler violated the Munich Agreement by invading what was left of Czechoslovakia, and the atmosphere changed. The promises of Munich were shattered. With Czechoslovakia down, Poland was next. War looked inevitable. With public opinion turning anti-German, it seemed that Herschel might be acquitted. Grimm began pushing for delay of the trial. And when Hitler did indeed precipitate the Second World War by invading Poland, Grimm informed the team in Berlin that if Herschel were to be tried at that time, the boy could be acquitted for no other reason than that he was a Pole.

But the French government—or at least that part of it Bonnet and his allies in the Ministry of Justice represented—did not want any trial at any time. They feared acquittal as much as they feared conviction. Acquittal would enrage Hitler. Conviction would enrage anti-Nazi opinion. Weill-Goudchaux, who was working with Herschel every day, put it clearly after the war: "The trial could have been presented to the criminal court in July 1939, but Georges Bonnet, the minister of Foreign Affairs, whose efforts to accommodate the Germans were already evident, did not wish it, for he feared acquittal."[19]

Yet the defense had also been reluctant to go to trial, especially in the early days. When conviction seemed likely, Weill-Goudchaux and Moro-Giafferi began to search for some strategy that would save the boy's life and at the same time humiliate the Germans *without* the political trial that seemed so risky.

They did not have far to look. It seems that gossip had reached the legal team that vom Rath had been a homosexual. This gossip was unfounded; we know from elaborate investigations following the war that there was no evidence for the charge at all. Certainly Moro-Giafferi had no evidence to that effect. But for Moro-Giafferi, as for widespread circles of gossip, it was enough that vom Rath had been a good-looking twenty-nine-year-old who lived alone. And despite his look of innocence, Herschel was a sexy, even sultry looking boy . . .

Eureka. Moro-Giafferi saw that he could accomplish his dual goal of saving the boy's life and humiliating the Germans through the simple expedient of wiping away the entire political context of the crime—that is, by not even referring to the Nazi crimes, but presenting the jury instead with a crime of passion. This *crime passionel* was pure fiction, and concocted in Moro-Giafferi's fertile legal imagination, but it was very convenient fiction. Suppose that vom Rath had been a homosexual using Herschel sexually, and at a certain point something happened that so enraged Herschel that he went to the embassy and shot him? The case would be radically changed. And what would serve as the something that happened? Perhaps Herschel had been prostituting himself for money, and the boy reached the boiling point of murderous rage when he realized that vom Rath did not intend to pay him. This narrative was a bit simple, and the effort to portray Herschel as a boy prostitute was troubled by a certain implausibility: He may have had a sexy look, but everything about this depressed, elfin child seemed to proclaim innocence. Early on, Herschel had confided to Weill-Goudchaux that he was sexually a virgin.[20]

From Moro-Giafferi's perspective, a French jury would treat what the homophobic world of 1938 would see as a Nazi sexually molesting a seventeen-year-old boy very differently than it would treat a cold-blooded political assassin, however young, who had threatened the peace of Europe. Herschel could expect a suspended sentence, and perhaps even time served or outright acquittal. Second, the homosexual fiction would humiliate the Nazis in a thoroughly satisfying way. Hitler and Goebbels had just completed glorifying vom Rath as a shining hero of the New Germany, using the outrage of his death to justify the most vicious pogrom in history. This "revelation"— false as it was—would make headlines around the world.

That it was all fictitious did not trouble Moro-Giafferi at all. He could claim that the perverse relationship between vom Rath and Herschel had been completely secret: that nobody at the embassy knew anything about vom Rath's tendencies and nobody in Herschel's circle had an inkling that he would or could satisfy them. Only two people knew anything about it, and one of them was dead. The survivor could tell the tale without the fear of being challenged or contradicted by anyone.

True, Herschel would have to retract all his pervious testimony about protest and the Jewish people. But that was simple. He could claim that he had invented it to cover up his shameful secret.

All Herschel had to do to accomplish this legal miracle—saving his own life and humiliating the Nazis—was lie. But first they would have to explain the strategy to the boy. The two lawyers went to Fresnes for a conference with their client. Weill-Goudchaux, as usual, did the talking, speaking in German. *Le petit* listened expectantly.

It seemed that a certain oddity in the life of Herr vom Rath had recently come to the lawyers' attention. It was an embarrassing fact, but one that might be very useful in Herschel's defense.

Ernst vom Rath, they explained, seems to have been a homosexual.

Herschel returned an uncomprehending blank stare. Homosexual? He did not seem to understand. Repeating themselves, the lawyers realized that Herschel had no idea what a homosexual was. He would have to be told.

So they told him.

There was a long silence in the visitors' room. The brown doe-like eyes of Herschel Grynszpan were wide. Then the boy broke that long silence by bursting into laughter.[21]

He had never heard of anything so absurd. And how could this "oddity on the life of Herr vom Rath" possibly help him in his defense? What role could anything so . . . so ridiculous possibly play when they got to court?

They explained. It would be the end of grandiosity. He would no longer be God's pawn. David to the Nazi Goliath. He would be a prostitute. A boy prostitute, to be sure, but a prostitute.

And of course he immediately refused. Whatever story he told in court would be the political truth. He went to the embassy to protest and avenge the deportation of his family and many thousands of other Polish Jews. Protest and vengeance: Those were his motives. As for Herr vom Rath and the "oddity" in his life, Herschel had never before seen or heard of the man before he walked into this office and pulled out his gun. When he testified before the examining magistrate the day after the shooting, it was obvious that he did not yet know even the name Ernst vom Rath.

No. He would have nothing to do with this dirty fiction.

Weill-Goudchaux and Moro-Giafferi did not give up easily. First of all, Herschel should realize that this story would save his life, or at least spare him a long prison term. Didn't he want to protect the Jews still being held hostage in Germany? Didn't he want to live? Didn't he want to do damage to the Nazis? Yes, it was a lie. A big lie. But such an *effective* one. Except for being completely unacceptable to the defendant, the strategy was brilliant.

—

Herschel wouldn't budge. Moro-Giafferi is sometimes quoted as referring to Herschel as "this *seemingly* weak child." It was over his client's stubbornness in his own defense that inspired Moro-Giafferi to use the phrase.

The words of a witness closer to the event than Gerald Schwab amplify Moro-Giafferi's role in the invention of the imaginary *crime passionel*. In 1960, Ernst vom Rath's younger brother, Günter vom Rath, by then a distinguished attorney in Wiesbaden, sued one Michael Alexander Soltikow for libel after Soltikow published an article repeating the homosexual fiction as fact. In Germany, unlike the United States and the United Kingdom, it is legally possible to libel the dead. One purpose of such a suit is to establish the truth. Vom Rath's case against Soltikow dragged on for twelve years: During that time, Soltikow was unable to produce any evidence acceptable to the court that Ernst vom Rath had been homosexual or that there had been a relationship of any kind between vom Rath and Herschel. Though his conviction was later overturned on a technicality, Soltikow was found guilty.

In 1964, as the trial played out in the European press, Günter vom Rath received a letter from a man named Erich Wollenberg, who during the early thirties had been a communist activist who played a role in the mock trial of the supposed arsonists of the Reichstag. He had become acquainted with Moro-Giafferi at that time.

The letter from Wollenberg came out of the blue; Wollenberg had merely been following the case in the press. In the letter, he unmasked the homosexual fraud by quoting a direct personal encounter with Moro-Giafferi:

> One day, and unless I was mistaken it was in the spring of 1939, I met de Moro-Giafferi on boulevard Saint-Michel and I asked him for news of Grunspahn. [sic] . . . He had just come from consulting him in his cell and was still revolted by the attitude of his client.
>
> "That young man is a fool, infatuated with himself," he said. "He

refuses to give a nonpolitical character to his act by saying for example that he assassinated vom Rath because he had had money quarrels with him following homosexual relations. Yet such an attitude in regard to the murder of vom Rath is necessary in order to save the Jews of the Third Reich, whose lives are becoming more and more precarious in regard to their property, their health, their future, etc."

De Moro-Giafferi appealed to the conscience of Grunspahn, implying that he was responsible for the persecution of the Jews by his act which made Jewish blood flow. "If only," he added, "he would deny the political motives of his crime and assert that he only had personal vengeance in mind, vengeance as a victim of homosexuality, the Nazis would lose their best pretext for exercising their reprisals against the German Jews who are victims of his fit of madness and now of his obstinacy."

I asked him if Grunspahn really had relations with vom Rath. He replied, "Absolutely not!" I said to him then, "But as defender of Grunspahn shouldn't you protect not only the interests of your client, but his honor as well?"

It was at that moment that de Moro-Giafferi exclaimed, "Honor! Honor! What is the honor of that absurd little Jew in the face of the criminal action of Hitler? What does the honor of Grunspahn weigh in the face of the destiny of hundreds of thousands of Jews?"

And was vom Rath homosexual? Wollenberg wrote, "Moro-Giafferi added, 'whether vom Rath might be a homosexual or not I don't know, and besides it doesn't interest me ...'"[22]

So much for the higher justice.

12

The Phony War

According to his guards at Fresnes, Herschel would sometimes wake in his cell during the small hours screaming or sobbing, crying for the comfort of his big sister, Berta. The frightened child who cowered beneath the pretense of being a grand and grown-up public figure seems to have returned at night and in solitude. That is when terror struck him. During the day, he was a fighter, and proud: fierce on the prison soccer field and a competitive whiz at Ping-Pong and other forms of amusement for the incarcerated. He gave many interviews. ("I did what I had to do," he solemnly informed the mainly sympathetic reporters.) He corresponded with his family and his many sympathizers. His mail included a sprinkling of love letters and many offers of money, which he invariably turned down. He would stride like a man into meetings with his lawyers or prison officials or the psychologists assigned to examine him, shaking hands all around and trying to radiate a confidence that one observer said was undercut only when those large, limpid eyes of his darted from person to person with the scared, shifting glance of a hunted animal. He was nervous—a nail biter. He spoke his three languages—his mother tongue, Yiddish; ungrammatical but fluent German; and passable French—with a slight lisp. He was also, at least in the opinion of his lawyers, smart. Moro-Giafferi told Gerald Schwab that Herschel was "one of the brightest kids he had ever known," and Weill-Goudchaux called him "an extremely intelligent autodidact."[1]

Bright or not, he was unmoored from his own reality. This is perhaps understandable in a boy who was even more given over to fantasy than most adolescents, especially one who had passed overnight from being what the wide world saw as a plainer-than-plain nobody to being a somebody who was somehow a pivotal pawn in the big history of his era. Like Narcissus, he drank deep from the shimmering reflection of his own importance. Meanwhile, he held on tight to the dubious fantasy that he was certain to be acquitted. While it is true that his acquittal or a reduced sentence became increasingly plausible as France moved toward war and popular hostility to Germany mounted, if he had been tried any time before March 1939, Herschel would almost certainly have been found guilty as charged, and perhaps guillotined. If in those days he believed he would never confront execution, he was dreaming; the delusion was probably linked to his daytime image of himself as an all-but-biblical modern-day David, the boy warrior guided by God, a rescuer of his people, a doer of glorious deeds. Remember that in March 1939, Herschel would have just turned all of eighteen. He was a child, and bright as he may have been, he was not an especially mature one.

Like many who are unmoored from reality, he became a (selective) liar. As the investigations of the examining magistrate proceeded, he never wavered from the truth of his basic claim: that he had taken a gun to the German embassy to do something spectacular enough to draw the world's attention to the Nazi persecution of his people. But that spectacular something changed with progressive reiterations. He may even have partly believed his many variations on the theme; partial belief is common enough among chronic confabulators. At one point he insisted that he had never intended to kill anyone: He wanted only to wound. Later, he claimed that he had acted in a kind of trance, beyond his conscious will. At another point, he claimed that he never intended to hurt anyone: He had taken his pistol to the embassy simply to blast Hitler's portrait off the wall. At another, he claimed that his plan had been to commit suicide, sometimes with, sometimes without also shooting down the portrait. Sometimes he spoke of wishing to kill the ambassador; at other times he said the identity of his victim was unimportant.[2] While he was in prison, psychologists and social workers repeatedly examined him. None was impressed with these fantasies. Their prime task was to produce the answer to two legal questions: Was his crime premeditated? And did he commit it while compos mentis, so that he was legally responsible for his action? Their answer was unequivocal; he was legally responsible for a premeditated act of murder. There was no way out. Herschel faced the supreme penalty. At least at first.

Whether the inventors of the fraudulent homosexual strategy were complicit in some of his kookier claims—shooting the portrait, for example—may be doubted. Nonetheless, as time went on and the long-anticipated Second World War drew near, acquittal became conceivable, and the lawyers encouraged Herschel's faith in his own invincibility. "I am sure this will be a short war," Weill-Goudchaux wrote his client in 1939. "After our victory, [sic] I will do my best to prepare your case, and march toward the glorious acquittal that you are waiting for."[3]

With prison time on his hands, Herschel wrote a great deal. It was part of Fresnes's progressive penology that the prisoners keep a personal diary in which the youths would write their stories, thoughts, and feelings for the benefit of prison psychologists and the examining magistrate. Herschel took to his diary with such enthusiasm that a British journalist named A. R. Pirie offered to go to Poland and bring the Grynszpan family back to Paris with him—in exchange for the right to publish the diary in a London newspaper. Herschel was horrified: He wrote his family demanding that they refuse to cooperate, even if it meant staying in Poland. The journal does not seem to have survived; after the French debacle, it fell into the hands of Grimm and the Germans. Only a few passages of it are known, selectively quoted by Grimm in *L'Affaire Grynszpan*.[4]

His sense of his own importance grew uncertainly but steadily. Months after the shooting, he seems to have believed that the eyes of the world were still on him and that whatever he did and said would still be news. This led to empty threats. When it became clear that the Ministry of Justice was in no hurry to put him on trial, he twice tried to scare them into action by threatening to go on a hunger strike—a menace the ministry twice ignored, and on which he never acted. He took to signing his correspondence with his surname only—just Grynszpan—and his signature became elaborate and pretentious.[5]

At the time of Herschel's arrest, Abraham and Chawa Grynszpan both had been arrested and put in jail. At first the police suspected they might be their nephew's accomplices. That suspicion eventually faded, but Abraham and Chawa remained indicted for having given asylum to an illegal immigrant: victims of the "decree laws" passed in the spring of 1938. France's longstanding national obsession with immigrants both legal and illegal was in one of its periodic crises. French press coverage was at least as focused on Herschel's illegal status as it was on the theme of anti-Semitism. But then, in 1938, the two issues were the same. Abraham and Chawa were charged under a hastily formulated law passed a mere seven months before as part of the crackdown on the immigrants who at that moment were the shared obsession of both Hitler and the French right wing: namely, the throng of fifty thousand dubiously documented refugees from Germany and Austria, the vast majority of whom were Jews. Despite an erudite, thunderous, and above all plausible defense by Moro-Giafferi, Abraham and Chawa were convicted under this law, even while they were still being held as possible accomplices. The punishment meted out to them for harboring an illegal immigrant, however, wavered in such a way as to suggest that the Ministry of Justice may have been at least politically unsure and perhaps even a little ashamed of itself. At the trial, Abraham and Chawa were sentenced to a nominal fine and four months each in jail. Once it was clear that they knew nothing about their nephew's crime, they were released on bail pending an appeal. Under the appeal, Abraham's sentence was increased to six months and Chawa's reduced to three, but after less than a month in renewed imprisonment, both were, as Schwab puts it, "discreetly freed."[6]

In other words, their slap on the wrist was delivered with fumbling uncertainty. Yet there was a more ominous part of their sentence for harboring Herschel. As legal residents—but not citizens—they were to be expelled from France, a punishment that might have been catastrophic for them. Where could they possibly go? Germany? Poland? Luckily, the sentence turned out to be illusory. Their expulsion from France was stayed until the completion of Herschel's trial. That saved them.[7]

They were never expelled from France because Herschel Grynszpan was never tried.

He never went to trial because with every new Nazi outrage, the acquittal, or mitigated sentence—and offense to Hitler—that appeasers in the government feared became more and more likely. Talk about the right to a speedy trial! Herschel Grynszpan was held without trial, without even being indicted, for twenty months: from November 1938 until June 1940. And during nine of those months, September 1939 until June 1940, France was at war with Germany. As 1939 moved toward the spring—especially after Hitler cracked open the Munich illusion by invading Czechoslovakia in March—a mitigated sentence seemed probable. And with the coming of autumn and the start of the Second World War on September 1, Grimm reported to Berlin that outright acquittal seemed a virtual certainty. With the country at war, a French jury was likely to look with a new kind of sympathy on a desperate bit of boyish madness provoked by vicious mass deportations and heightened by the incomparably more heinous crimes of the Kristallnacht.[8] By October and November of 1939, shooting Nazis had become . . . understandable.

That was the problem. Herschel's acquittal would be an insult to Hitler that the French Foreign Ministry under Georges Bonnet feared. Bonnet would remain devoted to appeasing Hitler no matter what happened, and to the bitter end, keeping at it virtually until the Wehrmacht had massed its troops on the borders of Belgium and France, ready to invade.

Once the war that everyone saw as inevitable did come to Europe in September 1939, it would be almost a year—from September 1939 through May 1940—before the "phony war," or as the French called it, the *drôle de guerre*, became genuinely warlike and Hitler, after having conquered Eastern Europe, directed his violence westward. But Schwab is surely right to say, "Probably nothing better characterizes that unreal period [the phony war] than the strange developments of the Grynszpan case."[9]

With the coming of war, Friedrich Grimm decamped for Switzerland, where he became consul general in the German legation in Berne. This job was a front: Both before and after the debacle, Grimm was a senior propagandist for the fascistic way in France, and in that capacity he maintained contacts with the many French publications and politicians that tilted toward Hitler. Grimm's contacts included warm relations with those French politicians under the influence of the fascist model—the very politicians who would dominate the successor to the Third Republic in Vichy. Grimm was, in short, a German contact man with potential collaborators.

The blunt fact is that Grimm and Abetz, going further than Hitler himself, were leading ideologues promoting a Nazified France. As the saga of Herschel Grynszpan continued—for Herschel's saga was only beginning when France fell—Grimm would remain a rising figure in the hierarchy, senior enough not only to have access to Bonnet, but also to have the former minister's rapt attention. But Grimm's ranking among French collaborators stood even higher than that. Not long after the armistice, he was Abetz's personal representative in extended talks with Pierre Laval, a leading politician in Vichy—destined to be premier—and who, among French collaborators, favored more rather than less cooperation between Vichy and Hitler. For hours, Grimm and Laval negotiated the fate of a nation—after all, Laval claimed, the interests of France and Germany were now all but identical.[10]

If it is not quite true that France was facing a possible civil war between democrats and fascists in the midthirties, it is also not quite true that such an idea was unrealistic to the point of absurdity.[11] After France fell, government under the leaders of Vichy—such as Philippe Pétain and Laval—was rightly feared by democrats well before the German army was marching down the Champs-Élysées. This is one way of understanding the Vichy government that was put in power by the German invasion. What was established at Vichy was the government of collaborators that might well have emerged from just such a civil war if the fascists and extreme right had been victorious. The German invasion essentially ratified a quasi-fascistic victory in a civil war that never quite took place. And while he supervised the German relation to the propaganda around the trial of Herschel Grynszpan, Grimm's larger task had been to cultivate contact with the people who would run that treacherous government-to-be.

But observing France from his safe Swiss perch during the *drôle de guerre*, Grimm became convinced that any effort to try Herschel during that period would result in acquittal. He was also aware that if it took place during the time that France and Germany were, at least in name, at war, any Grynszpan trial would probably result in the revelation of Nazi crimes both over the deportation of the Polish Jews and the even more outrageous crimes of the Kristallnacht. There had been a change in Paris: Before that war, Judge Tesnière had quietly assured Grimm that, since they had occurred after the shooting, the events of the Kristallnacht would be deemed irrelevant to Herschel's trial. With the approach of war, Judge Tesnière had changed his view: Herschel had been motivated in response to German anti-Semitism, and therefore evidence of German anti-Semitism was admissible. A simple switch.[12]

Faced with these bad propaganda odds, Grimm became determined to find some way of preventing the trial from taking place at all. He arranged for a mission to Paris on the part of a compliant Swiss lawyer, a gentleman with a very neutral look: Marcel Guinand. And with whom would Guinand meet? None other than Georges Bonnet, who after war was declared was moved in the cabinet: He ceased to be minister of foreign affairs, and became minister of justice—once again perfectly placed to decide Herschel's fate. And Bonnet was one of those French politicians who were Grimm's specialty: the ones who tilted in the German direction.

Charged with the mission of stopping the trial, Marcel Guinand left Switzerland for Paris on October 19, 1939, a little more than six weeks after war broke out. Grimm was concerned: Herschel had sent another letter to the minister himself—probably ghostwritten by his lawyers—seeking release from prison. "I know that France is passing through a tragic period. I therefore request that you allow me to enlist in the French Army. I wish to redeem the act which I committed with my blood, and thus repair the troubles which I have caused the country which accorded me its hospitality."[13] The recipient of this request was Georges Bonnet himself, and the Associated Press reported that "informed legal sources"—Moro-Giafferi?—believed that such a release was "highly improbable." But of course it was improbable. Someone—someone who knew perfectly well that release was improbable—had had the letter sent to Bonnet, and in the process informed the press. The propaganda value of Herschel's plea was obvious. The boy who everyone claimed had threatened the peace now wanted to join the war.[14] The danger of acquittal was more urgent than ever. Some countermove was called for. Grimm's countermove was the Guinand mission.

The Guinand mission serves as one small measure of the degree to which pro-German and/or fascistic sympathies lingered in certain sectors of the French government even after war was declared. It was arranged for Guinand to carry his message to a high official of the Ministry of Justice in Paris: the director of the Section for Criminal Affairs, one M. M. Batestini. Be it war, no war, or phony war, Batestini proved sympathetic—more than sympathetic—to the German case. He agreed: If Herschel were to be tried under present conditions, the deplorable result would be that he would be acquitted. Batestini also agreed that such a trial would almost certainly become a forum for anti-German "smear" propaganda—a result which, speaking as an official of the Ministry of Justice, he would find "scandalous."[15]

But the director of the Section for Criminal Affairs was flummoxed. How would it be possible to convict Herschel Grynszpan and avoid "scandalous" "smear" propaganda from being presented to the court? Batestini suggested that the problem was knotty enough that it should be put before Minister Bonnet himself—the same Bonnet whose influence had delayed the trial steadily until the start of the war.

And so a meeting at the top was proposed with the express purpose of finding some way to block what Dorothy Thompson called "a higher justice" in the trial of Herschel Grynszpan.

The meeting with Bonnet had to be rearranged at the last minute when Bonnet's brother, Charles Bonnet, was killed in an accident. Rather than postpone the meeting, a conference was arranged with a man named Victor Dupuich, who was Bonnet's *chef de cabinet* and right hand. We may assume that Dupuich spoke with Bonnet's voice.

It was a strange meeting for representatives of two countries at war.

Dupuich was not deceived by the charade of the vom Rath family as the *partie civile*. He knew perfectly that he was conferring with a representative of the German government. This does not seem to have troubled him. After all, a German diplomat *had* been shot inside the German embassy; the German government *did* have an interest in the course of Grynszpan justice. Guinand came clean; he openly admitted that he had been sent by Grimm, and suggested that if the two of them were able to settle the Grynszpan problem to their mutual satisfaction, other outstanding issues between France and Germany—for example, the exchange of prisoners of war—might be discussed simultaneously. He was ready to negotiate, government to government.[16]

In his written report to Grimm, Guinand described his success in rosy terms. He was struck by the remarkable cordiality with which he had been received and delighted by the readiness of the French officials to cooperate with their German foes. Everyone understood perfectly: There was a clear and present danger that if a Grynszpan trial were held during this time of war, it would be used as a platform for anti-German propaganda. That—everyone agreed—must be avoided. Fortunately, the Ministry of Justice was in a position to avoid it, and Dupuich promised to do "whatever was necessary" to see to it that it was avoided. The means? Simply do not hold the trial. Such was the view of the Ministry of Justice in wartime.

Grimm had every reason to be reassured: The Guinand mission could not have had a better outcome. A little later however, Grimm once again became nervous. In January 1940 he learned through his sources in France that a propaganda film was being planned claiming that the Gestapo was behind the vom Rath murder, using Herschel as its pawn. Not long after Grimm learned about the film, he learned that a series of radio broadcasts featuring anti-German propaganda was scheduled, with Moro-Giafferi as one of the featured speakers. There was now an urgent danger that the Grynszpan story would enter the stream of anti-German propaganda flowing from France.[17]

Then a final bit of information left Grimm truly alarmed. Herschel had once again petitioned the ministry for an early trial, once again giving as his reason his desire to leave prison and join the French army.[18]

So in early January, just as Herschel was threatening to stage another hunger strike, Guinand was once again dispatched to Paris. It is a measure of Grimm's typical role in the realms of German intelligence that Guinand's twelve-page report on this mission was mainly devoted to "political, economic, and military intelligence aspects, troop movements and morale, and public opinion." In short, the ordinary scut work of intelligence. Yet he did meet once again with "authorities" from the Ministry of Justice, who, while not as fulsome in their reassurance as they had been in October, did assure him that whatever might happen, the interests of the *partie civile* would be "safeguarded." Guinand correctly reported that he took this to mean, in practice, that no action of any kind was contemplated.[19] And sure enough, no trial would be held.

Ever.

13

"I'm Herschel Grynszpan! Arrest Me!"

One might suppose that the coming of the Second World War would discredit Georges Bonnet. It didn't. As foreign minister, his policy had been more or less abject appeasement of Hitler's plans for conquest in Eastern Europe, to be clinched by some sort of special relationship between France and Germany—perhaps something not entirely unlike Spain's or Italy's quasi-fraternal bond to Nazi fascism, or for that matter, the quasi-fraternal bond between Nazi fascism and Vichy. Yet when September 3, 1939, pulled the rug out from these compromises and fantasies, Georges Bonnet had landed on his feet, as minister of justice, the executive in charge of Herschel Grynszpan's fate.[1]

As a foreign minister, Bonnet had always tried to avoid offending the Nazi dictator. He had assumed that Herschel's acquittal, or for that matter anything short of the guillotine for this pawn of the World Jewish Conspiracy, would offend Hitler mightily.

But after September 1939, was it *still* important to avoid offending Hitler? Bonnet's answer was, as usual, a duplicitous yes and no. During the phony war, Bonnet's pro-German ideas were very much alive in France.

The standard Bonnetiste right-wing claim was that going to war over the German invasion of Poland and Eastern Europe had been "unnecessary,"[2] and after the fall of France in June 1940, the notion that there ought to be a special bond between France and Nazi Germany took on a whole new complexion. France—or at least the French government—changed overnight from being an antifascist republic to being a quasi-fascist dictatorship. The relation of victor to vanquished meant collaboration, and not surprisingly, Bonnet made the transition from opposition to collaboration with seamless ease, becoming a member of Vichy's "National Council," which had been created to draft a constitution of a German-dominated France, all the while angling for some important diplomatic position under the New Order.[3] So after the fall of the Third Republic, Bonnet once again landed on his feet, this time in Vichy. In 1940, Vichy must have looked, *faut de mieux*, rather like the catbird seat, since Bonnet was pretty sure (not to mention hopeful) that England would be conquered quickly, just as France had been conquered quickly, and Germany would have won the war in Europe.[4]

Under Bonnet, the French Ministry of Justice did not bestir itself even to indict Herschel until the exact moment when the phony war was metamorphosing into a very real battle to the death. Herschel Grynszpan was indicted for the murder of Ernst vom Rath on June 8, 1940—a full twenty months after the crime was committed, but only three days after the evacuation of the British Expeditionary Force at Dunkirk and two days before the French government, sliding from complacency to catastrophe, abandoned Paris and fled south, a few hundred kilometers ahead of the conquering Wehrmacht.[5]

The timing of Herschel's last-minute indictment remains bizarre. Why a government facing collapse should have paused in the midst of the debacle to fuss with this detail defies easy explanation or even speculation. The German enemy was at the gates. The nation was on the verge of anarchy. The Germans were obviously the sure winners. Already, major figures in the government—including Pétain—favored capitulation and armistice. Why was *this*, after an unconscionable delay of a year and a half, the moment to hand down an indictment against Herschel? An impartial trial was obviously impossible. Did Bonnet *want* to put Herschel in German hands?

What Bonnet wanted no longer mattered. The Germans were far from having forgotten about the assassin, but they no longer had any interest in seeing him tried under the auspices of French justice, even assuming French justice would dutifully convict and behead the boy, no questions asked. Beheading was not enough. The order had gone out; advancing with the German army was a special unit of the Gestapo assigned with one simple task: to find Herschel Grynszpan, arrest him, and bring him to Berlin, secretly and—above all else—*alive*.[6] Hitler had his own plans for Herschel, and they were startling plans that went way beyond mere guillotining.

The German army marched into Paris on June 14, 1940. The next day, Friedrich Grimm arrived in the capital at the side of his immediate superior, Otto Abetz, the "ambassador" who would be in effect the new Nazi viceroy of France. Grimm ordered the Gestapo to scour Paris for every document relevant to the vom Rath murder.[7] Moro-Giafferi and Weill-Goudchaux's homes and offices were ransacked. The files of every Jewish—or Gentile— organization that had shown any interest in Herschel's fate were pilfered. Grimm was sure—*sure*—that if he dug deep enough, he would dig up the World Jewish Conspiracy behind it all. After all, they ran the world. Didn't they? Maddeningly, the Ministry of Justice dossier on the boy assassin could not at first be found, but everyone with any connection to the killing was interviewed. And of course, the Gestapo was dispatched to Fresnes prison, hoping to seize the assassin himself while he was still locked in his French cell.

But when they got to Fresnes, Herschel's cell was empty.

In early June, once it was obvious that Paris was doomed, and right around the time that Herschel was indicted, Bonnet's Ministry of Justice decided to move its judicial administration south to the town of Angers, and to disperse its more important prisoners over various jails across the country. Herschel was dispatched with a group of other high-profile inmates from Fresnes to the town of Orléans, which lies about one hundred kilometers due south of Paris.

One hundred kilometers was not far enough. Orléans was also doomed. On June 15, the day after the German troops entered Paris and paraded down the Champs-Élysées, Herschel was sent by some sort of "convoy" (buses? a train?) along with ninety-six other prisoners heading due south, out of Orléans, this time toward the town of Bourges.

As it crept toward Bourges, this convoy of malefactors was bombed and strafed by the Luftwaffe. In the bashed and burning vehicles, ninety-six prisoners realized that this was the moment for their escape. The guards lost control—or more likely, gave up control. Given the vast scale of the debacle, their mission must have looked like an exercise in futility. These French prisoners would soon be German prisoners no matter what they did. They were running, but the black shadow of defeat was surging after them, and it was catching up. Their doomed southward flight could end only in defeat at the Mediterranean. Everyone—at least everyone except Herschel—sensed that the game was lost. Soon ninety prisoners were tumbling out of the wreckage, running free under the June sky, plunging into the surrounding fields and woods. By the time they had vanished, only six of the ninety-six inmates were still under the guards' control.

Herschel seems to have been one of those six inmates. He refused to run. He did not want freedom in the open air. He wanted to remain a prisoner of the French Republic, and he insisted that the dazed guards keep him in their custody.[8]

In retrospect, this request may seem almost incomprehensible, even a little mad. Freedom beckoned. Chaos was swirling around him. Why not take his chances with flight? Various chroniclers see his decision in various lights. For French physician Alain Cuénot, the gesture is evidence of a callow and unimaginative adolescent mind, unable to seize an obvious opportunity.

Schwab sees it more sympathetically. Herschel's lethal enemies were over-running France. The boy assumed—God knows, with good reason—that if he were to fall into German hands, he would be a goner. With his famous face and name, shaky French and thick German accent, throwing himself on the mercy of the countryside might amount to little more than asking to be betrayed and captured. On the sixteenth or seventeenth of June 1940, he probably had no sense of the scale of the defeat. He surely didn't know that the French government was about to be transformed. The French were the enemies of the Germans. Weren't they? So surely they would protect him. Wouldn't they? It was a guess, and it turned out to be a very bad guess. But it was a very understandable one.

The chase was on.

On June 19, Grimm informed the German Foreign Ministry that the Gestapo had found Herschel "illegally" removed from Fresnes, and that "a special troop of the Secret Field Police is following his trail."[9] The Gestapo had swept from Fresnes to Orléans only to find him gone, on his way to Bourges. They followed, speeding south.

The Gestapo squad was still on its way when the guards from the wrecked convoy appeared in Bourges shepherding their strange, straggling little band of trusties. Led to the prison officials, Herschel boldly announced that he was Herschel Grynszpan and demanded that he be arrested and put into custody.

His demand was greeted with consternation. The Germans would be there at any time. The other five inmates still in custody were probably not figures of even slight interest to the Gestapo. They could be held without complications. But Herschel? To hold him was at once dangerous and futile. It was dangerous, because to be found giving refuge to one of the conquering army's most wanted fugitives risked reprisal. It was futile, because it meant that Herschel would soon, and certainly, be in German hands, facing lethal danger that he might escape running through the French fields. Both for his sake and their own, the Bourges officials wanted him out of their hands. They wanted him to vanish from Bourges, and vanish without a trace.

Doubtless hoping he would run to freedom, the officials' decision was to make no record of his presence in Bourges and send him—it appears on foot—to the next town south, a place called Châteauroux. Exactly how Herschel traveled the sixty-five kilometers from Bourges to Châteauroux remains murky. It seems likely that he hitched some sort of ride on the roads clogged with the fleeing French.

In any case, when the Gestapo got to Bourges, Herschel had eluded them once again. Though the warden and public prosecutor had left no sign of Herschel's presence in the prison records, the Gestapo interrogated everyone, then rushed to Châteauroux, where once again they did not find Herschel. It seems that the Germans suspected, quite mistakenly, that the public prosecutor in Bourges, a man named Paul Ribeyre, knew the boy's true whereabouts and that he had helped Herschel to go into hiding somewhere other than Châteauroux. The Gestapo was afraid to report to Hitler that they had lost Grynszpan's trail. They proceeded to interrogate two people whom they suspected might know where the elusive prisoner was hidden. The first was Paul Ribeyre. The second was Pierre Cavarroc, who was no less than the attorney general of the republic.

Ribeyre was repeatedly questioned in Bourges, until in July he was taken to a military prison in Paris—Cherche-Midi, where Dreyfus had been held—and was subjected to the more brutal investigations of the Gestapo, varieties of what would later be called "enhanced interrogation." They included, on July 11, 1940, being brought to an interrogation room where he faced a pistol lying on a table. He was told that he would be allowed to write a last letter to his wife, after which he was to turn his face to the wall and wait for a bullet through his brain. It was under the threat of this death that Ribeyre at last confessed the simple truth: that yes, he had seen Grynszpan in Bourges, kept his name out of the prison records, and sent him on, anonymously, to Châteauroux. That simple truth was perhaps too simple for the

Gestapo. They had, after all, already been to Châteauroux, where once again they had found nothing. But the confession did save Ribeyre's life.

The interrogation of the former attorney general of the republic, Pierre Cavarroc, did not include the threat of death, but it did include the threat of arrest.[10] In truth, Cavarroc knew less about Herschel's whereabouts than Ribeyre knew, but he did have some idea about the whereabouts of something else that the Gestapo very much wanted: Herschel's Ministry of Justice dossier.

When Paris fell and was occupied, the attorney general had assembled a set of the most sensitive dossiers on criminal cases then before the ministry, including the ministry's dossier on Herschel Grynszpan. He crammed all these dossiers into a largish suitcase and managed to squeeze it shut, but before he closed it completely he also stashed inside the state seals of the French Republic, which had been left behind, lying on a table in the abandoned ministry. He then gave this heavy valise to a certain Monsieur Menegaud, an employee, and told him to get it south to what it was hoped would be the ministry's new home in Angers.

Menegaud then left Paris driving his own car, the precious suitcase in the trunk. The roads were jammed with soldiers from the defeated army and the fleeing population of Paris, all vulnerable to Nazi Luftwaffe attacks that flew over regularly, engines screaming, as they swept down to strafe the columns of defeated traffic. Just outside of Orléans some of this strafing hit Menegaud's car and left it completely disabled. Taking the heavy suitcase in hand, Menegaud made his way on foot, carrying the Grynszpan dossier and the great seals of France to the offices of the Ministry of Justice in Orléans, where he left the bag and its contents in the care of the concierge of those offices, and then turned around and began to make his way back to Paris, there to report the disaster he had encountered.

Attorney General Cavarroc was just about to be arrested after long and fruitless interrogation by the Gestapo when Menegaud appeared in Cavarroc's office, and the secret was out. The Gestapo rushed to Orléans, where they found the fateful suitcase exactly where Menegaud had left it, in the hands of the local concierge.

So through Cavarroc, the Gestapo was able to retrieve Herschel's Ministry of Justice dossier and, incidentally, the great seals of the French Republic. And through threatening Ribeyre with death, they were put back on the trail of Herschel himself.

Not that it helped much, since when the Gestapo squad raced to Châteauroux, Herschel had vanished once again.

Where was he? Herschel had been refused confinement in Châteauroux on June 18, and he seems to have left that little town on foot the same day. His odyssey ended five days later, on June 23, in the largish city of Toulouse, some four hundred kilometers due south.[11] During the five days between June 18 and June 23, France was transformed. The French Third Republic had died, and the collaborationist government of France known as Vichy had been born. The new regime, acceptable to the Germans under Marshal Pétain, had sued for an armistice, and on June 22, that armistice had been signed in Compèigne—in the same railroad car in which Germany had surrendered to France in 1918. Hitler had been present, jubilant, literally dancing a jig. The French government was now allied with Herschel's enemy. Herschel had arrived in Toulouse exactly one day too late.

But how did he get from Châteauroux to Toulouse? What took him five days? The most plausible answer to that question comes from one of the heroic figures in the modern history of tyranny: an American newspaperman named Varian Fry. Fry was an almost absurdly presentable WASP (with a father on Wall Street, educated at Hotchkiss and Harvard) who was chosen to go to new France of Vichy, representing the Emergency Rescue Committee, a group in New York formed in response to a clause in the armistice—article XIX—requiring the Vichy government to "surrender on demand" any German wanted by the Nazi regime. There had been fifty thousand German-Jewish refugees in Paris when the battle of France began. All of them were potentially in danger of deportation under article XIX, and the more prominent among them were in grave danger. All were seeking some way out of the France that had been their uneasy refuge in the years since Hitler took power. Fry was the real-life figure networking the kind of escapes from Vichy immortalized in the 1942 film *Casablanca*. He managed the rescue of something like two to four thousand Jews and refugees from Vichy.

When he got to Marseilles, Varian Fry heard from one of these refugees the story of how Herschel Grynszpan was finally captured by the Gestapo, and Fry recounted the story in his book *Surrender on Demand*.

It seems that after leaving Châteauroux on June 18, Herschel somehow traveled the 122 kilometers to the town of Limoges. Did he walk? Hitch rides? The trek took a while: It is likely that he arrived in Limoges only on June 21 or even June 22. When he reached Limoges, he once again marched into the local prison and announced that he was Herschel Grynszpan. Once again, he asked to be taken into custody. Once again, he was refused. But the public prosecutor in Limoges assigned Herschel a false name and put him in the custody of two gendarmes who were instructed to escort him to Toulouse, which was 250 kilometers due south as the crow flies. This they did, arriving in Toulouse on a Sunday, June 23. Since it was a Sunday—and one day after the death of the French Republic—they found the prefecture of police closed. At this point, the gendarmes told Herschel to find a room for the night and come back to the prefecture in the morning.

Find a room for the night and come back in the morning? Such instructions were bizarre, almost incomprehensible, and Herschel clearly did not grasp their import.

According to Fry, the gendarmes holding Herschel were expecting him to run; they assumed—they *hoped*—that he would simply not appear the next morning. "Grynszpan's case," Fry wrote, "is typical of the attitude of the French authorities; they would give a man a chance to escape before they arrested him, but if he didn't take it they would arrest him and turn him over, in obedient fulfillment of the terms of the armistice."[12] Herschel waited through the night, and when the cops returned in the morning, he was still there, still eager to be taken into custody.

Probably disappointed, the cops obliged him.

He was once again a prisoner of the French government, unaware that as of thirty-six hours before, the French government had been invisibly transformed into a regime that was collaborating with his enemies, and Herschel had turned himself over to those collaborators.

Still using the false name he'd been given in Limoges, Herschel was held for a month in the gloom of the Toulouse prison—a far cry from the soccer fields and Ping-Pong tables of Fresnes. When the Germans realized what had happened, Herschel Grynszpan was the very first person the Germans demanded be returned under article XIX. He was their most wanted man.

The irony of Herschel in Toulouse did not stop there. He was also unaware that at the moment he arrived, Toulouse was swarming with Jews and fugitives from the Nazi regime looking for means of escape from France. They were often finding it. Toulouse was Casablanca. If Herschel had tried to escape that night, he would have run into countless people like himself, all in flight and all in jeopardy from the Nazis. He might even have run into Uncle Abraham and Aunt Chawa, who had fled Paris as the Nazis advanced. They all were a few miles away when he turned himself over to the gendarmes. Not only were his aunts and uncles all in Toulouse, but also one of his lawyers, Maître Frankel, was with them. Moro-Giafferi himself, who ultimately escaped to Switzerland, was at that moment taking refuge in the nearby town of Aiguillon. When Herschel demanded to be made a prisoner, possible freedom and the people he loved most were only a mile or two away.[13]

The false name bestowed on him in Limoges served him well—for a while. The Gestapo had followed Herschel's trail into Vichy, but it took time and some frustrated searching before they became aware that the anonymous prisoner in the Toulouse prison was really Herschel Grynszpan. When they did, the "demand" was made for his surrender to the Germans, and the Vichy Ministry of Justice ordered him transferred from Toulouse to the city of Vichy. From the town of Vichy, on July 18 he was taken in handcuffs to the little town of Moulins on the demarcation line. There, on July 18, 1940, the French police led him across the line and handed him over to the waiting squad of Gestapo officers.[14]

He had become a crucial prisoner of the Third Reich. He was nineteen years old.

14

Herschel the Captive

Hitler now held the pawn in his hand, and he and Goebbels were able to
lay their plans on how to play him. They were sinister plans, and so bizarre
that in the twenty-first century it takes a leap of the imagination to understand them at all. They intended to use Herschel as the prime defendant in
a great propaganda trial proving that "international Jewry" was responsible
for starting the Second World War. And having "proved" that crime, they
planned to use it as part of the radical new anti-Semitic propaganda campaign masking the Holocaust.

Many assumed what Herschel himself assumed: that once he was firmly
in German hands, his execution—more properly, his murder—would
swiftly follow. There would be a firing squad, a gallows, a bullet through
the brain, something—and when he vanished he left nothing but rumors.
Weill-Goudchaux, a serious but impressionable jurist, somehow got it into
his head that during that summer of 1940, Herschel had been beheaded
by someone in Toulouse, where the French held him in their last lockup.[1]
Meanwhile, Maître Isidore Frankel, another member of Moro-Giafferi's defense team, in the course of making his own escape to the United States,
learned that Herschel was being held in Toulouse, and made an effort to see
and perhaps free him. By the time Maître Frankel acted, it was too late.[2]

—

The indisputable reality was that by July 1940 Herschel was a prisoner in Berlin, and instead of being tortured or killed, he was being treated—as prisoners go—with every consideration. Not a hair on his nineteen-year-old head was to be harmed. Not yet. Once Vichy and the Gestapo had him in their clutches, once he crossed, handcuffed, over the demarcation line between Vichy and occupied France, he had been spirited in haste to Paris, passing through the fallen capital without being allowed to see anyone, even enemies of such importance as Friedrich Grimm.[3] Instead, he was hustled onto a secret night flight and flown from Paris to Berlin, where he was taken direct to Gestapo headquarters on Prinz-Albrecht-Strasse and locked into the subterranean prison the Gestapo maintained in its basement, a boutique dungeon reserved for prisoners of exceptional importance. All this was done sub rosa. Goebbels saw to it that the German media had no clue that the assassin of Ernst vom Rath was now a prisoner of the Reich. Meanwhile, the French and Anglo-American newspapers—insofar as they cared about the baby-faced killer any longer—were stuck with substanceless rumors and what little they could gather about his southward flight to captivity. *The New York Times* got wind of his odyssey from Paris to Orléans to Bourges to Châteauroux to Toulouse, begging to be imprisoned at each stop, and published an amused little feature about it—a scrap of levity in the midst of the heavy debacle. But after that, it seemed that Herschel Grynszpan, a fifteen-minute celebrity from a bypassed political moment, had simply vanished.[4]

In fact, he was being prepared for a new and politically much more important level of visibility, and he knew it.

We know this from his own words.

During the spring of 1942—almost two years after he was taken prisoner by the Nazis—Herschel devised (in his head!) an alphabetical code that he used to encrypt and dictate his personal testament to his cellmate, whom he believed to be some sort of political prisoner of the Nazis.[5] This testament is his own account of his ordeal, and it is the most remarkable document in this remarkable story.[6]

By the time he dictated his testament, Herschel's privileged status as a prisoner was over. He had attempted suicide twice, and to prevent a third attempt, he was bound and chained in his cell, so that he was physically unable to write. Hence the need to dictate; hence, the need for a code. He had only his native ingenuity to rely on, and his only hope was that the document might somehow be found, deciphered, and published after his death.[7] Gerald Schwab writes: "There is no indication what type of cipher Grynszpan utilized. However, it must have been one that he was able to develop and keep in his head, such as a simple numerical code or one consisting of transposed letters, since his fellow prisoner obviously did not have the key."[8]

Slowly, arduously, Herschel dictated in German a series of six daily entries, letter by encrypted letter. At first, he managed to get down only twenty words or so per day. As time went on, as he became more adept with the cipher, he managed to work his way up to sixty or more than a hundred.

This astonishing document is Herschel's final statement of his understanding of what had happened. "When France extradited me to Germany," he wrote, "I thought that there would be no trial in that the Gestapo would murder me." Expecting to die, and die quickly, he was at first bewildered to find himself alive. "The French did turn me over to the Gestapo as a prisoner, but they treated me exceptionally very well." Why? His fellow prisoners quickly set him straight. "I heard there from other prisoners one is treated well by the Gestapo only if one has special plans for that person. In my case, this could only be a propaganda trial."[9]

Herschel guessed rightly about the propaganda trial. The legal extravaganza Hitler and Goebbels had in mind would be held in Berlin with Herschel in the dock. It would dominate the headlines. It would be broadcast live on German radio and it would be held in the biggest courtroom in Berlin, which would be packed with press from around the world—especially press from occupied countries—and crowded with fascist cultural celebrities such as Céline. Hitler was assured that the trial would "neutralize foreign compassion for Jews."[10] Specifically the trial would be designed to prove that the murder of Ernst vom Rath had been part of a Jewish conspiracy to sabotage the Franco-German entente that Bonnet and von Welczeck were arranging when this small person, this boy, committed his crime, which in turn somehow fomented the war. The claim seems ludicrous on its face, but something like that same lie had worked in the Kristallnacht, and Goebbels was sure it would work again. In 1940, with the fall of France still inexplicable and unbearable in the eyes of the world, Goebbels's faithful servants Friedrich Grimm and Wolfgang Diewerge were able to put together an array of fascist and fascist-fellow-traveling witnesses, including some who would attract world headlines, all prepared to come into the court and swear that the theory was true. The Jews had started the Second World War.

This legal charade was designed to serve a larger purpose. By late 1941, German anti-Semitism had moved far beyond the pogroms of the Kristallnacht. Mass murder was imminent. Historians of Herschel's life agree: His trial was to be a propaganda link to nothing less than the Final Solution. Pointing to the presence of Adolf Eichmann on the planning committee, Gerald Schwab writes about the trial, "The 'guidelines' called for the trial of Herschel Grynszpan to fix blame on 'World Jewry' for the outbreak of the war and to call for the destruction of the Jews as a pre-requisite for the coming new order. The trial, in other words, was to justify the 'Final Solution' . . ." Schwab adds: "Had the trial taken place as scheduled, it would have coincided with the Wannsee Conference (January 20, 1942) called to discuss the logistics of killing some 11 million human beings."[11] Note well that Adolf Eichmann likewise played a leading role at the Wannsee Conference itself. He was present for planning it all.

Alan Steinweis reaches the same conclusion. Against the background of the Wannsee Conference, "the trial planners clearly understood their project as a method for legitimizing the 'Final Solution' . . . There can be little doubt, then, that at the very highest levels of the Nazi regime, the planning for the Grynszpan trial was understood in connection with the unfolding mass murder of the Jews."[12]

Of course Herschel could not possibly have imagined exactly how monstrous the purpose of his trial really was. His mind had already been seared by the great pogrom of November 9–10. Not even he, with his fiery adolescent imagination of disaster, could possibly foresee Auschwitz. All he could see were "more bloody pogroms." They were enough.

In Paris, Herschel had reacted to his grim celebrity like the seventeen-year-old that he was: shallowly. Even his penance—penance for having jeopardized his people, and even for having killed vom Rath—was counterbalanced into shallowness by his egomania, his self-importance, and his boyish sense of himself as God's pawn. He may have grieved over the Kristallnacht, but he did love his celebrity. Now that he was captured and held in secret, all that changed. His name was no longer in the newspapers. He was no longer on the evening radio news. No reporters were making their pilgrimage to Fresnes to flatter him. In Germany, he understood something that he had never quite understood in France: that his life was at an end.

He saw that he would never leave German custody alive. That knowledge changed him, and in its death-directed way, made him grow. While he was still in France, his self-importance could be animated by hope. From his lawyers' perspective, it was foolish hope, but it is what gave Herschel the boyish swagger he had when he strode into meetings with those lawyers, or the police, or psychiatrists or journalists; handshakes all around, proud to be the boy warrior, conscious of the glow of his strange celebrity. It is said that from the beginning—when to adult eyes, the guillotine seemed possible, and even likely—he believed that he was certain to be acquitted. Later, to be sure, during the anti-German atmosphere of the *drôle de guerre*, he did have genuine hope of leniency or acquittal. But before? Even Moro-Giafferi feared he was doomed. But in Herschel's vanity, he always assumed that he would be set free, always took it for granted that he would be rescued by some higher justice. What else could happen to God's pawn?

Even during his flight south as the Germans swept into a conquered France, he still had hope. What looked like the comedy of his effort to stay in the custody of the French was in truth a misled but deadly serious effort to find shelter and protection from what he assumed would be certain death at German hands.

But now, in the darkness of his German captivity, all hope was gone. As a result, Herschel developed an entirely new relation to his own survival, and therefore to himself. From this point forward, all his thinking was dominated by the need to prevent the show trial from ever taking place. He was no longer trying to save his own life. He assumed that he would die. Boy that he was, he saw himself as a dead boy walking, and that certainty was only confirmed when he was not summarily executed. Then he came to realize that he was being given special treatment merely to prepare him for the trial that would lead to his public execution, probably hanged or beheaded. In the words of the historian Michael Marrus, Herschel "almost certainly knew that he was only being kept alive for purposes of the trial, and that by subverting these plans he might have been signing his own death warrant."[13] Menaced in this way, the threat of death gave him something he had not had since he had so very foolishly shot vom Rath: a purpose. At seventeen, he had wanted to make the whole world see. He now sought invisibility. His task now was to defend his obscurity and die in it. He had to do something—anything—to prevent the Nazis from putting him in the dock.

In his testament, he wrote that summary execution—his murder—"was naturally more to my liking than a grand propaganda trial which undoubtedly would have resulted in bloody pogroms . . . This [the trial] I wanted to avoid in any event in order to prevent any possible pogroms which could result through my trial and so that I personally would not be misused as a tool of German propaganda."[14]

—

Herschel was held in the prison of Gestapo headquarters for six months—from the time Vichy released him into German hands in July 1940 until January 1941. During this time, Grimm and Diewerge wanted their prisoner to be kept close at hand while they conducted their "investigations."

The two propagandists were not investigating the essential facts of the original crime. When Paris fell, the Gestapo searched and seized all the paperwork they could find, whether in lawyers' offices or police records or psychiatrists' files or the proceedings of the court, and dispatched this huge bureaucratic haystack to Berlin. Grimm and Diewerge had no doubt about exactly what had happened in the office of Ernst vom Rath that November morning. They had the complete French dossiers—several complete dossiers—on hand. The French investigation had been massive, and it left no room for doubt. Herschel Grynszpan had assassinated Ernst vom Rath motivated by his belief that he was protesting and avenging the Nazi dispossession and deportation of his German family and eighteen thousand other Polish Jews who were legal German residents. About all this, there was nothing new to investigate. Whatever questions they posed to Herschel in the basement interrogation rooms of Gestapo headquarters were focused on something else.

Because there was a needle in Herschel's bureaucratic haystack that Grimm and Diewerge were convinced *had* to be buried somewhere, and for which they spent those six months searching. They assumed—they were sure, absolutely *sure*—that somewhere in the murky background of Herschel's crime there had to be the invisible manipulating hand of a conspiracy. Not only a conspiracy, but *the* conspiracy: the conspiracy of "world Jewry." He *had* to have been the pawn of the Jews.

It appears that this assumption about the evidence and the lack of evidence—this assumption that the Jews who ruled the world must have covertly likewise ruled their young creature, Herschel—was sincere. Both Grimm and Diewerge seem to have gone to their graves convinced that Herschel could not possibly have acted alone, that he had to be in the service of that sinister Semitic higher power that in Himmler's words was the "driving force . . . the essence of everything that was negative."[15] They really believed their paranoiac myth. This sickening sincerity may partly explain why in their search for evidence of Jewry's hand guiding the world to war they did not concoct the "evidence," as Stalin's minions concocted "evidence" of the crimes of the old Bolsheviks who were tried in his great show trials of 1937 and 1938. They thought world Jewry was a real entity, and therefore whatever evidence they could dredge up would be genuine. Where they could find no evidence, that absence was in itself proof of how cleverly world Jewry was able to cover its insidious tracks.

And so they ransacked those heaping mounds of bureaucratic paper, seizing on any trace of Jewish influence or even interest in Herschel as conspiratorial. If a lawyer on Herschel's legal team turned out to be Jewish, that discovery became evidence of the grand plot. That Herschel admitted to having quite regularly read two Yiddish newspapers in Paris showed the stealthy power of "world Jewry" over his young mind. Any kind of support for Herschel in his situation—such as the support of the very Gentile Dorothy Thompson's Journalists' Defense Fund—was read as inspired and ordained by the Jews. In reality, many spokesmen for sundry Jewish organizations had done all they could to condemn Herschel's crime and distance themselves from him. To them, the Kristallnacht showed how the rash, reckless, infantile murder of vom Rath had merely sprayed gasoline onto the fires of Hitler's ideology. Many believed Herschel had been a pawn of the Gestapo. In fact, the Jewish community, such as it was, generally disapproved of Herschel.[16] That made no difference to Grimm and Diewerge. Any sign of organized Jewish concern for Herschel was brandished as part of a vast, coherent anti-German cabal.

Poring over the record, Grimm and Diewerge were able to piece together scraps of what looked to them like the tracks of this great conspiracy. Eventually all their material was published in both German and French in a kind of pamphlet of unconvincing but real facts and factoids woven into paranoid whole cloth by Grimm's inflammatory prose. This is a book of scraps. Nothing in it is capable of raising suspicions about some great conspiracy. It could convince only someone whose paranoid delusion was already in place.[17]

Herschel was kept in Berlin while this search of the documents went on. He was interrogated. In the first weeks of his captivity, he resorted to one of his more fanciful claims, saying that he had not gone to the embassy with the intention of killing anyone, but merely to shoot a bullet through the portrait of Hitler hanging there, after which he would awaken the world by committing suicide. He claimed that he shot vom Rath instead of himself in a distracted moment, only when the young lawyer had called him "a dirty Jew." Herschel even wrote out this fantasy confession in his own hand. Grimm and Diewerge brushed it aside as obviously untrue. The facts were clear and recorded unchangeably. The boy had gone to A la Fine Lame and bought a gun. With the gun in his pocket, he had taken the Métro to the German embassy on the rue de Lille. There he had asked to see "one of the embassy secretaries." He had been escorted to vom Rath's modest office, and sometime within the first minute after the door closed, pulled out the gun and fired the fatal shots. His actions were clear; the only mystery was whether they were the actions of someone's pawn.

The fact is that of course Grimm and Diewerge were never able to produce any connection to a great conspiracy. After the war, Otto Abetz, who was Grimm's immediate superior in Paris, wrote more honestly than his subordinate: "The search for possible accomplices produced no result, and it was impossible to establish whether Grynszpan had acted on his own or if he was only an emissary."[18]

In January 1941, after six months of being held in Gestapo headquarters, Herschel was transferred to the vast Nazi prison camp at Sachsenhausen, located some twenty-five miles north of Berlin in the city of Oranienburg. There he continued to receive unexpectedly gentle treatment by the SS.

There was a section of the prison camp known as "the Bunker." According to Schwab, the Bunker was reserved for high-profile prisoners. For example, the former chancellor of Austria, Kurt Schuschnigg, was held there.

And so was Herschel. He continued to be privileged in ways that suggested evil to come. He was not dressed in a prison uniform. He was allowed to wear ordinary street clothes. He did not have to display his prison number. His head was not shaved. He was not forced to eat prison fare; he ate what his guards ate. He was assigned jobs usually given to trusties, and it is said that his SS guards took a shine to him, giving him the nickname *Bube,* "little lad" or "scamp." They thought the kid was cute.[19]

He was a quick learner. By the time he arrived in Sachsenhausen, Herschel seems to have grasped that his concocted fictions about suicide and shooting Hitler's portrait were absurd and futile. They would never stop the trial. The only thing the Nazis cared about was the political motivation of his crime. Moro-Giafferi had been right. Herschel's sole hope of outmaneuvering Goebbels was to claim that he had killed vom Rath for something other than a political reason. That alone could stop the trial.

And Moro-Giafferi had handed him the perfect method. At Sachsenhausen, he decided to use the homosexual strategy, picked up where it had been left lying when he tossed it away in outrage. As he wrote in his testament, "in order to prevent [the trial] no means was good enough for me. I therefore utilized a touchy phase out of the life of Herr vom Rath which my attorney Godchaux [sic] acquainted me and out of this made up false testimony to the Gestapo." Using his delicate circumlocution, "a touchy phase in the life of Herr vom Rath," the boy expected to die. "I had hoped on the basis of this testimony that they would murder me so that no outsider would get wind thereof." Forbidden sex was secret, and Herschel hoped to die for it in secret.

It was a lie of course, and a daring one, but so long as it was properly told, it was not even important that it be believed. All that was needed was for the Nazis to believe Herschel might credibly claim it in court. Its success depended on the inflammatory power of scandal. Lie or no lie, Herschel's tormentors couldn't afford to let any plausible version rear its hot head long enough even to deny it. The world press would be watching; the gleeful anti-Nazi press would be waiting for any way to discredit the proceedings. GRYNSZPAN CLAIMS ILLICIT LIAISON WITH VOM RATH! CRIME OF PASSION! Vom Rath, who in real life had described Hitler as the antichrist, had been made into a National Socialist hero, proclaimed by Ribbentrop to be the "first casualty" in what the Nazis called the Jewish war against Germany. He could not be "exposed" on the front pages of every newspaper in the world as what their readers would see as a sexual predator given to molesting seventeen-year-old boys. The Nazis would never let it happen. Moro-Giafferi had earned his fee.

Thus determined to die, Herschel summoned his Nazi interrogator to Sachsenhausen and told him that after all this time, he had at last resolved to tell the shocking truth about the murder. It was humiliating. There was nothing heroic about it. Earlier, he had been too ashamed to let it be known. But now he was prepared to reveal the whole story.

He had been sexually entangled with vom Rath. That is why he killed him.

Herschel was quite ingenious fabricating the details of this lie, though this first version of the *crime passionel* was not as ingenious as he would eventually make it. But it made a good story. Even so, Grimm and Diewerge did not seem unduly concerned. Not at first. At first, Hitler was not even informed. Maybe even Goebbels wasn't. Sometime after telling it, Herschel was transferred "for protective custody" from Sachsenhausen to Flossenbürg concentration camp, where he confidently expected to be murdered, and murdered soon. Yet he lived on, privileged and perplexed. Meanwhile, the Nazis investigated his story and worked at refining their own great lie.

At first. Grimm and Diewerge worked amid competing bureaucracies, and the trial of Herschel Grynszpan was such a delicious morsel that every Nazi ministry was angling for a leading role in serving it up. The trial may have been Goebbels's idea, but in practical fact, he was not in charge. As the historian Michael Marrus puts it, "The various ministries supposed to be coordinating fell to quarreling with one another over the direction of the trial. The Propaganda Ministry, under Goebbels, wanted to heighten a campaign against 'International Judaism' by stressing the pre-war collusion of the Jews against Germany. The Foreign Ministry, under Ribbentrop, wanted the trial to accent the breakdown of relations with France. Representatives from the Ministry of Justice preferred a thorough, narrowly defined trial that would concentrate on the facts of the assassination."[20]

Nonetheless, a steering committee of Nazi bigwigs was formed, with representation from the various ministries. Its purpose was to hammer out some sort of schedule for the trial and above all some statement of its goals, something that could be submitted for highest-level approval by the Führer.

The most sinister member of this committee was none other than Adolf Eichmann, the thin-lipped, punctilious technician who would supervise the coming mass murder. Eichmann's presence was no accident. And the date set for the trial to begin—a date that was submitted to Hitler for his approval—was January 22, exactly two days after a vastly more important meeting in which Eichmann also played a leading role: the Wannsee Conference of January 20, 1942, at which tactical plans were laid before senior Nazis for implementing the Final Solution.[21]

Eichmann's presence was especially felt on October 19, 1941, when the committee prepared this six-point statement of goals to be submitted to the Führer. The trial would serve the following ideas.

1. The person of the assassin is basically of little interest ... World Jewry is in the dock.

2. The murder was World Jewry's signal for the start of the war against National Socialist Germany.

3. World Jewry drove the French people into this war against their own interests.

4. The bloodguilt of World Jewry is evident from numerous parallel cases, proof of which is available.

5.   Germany's battle against Jewry before the war, both inside and out-
     side its borders, was a battle for peace. *The destruction of Jewry is a
     prerequisite for the coming European new order* [my emphasis].

6.   The background of the murder demonstrates the overall responsibil-
     ity of Jewry, including the intellectual complicity of the Jews remain-
     ing in Germany after the [National Socialist] accession to power.[22]

*The destruction of Jewry is a prerequisite for the coming European new
order.* In this grim bureaucratic platitude echoes the language of the Final
Solution.

A few weeks later, a *Führermemorandum* was submitted to Hitler based on
these objectives. In it, the dictator was told that "the trial . . . offers the
possibility of proving before the entire world the decisive contribution of
World Jewry to the outbreak of the present war . . . All arguments have been
collected: they prove World Jewry's spiritual responsibility for the shooting
and its solidarity with the murderer . . . World Jewry will therefore sit in the
defendant's dock."[23]

In the same memorandum to Hitler, Goebbels and company played
their ace. Hitler was informed that they had lined up a witness whose testimony would dominate the headlines of the world, someone who could
give proof positive of the Jews' responsibility. This was none other than the
former foreign minister of France, Georges Bonnet. Grimm had arranged
it all: Bonnet was prepared to come from Paris to Berlin and swear before
the court that the anti-Semitic claims of the prosecutors were fully justified.
The Jews *had* started the war. Bonnet's testimony should not have come as
a surprise. The former foreign minister was, after all, an old acquaintance of
Grimm, that smiling friend of all the French near-fascists. The memorandum triumphantly told Hitler that "the (former) French Foreign Minister
Bonnet has prepared affidavits concerning the extent to which pressure was
exerted by World Jewry on the French government in 1939 to enter the

war. He is prepared to testify regarding these matters before the People's Court."[24]

But Bonnet had promised more. Around the same time, Grimm exulted that "Bonnet was willing to testify to being convinced that the assassination was not the act of a single fanatic, but a well-thought-out effort to sabotage Franco-German understanding and Ribbentrop's visit of December 1938." Hitler himself had been informed that "a connection between the Grynszpan trial and French foreign policy is above all proven by the Jewish attempts to undertake demonstrations during the visit [to Paris] of the Reich Foreign Minister."[25] Grimm's claim was that there was no daylight between Bonnet's view of the World Jewish Conspiracy and his own. Shortly after sending the memo to Hitler, Grimm rejoiced with a colleague that he "had discussed everything with Georges Bonnet in several long meetings, and M. Bonnet completely agrees with me on all points and is basically prepared to appear as a witness."[26] Goebbels, too, wrote in his diary that Bonnet's planned testimony "shows in what irresponsible fashion this war was started and how severely those must be punished who acted so irresponsibly." Later, he wrote: "the testimony of Bonnet, which will attribute war guilt primarily to the Jews, is prepared correctly so we can expect from it a great boost for our war effort."[27]

So Bonnet was ready to make world headlines in Herschel's trial.

Measuring the sincerity of Georges Bonnet's fascist fellow traveling—like measuring his sincerity on any subject—must be a matter for mere speculation. Substance and shadow merge. Did he truly believe in the New Order of Europe? Or were his many services to Hitler a matter of pure opportunism? Was he merely putting his money on the tyrant who, until 1942, looked like Europe's sure winner? Bonnet's avaricious wife, who was almost fanatically ambitious, dominated him. Many otherwise sensible people suspected them both of being German agents. Somerset Maugham thought they were, and tried without success to convince his brother, Frederic Maugham, Britain's Munich-besotted

Lord Chamberlain, of their guilt.[28] In 1939, a spy scandal, along with their friendship with Otto Abetz, brushed very near the couple. There was no proof, despite embarrassing circumstances.[29] There was never any proof. To grasp a fact among these illusions, it is at least certain that while he was minister of finance in 1937, Bonnet became convinced that in any head-to-head arms race or military confrontation with Germany, France would certainly lose. His policy therefore was always to maneuver around this perceived German dominance. Did that make him a fascist? Another shadow. But his promised testimony in Herschel's trial makes clear that he was an anti-Semite who was mightily impressed by Germany under National Socialism.[30]

In August 1939, when Hitler invaded Poland, in the senior reaches of the French government, Bonnet's voice was strongest against a declaration of war. With the coming of the *drôle de guerre*, Bonnet was banished from the Ministry of Foreign Affairs and appointed to the Ministry of Justice, where he became minister and, as the Guinand mission showed, the man responsible for keeping Herschel's case from ever coming to trial. Why was Bonnet retained in any capacity? Because he was a leader in a faction that was too powerful to be ignored. In office, Bonnet was busy with other matters besides being minister of justice. He was a leading member of a "peace lobby"—a who's who of the French politicians who leaned toward Germany. In March 1940, he met six times with that lobby to pressure the French government to appoint Pierre Laval—perhaps the most egregious collaborator—as foreign minister, the better to arrange "peace." Peace for the "peace lobby" meant French withdrawal from a war that the lobbyists called "unnecessary," while conceding Hitler's conquests in Eastern Europe and accepting the wartime status quo. "Peace," in short, would be a defeat without a battle.[31]

Then came the fall of France and the new German-dominated government in Vichy. Bonnet flourished under the new puppet government, while his former chief, Édouard Daladier, fled with numerous other officials of the Third Republic to French North Africa, where they hoped to establish a French government in exile. The effort failed; Daladier himself was arrested in Morocco by the Vichy police and brought back to metropolitan France, where he was imprisoned and charged with nothing less than treason—treason for having led a nation defeated by the Germans. The Nazis enthusiastically supported this charge and looked forward to a large show trial of Third Republic officials in the southern French town of Riom.[32] The Riom trial would be parallel to the trial of Herschel Grynszpan in Berlin, fixing responsibility for the debacle on the government that had the effrontery to declare war on Germany. In Herschel's trial, it was to be the Jews who had forced the French government into making this absurd, unnecessary move. In Daladier's trial, it was the "decadence" of the democracy the former premier represented. The anti-Semitic focus of the Grynszpan trial was of course going to be echoed in Riom: A prime defendant, along with Daladier, would be Léon Blum, who was Jewish and had been the premier of France in the years of the antifascist Popular Front. The Riom trial was intended to discredit French democracy. The Grynszpan trial was intended to discredit the Jews. Democracy and the Jews together had brought about the debacle. Democracy and the Jews were to be put on trial in preparation for a fascist France.

While his colleague Léon Blum and his former chief Daladier were facing trials for their lives, Bonnet was a senior statesman, being appointed to various eminent boards and commissions. Of these, by far the most important was something known as the National Council.

The National Council was composed of what might be viewed as the most distinguished profascist political and social figures in France. Defenders of Bonnet—and even in the twenty-first century, he has them—are quick to point out that despite the high-powered list of dignitaries who composed it, the National Council never actually met. For this reason they shrug off his membership in it as innocuous.

This is quite misleading. In 1940, Germany was using northern France as the staging ground for its attack on Great Britain. When and if the planned invasion of the island took place, that invasion would originate in France. The idea was that once England had fallen—and it was expected to fall quickly, just as France had fallen quickly—the Nazi occupation of France itself would segue into a profascist or near-fascist puppet government for the entire country. Vichy and all it represented would expand to the country's previous frontiers. France would become France again, but it would be France under the swastika, with its capital in Paris, run by Frenchmen who understood that the better part of Gallic valor was submission to Berlin.

The National Council was to serve as the constitutional convention for this fascist France. Once England fell, or was forced into an armistice that would be tantamount to surrender, the French could have their country back—at least in name—under a new fascist constitution.[33] The National Council, with Georges Bonnet as one of its most distinguished members, would draft this shameful document.

Why then did the National Council never meet? It never met for the simple reason that England never fell. England won the Battle of Britain. It survived the blitz. It did not seek that surrender through armistice that Georges Bonnet confidently expected and hoped the British would seek. As a result, a new French government allied with Hitler was never created.[34] From this stalemate Bonnet's defenders have attempted to create the appearance of innocence.

Nonsense. If Bonnet was comparatively inactive during the Vichy years, it was not through lack of trying to play an active role. Bonnet was still a vocal supporter of the treacherous Pierre Laval. In memoirs written after the war, Bonnet claimed to have had some sort of vague association with the anti-Nazi resistance. The standard historian of the era points out that "the German records tell a different story." In fact, "it would seem that Bonnet's retirement was much more active than might appear from his memoirs."[35] In 1941—when he was ingratiating himself with Friedrich Grimm, discussing his anti-Semitic testimony in the Grynszpan trial—

Bonnet was in contact with the Gestapo, angling for a position in a Vichy government under his friend and patron Laval.[36]

Later, once the Reich's defeat in Britain and Stalingrad burned away the glow of Nazi invincibility, and above all once British and American armies had landed in North Africa in obvious preparation for an invasion of Southern Europe—leadership in Vichy began to panic and defect. Bonnet remained faithful. He assailed the defectors as loudly as possible, "fulminating against dissident generals and politicians." Once again, he made contact with the Gestapo, emphatically assuring the Nazis that he had "never contemplated leaving France." Rumor clinched this treachery when "in the autumn of 1943, Bonnet and Albert Chichery . . . were alleged to be involved in a plan to prevent General de Gaulle assuming power in the event of a successful Allied invasion."[37] And once the Allied invasion did indeed take place, and once Vichy was doomed, Bonnet did leave France, departing for the safety of Switzerland in 1944, only returning in 1950 to the country he had so mendaciously betrayed.

In March 1941, Herschel at long last ceased to be a teenager. He must have been in Sachsenhausen when he turned twenty. Not twenty-one. Twenty. He had not even reached his majority, but he was finally becoming a grown man—albeit a grown man imprisoned, without hope, held captive at the center of a great lie. Arrayed against him were Hitler, Goebbels, Eichmann, Bonnet, Grimm, and Diewerge: personalities that in 1941 seemed to be armed with omnipotence. The large event in which these men intended to use him as their pawn was the radical consolidation of German anti-Semitism after the Kristallnacht, in preparation for the gathering horror of the Final Solution. The goal of his trial was simply stated: *The destruction of Jewry is a prerequisite for the coming European new order.* In memos to Hitler, reference to the coming mass murder was oblique. It did not need to be direct. The purpose of the trial, as Hitler was once again assured, would be to "strangle any feeling of pity among the German population for those Jews currently being deported from Germany."[38]

While these demonic plans were being laid, this very young man, so recently a child, confronted history—monster history—alone and entirely defenseless. There was no one he could turn to, no one he could trust. In prisons and concentration camps, he had gone from rash adolescence to the verge of fatalistic adulthood, certain he was going to die, with nothing but his wits to defend his choice of how to end his life.

And here is how he did it.

15

The Homosexual Strategy

The lie began as gossip. Perhaps it was inevitable; conspiracy theories crusted on the murder of Ernst vom Rath like barnacles on a wet rock. According to Goebbels, Herschel was a pawn of the Jews. To some on the left, he was a pawn of the Gestapo. Or of the British Secret Intelligence Service. Why not also the homintern? It is not really surprising that the gay gossip of 1938 should have been at its most inventive with this particular murder. At twenty-nine years of age, vom Rath lived alone, with no current girlfriend in evidence. Meanwhile Herschel's dark brooding face, seen above the fold on front pages around the world, was indelible: seductive with sullen but sultry good looks that seemed simultaneously to say "go to hell" and "come hither," pure innocence mingled with pure guilt. Gay fantasy ran riot. It has been repeatedly claimed, and without contradiction, that André Gide recorded the theory of their homosexual liaison in his diary, much amused that by taking Herschel as his lover, vom Rath had "sinned twice"—gay sex with a Jew—"according to the laws of his country." In fact, Gide recorded no such thing: The source of the gossip—and it was pure gossip—came to Gide via his friend Jean Schlumberger, and was recorded by Gide's intimate friend, Maria van Rhysselberghe in her secret diary, about which Gide knew nothing.[1]

From the beginning the whole cloth of the gay scenario was spun from tattling scraps and patches. Vom Rath, it was claimed, had met Herschel at a famous gay bar, Le Boeuf sur le Toit, where Herschel, a boy prostitute, was trolling for customers, and vom Rath was a habitué, a flamboyant queen known as "Madame l'Ambassadeur." It was squalid stuff, and all of it was false, contradicted by a complete lack of evidence, compounded by improbability.[2]

The original gossip focused on vom Rath. Moro-Giafferi had heard rumors—empty as air—that the young lawyer was gay. Those rumors seem to have sparked Moro-Giafferi's bright idea to concoct the larger lie that became the homosexual defense. The long shadow that the lie cast on the posthumous reputation of vom Rath, and for that matter the whole story of Herschel Grynszpan, has never lifted. Moro-Giafferi himself was perfectly aware of course that Herschel was not gay, but he was never quite certain whether the rumors about vom Rath were false. Not that he cared. Neither was Herschel certain about it; he seems to have believed there really was a "touchy phase out of the life of Herr vom Rath."

The truth is that the real Ernst vom Rath lead an exceptionally quiet life. It seems—if Karl Brandt's wartime testimony is to be believed—that in 1938 vom Rath was a very sick man, suffering and possibly dying from intestinal tuberculosis. This confirms his French landlady's report that the young lawyer's private life was notably sedate. He was, she said, "quite proper. He received only a few personal friends and in general led a retiring life." One of his friends at the embassy was a certain Herr Auer, who was the ambassador's private secretary. Auer testified that he and vom Rath "went out together occasionally, but rarely at night, primarily due to vom Rath's poor health." Auer added: "His private life was without incident. He was level-headed, not expansive, and he was always very moderate in the way he expressed himself."[3] The fantasy of vom Rath as a shrieking nocturnal sexual predator is one of gossip's more lurid fabrications, at odds with everything known about him.

As for Herschel, apart from his complete lack of experience in all matters sexual, the boy was intensely religious—almost religiose—and in every way more than proper for his class and time. He was an overprotected seventeen-year-old, whose seductive appearance belied complete erotic ignorance. At seventeen, he may have been standing on the verge of sexuality, but nothing at all had happened on the far side of that immaculate threshold. Despite his hot temper, he was shy and was probably especially so with girls. We know he loved going to dances, though he told prosecutors that he didn't know how to dance. He just watched, a wallflower.[4]

In Paris, once he understood the (to him) unspeakable idea that was being proposed, he had flung aside the homosexual defense proposed by Moro-Giafferi as not merely disgusting, but as a claim that would forever demolish the narcissistic image of himself as a hero—an image he had doubtless embraced partly to assuage his horror at having been used as a pretext for the great pogrom. But now, as a prisoner in Germany, all that changed. Now that he was older—all of twenty—and in the hands of the Gestapo, he was facing the certainty of his own rapidly approaching death, and his adolescent narcissism faded, or perhaps more accurately assumed a new and more somber form. The Nazi plan was clear to him. He was their prisoner; nothing could free him. Some sort of heroic action—another action so flamboyant that the whole world would *see*—was closed to him. Add to this impasse his highly realistic conviction that one way or another, whether as a pawn of Adolf Hitler or as a nonentity that the tyrant would throw away, the Nazis were sure to kill him. It is clear that he never believed that he might somehow be liberated. Even near the end, when he dictated his encrypted testament, his only hope was that it might be found and published after his death. Therefore, it seems he thought there *might* be a Nazi defeat. But it would not come soon enough to save him. Even though both hope and freedom were lost, he had to do something, say something that would make them call off the trial.

That's when he remembered the homosexual defense, which he had flung aside with such adolescent and (Moro-Giafferi's word) "obstinate" scorn. It returned to him now in new terms. It was no longer humiliating. It was promising. And it was just possible that if he tried it, it might work. But it would have to be told in a new and ingenious way.

Moro-Giafferi's plan in Paris had been crude, even surprisingly crude. Put simply, the plan claimed that vom Rath had either found Herschel as a boy prostitute—or possibly made him one—and that Herschel had killed him when vom Rath refused to pay him for his services. It was a story sure to stir incredulity, given Herschel's obvious naïveté and vom Rath's obvious wealth. In Germany, Herschel felt that he needed to invent a story that would be more ingenious than Moro-Giafferi's Parisian lie.

After Herschel was sent from Gestapo headquarters to Sachsenhausen, an official of the Gestapo named Jagusch was assigned to whatever inter-rogations remained to be done. It was during one of Jagusch's visits to his prisoner that Herschel sat down and quietly informed his interrogator that it was time that the real truth of the murder be told. Shame had silenced him since 1938, but the time for shame had passed. His reason for killing Ernst vom Rath had not been the reason he'd been telling the world for two years. He had known Ernst vom Rath, known him all too well, before he killed him. And the reason he killed him was not political. It was a crime of passion.

Jagusch sat and listened in shock to the piece of fiction Herschel was telling him. It was very different from the rough invention that Moro-Giafferi had concocted those many months before.

Herschel's new version was quite ingenious, and he seems to have made it up himself. It was designed to show vom Rath in an even worse light than Moro-Giafferi proposed, while retaining his own "honor" in the guise of vom Rath's sexual victim.

He told his interrogator that in the summer and fall of 1938, Herschel had been in the habit of hanging out around the Place de la République near where he lived with his aunt and uncle. One such Saturday, he was approached by an impressive-looking, handsome German—he was dressed in a light-colored overcoat—who started a conversation in German. What a welcome relief it was to speak German in Paris! The handsome German not only looked impressive; he was impressive. He was a member of an aristocratic family; his name was Ernst vom Rath. He freely explained that he was a diplomatic official with an office in the German embassy building on the rue de Rennes. The conversation soon drifted toward sex, then into a sexual proposition. Money was mentioned. Without any seeming hesitation, Herschel agreed to accept a cash deal and go where Herr vom Rath wanted to go. They got into a taxi and were taken to Montmartre, where the cab pulled up outside a seedy hotel where rooms for sexual assignations were rented by the hour. There, in some reeking little room, vom Rath initiated Herschel into homosexuality. Herschel hated it. It was only the money that had tempted him to act so radically against his nature, and he had accepted the money shamefaced, and with disgust.

He said that even though vom Rath asked for another rendezvous a few days later, Herschel's revulsion was so great that he stood up vom Rath and failed to appear. Frustrated—and it would seem, infatuated—vom Rath came to the Grynszpans' apartment building at 6 rue des Petites-Écuries, and haunted the sidewalk outside, obsessed, watching and waiting for Herschel to emerge, hoping to arrange another date. When Herschel came out and heard the new proposition, he refused with a curt insolence that made his revulsion vivid. Though vom Rath then left, he could not stop. He kept reappearing. He was stalking the boy. Herschel, now both panicky and outraged, afraid among other things that his aunt and uncle might find out about the dreadful thing he had done, decided to go to the embassy for some kind of showdown with his tormenter. With him he brought a gun. Shown into vom Rath's office, Herschel once again confronted the man. There was an exchange of insults that was so inflammatory that Herschel pulled out the revolver and shot him.[5]

There it was: the true story behind the assassination of Ernst vom Rath. Herschel gave times and dates. Taken into custody, he said that he had been too ashamed to reveal the sordid truth, and instead invented the story of being politically motivated by the deportation of his parents. Pure pretext. The truth was sexual shame and fear and passion.

Jagusch listened to this story alarmed, realizing at once the threat it posed to the show trial. He returned to Berlin and swiftly told it to Friedrich Grimm, who was now dividing his time between Berlin and an office inside the German embassy in Paris.

It is important to know that the Nazis never believed any part of the homosexual story. They were concerned about it, but its truth or falsehood was not what concerned them. They saw the story simply as a threat to their own show. It was essential that "enemy propaganda," as Goebbels referred to the democratic press, got no hint of this humiliation of the Reich and its canonization of vom Rath as a Nazi martyr. Herschel could not be permitted to tell this tale in open court. Which meant he could not be permitted to speak at all in open court. The anti-Nazi press around the world would seize upon his claim with gleeful delight, indifferent to verifiable fact. Truth, they assumed, would not matter to them, either. All that mattered was scandal.

In any case, Friedrich Grimm did not let Herschel's tight little tale of sexual obsession interrupt his planning for the trial, though he took the threat of the homosexual defense seriously enough to have the Gestapo investigate it. Foolishly, Herschel had supplied dates for the street pickup and vom Rath's supposed stalking of the Grynszpan apartment. They were jumbled dates. It turned out that vom Rath had not been in Paris when Herschel claimed the pickup had happened, and that the Grynszpans had not yet moved to their new apartment when vom Rath was supposed to have stalked him in front of it. Then there was the intrinsic improbability of the tale. No one could believe that someone in as delicate a position as vom Rath would have supplied a street pickup with his real name, address, and position in the world. Finally, the Gestapo was somehow able to determine that vom Rath had never owned an overcoat like the one Herschel described.[6] Once he got these reports, Grimm seems to have brushed aside the homosexual threat and proceeded full speed with the trial.

At some point after telling this first version of his tale, Herschel was transferred from Sachsenhausen to Flossenbürg, a huge concentration camp run by the SS farther from Berlin, near the Czech border in Bavaria, an exceptionally harsh camp where he continued to be granted privileges like the ones he had known at Sachsenhausen.[7] As he wrote in his testament, "I was placed in a single cell and was treated quite well. Almost every wish was fulfilled."

But the privileged treatment in Flossenbürg spoke to him in a newly menacing way. That his every wish was being fulfilled in Flossenbürg suggested to him that his plan had failed. If the homosexual strategy had succeeded, so he reasoned, the Nazis' next step would be to murder him. They would murder him in the dank anonymity of the concentration camp or the Gestapo cellar—murder him as he hoped to have them murder him when he invented the homosexual strategy, assuming that they would call off the trial and kill him in secret. A key element in his strategy was that the Nazis would naturally want to keep the story absolutely secret. They had made vom Rath a hero: He could not be "exposed" as a homosexual. For Herschel, it was essential that the outside world would never, as he put it, "get wind thereof." The whole fiction would vanish in the obscurity of his death. He expected to die. "I was very curious about [the special treatment] but did not believe that I would again leave the camp alive."

Yet every day brought continued life in his privileged cell. He was filled with doubt. He was sure he had failed. He had been certain they could not possibly proceed after he made the homosexual threat, but it seemed that they were going forward.

And they were.

—

Preparations for the trial lasted from July 1940 to October 1941: sixteen months. It is not quite clear why Grimm and Diewerge's preparations should have taken so much time. Perhaps the Nazis were holding off until the Wannsee Conference, when the Final Solution was about to begin in earnest. In any event, Herschel was not brought back to Berlin until October 1941, where he was held in Moabit prison, awaiting his trial, which at that time was scheduled to begin on January 22, 1942. With the trial date drawing near, he decided to give the strategy a second try. We know from the German records that somewhere around October 1941 Herschel startled his captors with a new version of the homosexual defense.

On October 15, 1941, a physician and psychiatrist named Victor Mueller-Hass—who was scheduled to be an expert witness in the trial—was ordered to interview Herschel and nail down what appeared to be yet another version of his story. The new version began very much as the old one had.[8]

In this version, Herschel had one day been lingering around a kiosk, paging through magazines, when a handsome German approached him and struck up a conversation. The conversation warmed up. It was such a joy to speak in German, and Herschel was fascinated to learn that the handsome German worked in the German embassy to Paris. He was some sort of official. Herschel's curiosity got the better of him: Was the gentleman important enough to protect a Jewish family in Germany from persecution?

Oh yes, that would be quite easy.

Could he protect Herschel's family in Hanover?

Certainly. A matter of a few phone calls.

And at this point the German diplomat invited Herschel back to his apartment and there, based on the promise to protect the Grynszpan family in Hanover, he proceeded to do all the unnatural things he wanted to do. And always based on the promise of protection for his family, this relationship continued for weeks, months, leaving the boy in an agony of shame that was nonetheless sustained by his belief that by letting his body be used in this way, he was saving his family from the Nazis.

But then in late October came the deportation of the Polish Jews and the dispossession of the Grynszpan family. When he received Berta's postcard telling of the family's destitution, Herschel realized that it had all been a lie. He had been prostituting himself for nothing.

And *that* is when Herschel Grynszpan went to A la Fine Lame and got his gun.[9]

This new fiction was even more ingenious than the first. Not that it was believed. There is no evidence suggesting that Goebbels or Grimm or Diewerge ever believed the story they were being told. "Insolent . . . a shameless lie," Goebbels seethed in his diary. "An absurd, typically Jewish claim," though he admitted that "it is thought out very cleverly and would, if brought out in the course of a public trial, certainly become the main argument of enemy propaganda."[10] The story did indeed have some shrewdly calculated features. First of all, it offered a reason why vom Rath would have tried to impress Herschel with his name and his position at the embassy. Secondly, if it made its way into court, it would have introduced into evidence the persecution of the Polish Jews, something Goebbels would go to any length to avoid. Thirdly, the story presented itself with a credible motive. Moro-Giafferi's version was crude. Herschel's own first version of the story, the one concocted in Sachsenhausen, which had been too easy for the Gestapo to discredit, again began with turning a trick for money and ended with Herschel defending his honor against the lurking presence of a stalker. This was far better than Moro-Giafferi's version, but it was so ineptly told that the lie crashed and burned. Herschel's final version of the tale retained Herschel's honor by portraying the sex in the story as selling himself not for money or for desire but for the sake of his family. All this new lie required was the presumption that vom Rath lived a secret life. He certainly would not have been the first seemingly impeccable person to do that. Meanwhile, the lie did everything that the lie was supposed to do: It would humiliate the Nazis; it would expose their persecution of the Polish-German Jews and make it part of the agenda of the court; and it would ensure that Herschel would have to be killed in secret.

Goebbels may have railed against this "absurd," "insolent," "cleverly thought-out" version of the story, but at first he did not see any need to cancel the trial. Goebbels saw the danger, but concluded, "I will therefore arrange for only part of the trial to be open to the public, while the rest will take place behind locked doors."[11] To be sure, this too-simple expedient begged the question of what the world press—"enemy propaganda"—with all its relentless curiosity, would make of a trial in which the defendant did not appear, or was at least not allowed to speak, forced to make his case, if he had one, "behind locked doors." Though his diary makes him sound complacent, Goebbels must have realized how unlikely it was that "enemy propaganda" would accept such an obvious cover-up without strident protest. The propaganda meister was a worried man.

Nonetheless, plans for the trial surged forward.

By the spring of 1942, Herschel had decided that his homosexual defense had failed, and that he was headed for the dock despite it. Still puzzled to be alive, he assumed that if his specious story had succeeded in making his captors abandon their plans for the trial, if it had made them see that he was no longer usable as their propaganda pawn, they would promptly take him into whatever cellar they used for murder and execute him in secret. Yet weeks and months had passed. Despite the lie, he was still alive, still being given his "special" treatment in his special cell. That alone seemed to him proof that the homosexual defense had failed. What he'd seen as his best hope of stopping the trial had slipped away.

"[They] evidently wanted to make a trial with me anyway," he wrote in his testament. "To prevent this I turned to the last available means which remained to me." He now had only one hope left, and that hope was suicide. One important purpose of the testament is to disavow the homosexual strategy. The first entry, dictated on April 24, 1942, begins with this disavowal. *I hereby declare that my second deposition which I gave to the Gestapo is untrue.*

At the same time, as if to clinch what he'd dictated in the testament, chained or not, he managed to get a piece of paper and scrawl in Hebrew a few words likewise asserting that the claims of the homosexual defense were false. Then he folded the paper and hid it in his clothing, wearing it like a talisman, apparently with the thought that it might be found on his body after his execution.[12]

The last entry in his testament reads: "I have entrusted this admission to three persons, in case they should someday wish to publish it so this is to serve as verification."

Who were the three persons to whom he had "entrusted this admission?" They are unknown; they have never surfaced. It seems likely that they were fellow prisoners. Who else in his surroundings could Herschel trust? Herschel was talkative; insofar as he had contact with other prisoners in Moabit, he may well have explained his dilemma to them. Certainly, he wanted his cellmate kept in the dark, though he had no choice but to entrust him with the cryptic dictation. It seems he wanted to keep his secret until after his death and he thought that somehow, somewhere in some different world, people he trusted might "wish to publish it."

As we have seen, loose talk about suicide was nothing new for Herschel. There had been a time when he would rather kill himself than spend another night under Uncle Abraham's roof. Another time, he would kill himself if he was forced to leave France. After he killed vom Rath, he claimed that his true intention had been to kill himself. In Paris, the thought of self-murder had been habitually on his mind. But was the threat really serious? Or was it adolescent hysteria and megalomaniacal bravado?

In any case, by 1942 in Berlin, suicide looked very different. A time had come to confront the final option in earnest and move toward it inexorably, without issuing any wordy threats. In his testament, he wrote that he tried to commit suicide twice. We have no idea what methods he used or how serious the attempts were. He says only that a man known to the record only by his last name—Hollmurg—foiled both attempts. A cellmate? A prison guard?[13]

The German files contain no record of Herschel Grynszpan having attempted suicide, but in his testament, on April 29, 1942, he vows to try killing himself again. "I have not given up the hope that I will still succeed." We do know, however, that after two unsuccessful attempts, the Germans protected themselves and made a third try even less likely to succeed. Around this time, Herschel lost his privileged status and was kept in his cell shackled hand and foot.[14]

By March 1942, it must have seemed to Herschel that he was running out of time, that the moment for his trial was drawing dangerously near. The trial had been postponed twice: What had been planned for January 1942 was moved to February, and then from February to still later, May 11.

In the early spring of 1942, two issues hovered over the planned show trial of Herschel Grynszpan. One of them—the homosexual defense—had the Nazis frightened. The other—Bonnet's promised testimony—had them elated. By March, they had not solved the problem of the homosexual defense, even though Herschel assumed that his continued privileged survival meant that his threat had failed, and that he was certain to be put in the dock.

On the other hand, the promise of Bonnet's testimony was an irresistible lure. On March 24 (four days before Herschel's twenty-first birthday, and a month before he dictated his testament), Hitler received a memorandum informing him that May was the ideal time to put Herschel in the dock. The memo was exultant. "It has been agreed with Foreign Minister Bonnet that he will testify about the intrigues of Jewish warmongers during the decisive days of September 1939 . . . He will submit his testimony in writing prior to appearing before the court."[15]

Yet Goebbels knew that even so delicious a feast as Bonnet's testimony could be ruined by the homosexual defense. That March, he was increasingly uncertain about going forward, and the date for the opening of the trial was coming up fast. What if the Jew Grynszpan really did deliver on his threat? There was no certainty at the top, and it would be at least six weeks until Herschel, convinced of his defeat, dictated his testament proclaiming the homosexual strategy to have been a lie. That confession would be discovered. Herschel believed that his cellmate to whom he dictated the testament had been imprisoned as an opponent of National Socialism. In fact, the man was a Nazi plant, and as April drew to a close and May 11 came closer, he promptly turned over the entire confession to his Gestapo masters.[16]

Herschel had been betrayed, but by the time his testament had been decoded, unexpected turns of events had changed everything.

16

Victory Unaware

Betrayed, manacled, and perhaps in despair because his show trial now seemed unstoppable, Herschel must have been increasingly certain that his worst fear would be realized. He had failed to stop the trial. He would be put in the dock. Once again, he would be used as a propaganda pawn to deepen the suffering of his people; once again, his fame would be a propaganda weapon in the hands of the Nazi enemy. He had done all he could to stop the trial, and the fact that he had written his testament indicates he believed he had failed. He was sure he would be tried despite the homosexual defense; in his name, there would be "more bloody pogroms." In the early spring of 1942, he thought the trial was going forward as planned, and that the only options left to him were suicide or silence: suicide before the trial, or silence in the dock.

About that, he was wrong.

Of course, Herschel had never intended to deliver publically on his threat to claim a homosexual relation with vom Rath. It does not seem that he ever *really* considered telling the story in open court. The sole purpose of the lie was to stop the trial from being held at all. He had hoped—and assumed—

that the fiction he'd invented would make holding the trial impossible. He had hoped—and assumed—that the lie would be kept a smarmy secret between himself and his enemies, something so shameful that the Nazis would do anything—including kill him—rather than let it be known. But after he invented the story, nothing seemed to change. The months of his privileged captivity wore on, with every indication that the trial was going forward as planned. He was sure he was doomed.

And yet, the homosexual defense had worked.

It just hadn't worked quickly. It had taken the Nazis four bureaucratically benumbed months to reach the conclusion that the threat of the homosexual defense meant the trial was not feasible. It was during those months of seeming inactivity that the youth decided he had failed. Yet from January 1942 until mid-April, Herschel's fiction had been making its insidious way through the Nazi mind. In the beginning, the senior players had been tempted to ignore it. Goebbels first heard the homosexual tale in January 1942, the very month that the Wannsee Conference was held. Hitler was informed at the same time, and after reading various memos from the Departments of Justice and Propaganda, the dictator "decided that the problem did not justify halting preparations for the trial."[1]

In the months that followed, Goebbels and the trial's steering committee dithered, without being able to produce any effective way to frustrate what the boy was threatening to do. While much of this time was spent in interagency squabbling, various counterstrategies were proposed, all of them futile. We know from a diary entry in January that Goebbels understood the homosexual defense but did not even consider canceling the trial because of it. He would arrange for Herschel's testimony to be heard "behind locked doors." Months later, Diewerge made a similar suggestion to the steering committee. The way to deal with any reference by Herschel to either homosexuality or the Polish deportations, he said, would be to have the judge cut off all discussion, denouncing it as "a dirty Jewish maneuver" and "a typical characteristic of Jewish squalidness."[2]

These suggestions were futile, even absurd. The Grynszpan trial, like the trial of Third Republic premiers in Riom, was to be a *propaganda* trial. Massive international press coverage was essential, and that coverage could not be limited merely to the controlled press in Germany and the occupied territories. The democratic press—"enemy propaganda"—also had to be present, and its reporters would be looking for any cracks in the façade of plausibility that Grimm and Diewerge so fondly imagined they were inventing. For plausibility, the Nazis still retained their ace: They were sure they had the promised testimony of Bonnet in their pocket. It would be a sensation; anti-Semites everywhere were sure to give the former foreign minister a sympathetic hearing. But Herschel? Perhaps their own paranoiac obsessions about world Jewry made Grimm and Diewerge believe they could convince the nations that the mad action of one small frantic child had really triggered a world war, but even they understood that if Herschel were denied the right to speak in his own defense, no representative of "enemy propaganda" could be expected to call the proceedings legitimate. Herschel had to be permitted to speak. And if Herschel were permitted to speak, their whole lie was lost. The dilemma was real. Without quite knowing it, Herschel had nailed them.

As the May 11 date for the trial drew closer, Goebbels and members of the steering committee grew more and more uneasy. There was a great deal of bureaucratic back-and-forthing. There was a great deal of evasion, conducted in Germanic officialese. But the approach of the trial date, hovering ever nearer, seems to have brought a certain amount of realism with it. On April 14, 1942—ten days before Herschel began his testament, and well after he had given up hope—Goebbels confided to his diary that he was sure the trial would be a great success, despite the risk of Herschel's homosexual testimony and raising the issue of the Polish deportations: "I will see to it that these two aspects are not discussed in court."[3] Two days later, Goebbels had reconsidered. On the afternoon of April 16, after a typically evasive meeting of the steering committee, Goebbels let it be known that he had the "gravest doubts about the advisability of the trial," and proposed that a memorandum be sent directly to Hitler exclusively devoted to the threat raised by the homosexual defense. No copy of this memorandum has ever been found. Either it was lost in the mountain of Grynszpan paper, or perhaps its substance was delivered orally. We know only that Goebbels's "gravest doubts" were conveyed to Hitler. And we know that Goebbels's last-minute case of nerves made Hitler change his mind. On April 17, the case was presented to Hitler. On April 18, 1942, a reply came from Martin Bormann, Hitler's mouthpiece. The trial should not be held on May 11, or any time soon. Was it therefore a dead issue? Almost, but not quite. Bormann's pronouncement included a caveat: "There is no question of dropping the Grynszpan case, but only of postponing it."[4] Postponed until when? No one could say. It was postponed indefinitely, and in actual practice, forever.

Six days later, knowing none of this, Herschel began to dictate his testament, asserting that the homosexual defense had been a lie and lamenting that it had failed to stop the trial.

He did not know it; perhaps he would never know it. But the homosexual defense *did* stop the trial. Herschel had won.

He had assumed the proof of the success of the homosexual defense would be his prompt execution. That probably did not happen. After all, in Hitler's mind, the trial was still a possibility. It had been merely "postponed."

Meanwhile that February, fascist complacency was given a jolt by the sister trial of high officials of the Third Republic in Vichy—the so-called Riom trial. In the French town of Riom, Édouard Daladier, Léon Blum, and Paul Reynaud—three former premiers of the French Republic—stood accused of having committed the crime of governing a France capable of declaring war against Germany. They had treacherously led France into an "unnecessary" war for which their policies had left the country unprepared. In this, all three were the pawns of "world Jewry." All three had criminally betrayed the French people. All three were guilty, ex post facto, of treason.[5]

The Riom trial, so elaborately prepared, was a propaganda fiasco. Blum and Daladier together made rhetorical mincemeat of their collaborationist

accusers, impressively turning the tables of accusation. Around the democratic world, press on the right, left, and center mocked the proceedings of
what looked so very much like a fascist kangaroo court. Within France itself, the essential dishonesty of it all mortified public opinion. After a month
of embarrassment upon embarrassment, Otto Abetz abruptly ordered the
trial suspended, never to be resumed. Not surprisingly, Hitler was enraged.

Though Riom shook Nazi confidence in the show trial as an instrument
of mass deception, it was hoped that the Grynszpan trial would somehow
recuperate some of the political and propaganda losses suffered there. Once
again, Bonnet's testimony was held to be essential. But Riom had given
everyone involved a taste of how even the best-laid plans might go awry in
the hands of a free press.

Interestingly, Georges Bonnet does not seem to have been slated to appear as a witness against his former chief in Riom. Nonetheless the spectacle
of the Riom fiasco may well have given Bonnet second thoughts about the
wisdom of serving the fascist revision of history quite as conspicuously as he
planned to do in Berlin.

This was especially true because by February 1942, the face of the war
was changing. Hitler's assault on Britain—the Battle of Britain, the blitz—
had failed. German armies were freezing and facing disaster in Russia; Stalingrad was not far distant. As of December 1941, the United States had
entered the war with a level of power and might that made it capable of
doing what Hitler could not do: conduct a two-front world war and win
on both fronts. When the Germans took Herschel captive in 1940, a Nazi
victory in Europe had about it the look of inevitability. By mid-1942, that
look was long gone. In 1940, insider opinion, to which Bonnet was so sedu-
lously attached, was sure of Hitler's victory. In 1942, the Wehrmacht was in
Russia, and losing, and nobody was sure of anything.

As for Vichy, complacency was becoming fear. Britain and the United
States in alliance were now sure to take the offensive, and it seemed likely
that massive Allied armies would launch that offensive from former French
colonies in North Africa, proceeding from there to an invasion of Southern

Europe that might well cut its swath directly through the South of France. Of Nazi Germany's sundry assets, Vichy might be the first to fall. And where would collaboration be then?

So Vichy's international standing was in the process of dramatic change just at the moment that plans for Herschel's trial were being finalized. With American entry into the war in December 1941, the Roosevelt administration's useful if hypocritical pretense of viewing Vichy as a fellow "neutral" nation—a charade maintained primarily as a means of preventing the French fleet in the Mediterranean from falling into German hands—was jeopardized. The United States was now a declared enemy of Germany, and Vichy was Germany's puppet. In the spring of 1942, all American pretense was jettisoned with Pierre Laval's ascendancy to power as premier. Laval assumed dominant power in Vichy in April 1942, the same month that Herschel's trial was debated and postponed. On April 17—the very day that Herschel's trial was postponed—President Roosevelt recalled his ambassador, William Leahy, indicating his displeasure at Laval's rise to power. Roosevelt now regarded Laval's Vichy, like Germany itself, as an overt enemy of the United States.

That being the case, many collaborators in Vichy began to look for a way out of the tricky wager they had made in 1940 about who would win the Second World War. Back in the halcyon days when it seemed Britain was sure to fall, Bonnet and Laval had been confident. In 1942, collaborators began to toy with defection. It was at this time that Bonnet himself—perhaps protesting too much—began loudly to assail those among his colleagues who looked as if they might turn away from the collaborationist regime, even going so far as to contact the Gestapo to assure them that he himself had no intention of leaving France.[6]

These tensions were making themselves acutely felt at exactly the same time as the Nazis' dawning recognition that Herschel's homosexual defense, if he were really to deliver on it, would make his trial an even worse disaster than the Riom fiasco. Herschel's trial was postponed while the Nazis were still confident that they had the testimony of Bonnet sewed up and certain.

To forego that testimony because of the homosexual defense must have been especially galling to Goebbels. The great anti-Semitic show trial with which he and Hitler proposed to "strangle" any possible sympathy for the Jews who were to be "deported" in the coming Holocaust had been called off through the maneuvers of one insignificant but clever Jewish boy. A child. A lying but shrewd child, using a "typically Jewish" trick. It was humiliating. On the day that Hitler made his decision—April 17, 1942—Goebbels wrote in his diary, enraged. After admitting that the homosexual defense was behind his doubts about the trial, he went on to rant that the homosexual defense was "a lie, dastardly and mean . . . One can here once again recognize how perfidiously the Jews act if one goes after their neck."[7]

Proponents of the trial could, for a while, clutch the consolation that postponement meant that the trial might soon be resumed. A month later, on May 14, Goebbels muttered to his diary that the postponement might be only "until autumn."

But the feeble promise of a return to the trial in autumn—or any other time—was cold comfort for the propaganda minister. His precious show had been ruined. In the same diary entry, Goebbels speaks of meeting with Ribbentrop and concluding that things had changed: It was now "no longer in the interests of the Reich's foreign policy to emphasize too strongly the role of former French Foreign Minister Bonnet."[8] This comment seems at first blush inexplicable. There is no evident reason why Bonnet's anti-Semitic testimony should have lost its usefulness to Goebbels merely because of the new attitude of the Roosevelt administration. But perhaps after April 1942 Bonnet, sensing shifting winds, decided to produce testimony that was not so anti-Semitic. There is ample reason to wonder if perhaps the looming threat of Allied invasion of Southern France and the downfall of the Vichy regime struck Bonnet as a possible scenario for his own future. Perhaps making himself the most conspicuous witness in a major propaganda trial linked to the worst of Nazi crimes was . . . unwise. Allied liberation of France easily could—and did—bring with it war crimes trials for the most active

collaborators. For Bonnet, these would brush close to home. After the liberation of France in August 1944, his friend and fellow collaborator Laval
would be convicted of treason and executed by a firing squad. Outcomes
like that were beginning to frighten many of the collaborators in Vichy.
Bonnet may have been among them. Something in the prospect of an Allied
occupation seems to have brought Bonnet's mind into very sharp focus.

In any case, he changed his mind. In 1940 and 1941, Bonnet and Laval had
been convinced that Germany was the sure winner of the war. But by 1942,
something had made Bonnet turn around. The German records contain
a memorandum dated about two weeks *after* Hitler decided to postpone
the trial, lamenting that Friedrich Grimm in Paris had run into a serious
snag in his conversations with the former foreign minister. There had been
a time when Bonnet was eager to testify on the subject of the nefarious role
of world Jewry and its pawn Herschel in France's downfall. He enthusiastically endorsed Grimm's theories; he was quick with his cooperation. Now
suddenly, at the end of April 1942, he seemed to have lost all interest in discussing the subject. In his various visits to the former minister, Grimm had
once again brought up world Jewry and the French debacle, but he couldn't
seem to extract any more anti-Semitic pronouncements out of the old fox.
Without anti-Semitism, Bonnet's testimony would be worse than useless.
He and Grimm were at an impasse. Bonnet had gone so far as to express
"grave doubts" about the "advisability" of his going to Berlin at all. In fact,
he had in effect reneged on his promise to be the star witness in the great
anti-Semitic trial of the war. Why? It is clear that Grimm and his masters
attributed Bonnet's defection to "the attitude of the United States, and obviously the attempted intervention of the Chief Rabbi."[9] With Bonnet's decision not to testify joined to the homosexual defense, any hope for making
the trial a successful piece of propaganda collapsed.

And so the trial that was to serve as a mask of the Holocaust was never held. In April 1942, the homosexual threat stopped the trial from going forward. In late April 1942, Bonnet's defection made it into something that was impossible to resume.

Is it some sort of irony, or is it merely a striking fact, that most of the Grynszpan family survived the Holocaust? The treacherous event that drove Herschel to murder, the Polish deportations of 1938, forced Sendel and Rivka Grynszpan to leave Germany; they were driven into Eastern Poland, where they were living when the war began, safely within what became the Soviet zone. In fact, Herschel's older brother, Mordecai, was able to join the Red Army, and after Hitler's invasion fought the Germans for the duration of the war. Herschel's beloved sister, Berta, was not so fortunate. When the German armies crossed Poland and advanced into Russia, Berta fell into German hands, and, according to Jonathan Kirsch, was brutally murdered.[10] But Sendel and Rivka lived: They were evacuated to Astrakhan on the Volga River, and after the war they moved to Israel, where they were reunited with Mordecai in 1948.

Meanwhile, the Holocaust, which Herschel's trial was intended to mask, was not only in preparation; it had begun. In the spring of 1942, Bonnet's ally Pierre Laval, having reached the pinnacle of his power under Marshal Pétain, was soon under pressure from the Germans to assist in the deportation of Jews in France—especially foreign Jews—to the death camps in Poland. As the historian Stanley Hoffmann writes, "There is no doubt that Vichy was not only willing but eager to help the Nazis by agreeing to their demands—which kept increasing from the spring of 1942 onward—for the deportation of France's foreign Jews."[11]

In all of France, some seventy-five thousand Jewish individuals were arrested and sent to killing camps. In 1942 alone, forty-two thousand French Jews were sent to Auschwitz. On March 27, 1942, three weeks before Herschel's trial was postponed, the first convoy of Jews being deported left Paris for Auschwitz. A little after that, in the unoccupied zone of Vichy, many thousands of foreign Jews, including those refugees from Nazi Germany, who since the debacle had been held in the huge and horrendous French concentration camp at Gurs, were "re-arrested" by the Vichy police and put onto convoys that transported them through the occupied zone and then on to the camps.

When Paris fell in 1940, Abraham and Chawa were among the tens of thousands who fled south, hoping to escape the conquering army. They were in Toulouse when Herschel was also there, conniving with the French police for his own imprisonment, unaware of his aunt and uncle's presence. Would anyone have been saved if in those hectic streets Herschel had crossed paths with his aunt and uncle? There were a few days, perhaps more, when such a meeting would have been conceivable. Is it possible that they all might have escaped France? Perhaps, and perhaps not. But it was not to be. Abraham and Chawa—like their nephew—fled into captivity. They were arrested by the Vichy police and sent to Gurs, where they were held for two years, until 1942, when Laval made his decision to assist the Germans with their Holocaust. Though Chawa was left behind, Herschel's Uncle Abraham Grynszpan was one of the foreign Jews "re-arrested" in Gurs.

He was put on a convoy. It carried him east to Auschwitz. There he vanished into the anonymity of mass murder. Abraham Grynszpan was never heard from again.

17

Oblivion

And Herschel himself? Herschel perished in some unique darkness all his own.

There can be no doubt that somehow, somewhere, he died before the war ended, while still held in German captivity. There have been sundry theories that he survived the war. Each has been discredited again and again. Yet how he really did die is unknown. After the postponement of the show trial in the spring and summer of 1942, Herschel Grynszpan vanished into the trackless murk of history. The archival record fell silent. Steering committees no longer met. Memoranda were no longer prepared for the Führer. Construction work preparing the show trial's great courtroom stopped. Only a few final scraps of bureaucratic detail remain. For example, it's known that once the show trial was postponed, Herschel was transferred from the Moabit prison in Berlin to the concentration camp in Sachsenhausen, where interestingly he was once again incarcerated in "the Bunker," that privileged facility reserved for high-profile prisoners of special importance, as if awaiting the trial's resumption.[1] Goebbels may have thought the trial might be postponed "until autumn," but it was not resumed in autumn. Or ever.

There are two schools of thought about how the boy met his end, each powerful but less than persuasive, neither able to marshal the evidence needed to carry its suppositions all the way to conviction. One view holds that the Gestapo probably murdered Herschel in or near Sachsenhausen during the late summer or fall of 1942. In fact, that amounts to something like the official view. Hans-Jürgen Döscher, Alan Steinweis, and Sidney Smeets, all three of whom differ on other subjects, are in agreement about the late summer or fall of 1942 as the likely date of Herschel's death. In their eyes, postponement or no postponement, Herschel was done to death once his usefulness in the dock of the show trial was at an end. The Nazis washed their hands of him. The archives fell silent because there is nothing more to say.

This supposition may well be correct. It fulfills Herschel's own expectation that he would be killed secretly and soon if the homosexual strategy succeeded. We know that either near the end of summer 1942 or "on or about September 26, 1942," the Gestapo came to Herschel and announced that he was being transferred from Sachsenhausen to another concentration camp in Magdeburg.[2] There was speculation among the inmates that the transport to Magdeburg was a "fake transport": that Herschel would either be murdered at Sachsenhausen itself, or that the car that took him from the concentration camp was really headed to a place called the "Industriehof"— the camp's killing field. Herschel himself believed that the moment for his murder had come at last. Before he was taken away, he "secretly" confided to his fellow prisoners "the time has come. They want to kill me."[3]

But did they?

A second school of thought, whose most notable proponent is Gerald Schwab, is skeptical about such an early date. Several factors challenge it. The Nazis kept their records with Teutonic punctiliousness, but there is no record of an autumn execution or of who might have dared to order it. Until a few weeks before, Herschel had been under the special protection of the Führer himself, and it was Hitler's mouthpiece, Martin Bormann, who ordained that the trial had not been canceled, but merely postponed. Since a September 1942 execution would have made the autumn resumption of the trial impossible, the order to execute Herschel would have had to come from the very top—probably Hitler himself—as part of a decision to sponge the trial once and for all. There is no record that such a decision was ever made. That fact is not necessarily decisive: The Nazis may have wanted to hide the killing in the bureaucratic dark, or the records may have been lost or expunged. But it is a little strange.

Meanwhile, Schwab cites a high-level counselor in the Nazi Foreign Ministry named Fritz Dahms, who later testified that "the death of Grynszpan occurred shortly before the end of the war, but I am no longer able to say if he died of natural causes, or if he lost his life by violence." Dahms was in a position to know, and according to him, the case was never closed. "In keeping with the directives of May 1942, it was regularly resubmitted for review until the end of the war."[4] And one scrap of archival evidence suggests that Herschel may have been alive after September 1942: a Foreign Ministry memorandum of December 7, 1942, orders that all the pretrial material Grimm and Dieweige gathered be "widely disseminated" for use as propaganda "even though, *for the time being*, the trial does not take place."[5] [My emphasis.]

Dahm's claim may be reinforced by the testimony of Adolf Eichmann, who was asked about Herschel during his 1961 trial in Jerusalem. Eichmann replied that he had been ordered to interrogate Herschel in 1943 or perhaps 1944, still trying to unearth his nonexistent coconspirators. Eichmann remembered that he saw Herschel for the first and last time "late in the war."

> I received an order that Grynszpan was in custody in Prinz-Albrecht-Strasse 8, and he had to be further examined concerning who was likely to have been behind the scenes. Accordingly I gave instructions to bring Grynszpan no, not this way—accordingly Krischak gave orders—Krischak was dealing with the matter—to bring Grynszpan and . . . either way it would have been useless, I said to myself. I still remember exactly, for I was curious to see what Grynszpan looked like, and I still said: . . .

If they had not found this out during all those years, then . . . this examination will also be pointless, this would be useless. But an order was an order . . . Krischak questioned him and took notes.

Nothing, obviously, emerged from the whole thing, and I merely said then to Krischak that if he had completed the interrogation, I wanted him to bring him to me upstairs, for I very much wanted—for once—to look at the man Grynszpan. I wanted to talk to him. And I did then exchange a few words with Grynszpan. He was very brief and brusque, was indifferent and gave short replies to all the questions. I wanted to ask him, since I had no knowledge at all of the whole matter, where he had been and things of that kind.

On the whole he looked well, he was small—he was a smallish lad . . . he was such a little man—What happened then I don't know. Again I delivered my report, that is to say, the report was again conveyed through the service channels by Krischak. It was a short report—because nothing came of it. This is still preserved in my memory, and then he was again returned to custody in Prinz-Albrecht-Strasse 8. I don't know what . . . what happened to him. I did not hear anything more. I didn't hear anything more about it.

And so it was that history's pawn exchanged a few words with the architect of the Holocaust.

Those who believe Herschel died in September 1942 argue that when Eichmann claimed to have met him "late in the war," his memory must have been deceiving him. Perhaps, and perhaps not. Eichmann spoke of the futility of the interrogation: "If they had not found this out during all those years," he said, "this examination will also be pointless." Yet in the absence of firm information putting Herschel's death in 1942, there is no particular reason to doubt the accuracy of Eichmann's memory. "Late in the war" was late in the war. It was that lateness that made the examination pointless.

Finally, there is the mystery of "Otto Schneider." After the war, a writer with the pen name Walter Hammer, a German anti-Nazi resister, reported that in 1940 he had come to know Herschel by sight when they were both being held prisoner in the basement dungeon of Prinz-Albrecht-Strasse 8. Hammer added that he had encountered Herschel again in Sachsenhausen, and later still in the Brandenburg concentration camp.

After the war, Hammer established an archive documenting the German resistance and the wartime concentration camps in Germany. How and where Hammer got his information is unclear, but he claimed to have learned that as late as January 1945, Herschel was being held prisoner in the Sonnenburg concentration camp under the (Gentile) name of Otto Schneider. "Otto Schneider" was registered as a tailor by profession, and his date of birth, March 28, 1921, was also Herschel's date of birth. Hammer was quite certain that Otto Schneider and Herschel Grynszpan were one and the same person.

What happened at Sonnenburg in the sub-zero spring of 1945 is yet another terrible story from a terrible time. Sonnenburg lay on the frontier between Germany and Poland, directly in the path of the advancing Red Army. Prisoners in the camp included 685 political prisoners and Soviet prisoners of war. Rather than surrender these people to the conquering Russians, the SS gathered all 685 into the prison courtyard and machine-gunned them to death. Then they fled. When the Soviets came to liberate the camp, they found nothing but 685 frozen corpses.

Yet, according to Hammer, "Otto Schneider," though he was certainly a political prisoner at Sonnenburg, was specifically singled out *not* to be a victim of this massacre. Before the killing started, he was taken from his cell, "shackled hand and foot," and driven deeper into the rapidly vanishing safety of the Germany that had not yet been conquered by the Allies. His first stopping place was the temporary refuge of Brandenburg penitentiary, where he was held under conditions of great security. It seems that Hammer encountered him again and presumably recognized him. Two days after that, the Gestapo transferred "Otto Schneider" to penal barracks at Magdeburg.[6]

In Magdeburg, he vanished. He may well have died there. It was the end of the Third Reich, and at that moment in 1945, it was remarkable for anyone to survive in Magdeburg. It was the scene of some of the most brutal assaults of the war. The British were carpet-bombing the city; the carnage was complete. At one point, when the prison itself was being heavily bombed, the SS ushered the prisoners out of the building and herded them into a nearby sports arena. But when the sports arena itself began to be bombed, panic ensued, both among the prisoners and their guards. Killing spread everywhere. In an epoch of massacres, it was yet another massacre. And "Otto Schneider" may have died there. Or maybe not. In any case, there is no record anywhere of "Otto Schneider's" death.

But was "Otto Schneider" really Herschel Grynszpan? And was Magdeburg really where he met his end? Pure speculation. There appears to be solid evidence that someone named Otto Schneider really was removed from Sonnenburg before the massacre there started, transferred first to Brandenburg and then to Magdeburg. And it is true that this "Otto Schneider" did indeed have Herschel's date of birth. That is suggestive, but hardly conclusive. The *lack* of evidence is almost as compelling, and no outside documents confirm Walter Hammer's version of events.

But then all the Herschel sightings after 1942 are shadowy. What about Fritz Dahms's claim that the case was never closed and was periodically reviewed? That would give some credibility to Eichmann's testimony about being ordered to interview Herschel yet again "late in the war." Yet while Herschel's bulging German dossier before 1942 contains every trace of every tiresome committee meeting and redundant memorandum, no scrap remaining in the German archives indicates that periodic reviews, or any review of any kind, ever took place. Why not? Adolf Eichmann claimed that his associate filed a report, brief but official, on their pointless interrogation. With whom was such a report filed? Who ordered the investigation? Nothing remains. Someone high up must have been behind it. After all, Eichmann himself was very high up, and someone superior to him must have given the order. As he dryly remarked, "an order is an order."

On the other hand, if those who believe that Herschel must have been executed in the late summer or early fall of 1942 look to the archival record, they, too, confront a universal blank. Herschel was a living figure in the Nazi imagination. He had a kind of fame. Eichmann himself wanted to meet him. Wouldn't his death have been noted somewhere? The absolute absence of documentary evidence after 1942 is in itself a kind of mystery. Since authorization for an execution would have had to come from a high level, wouldn't Goebbels, or Grimm, or Diewerge, or someone on the steering committee, many of whom survived the war, have known about it? But nothing remains.

If he indeed lived through most of the war, he was glimpsed only here and there. We see—or think we see—mere flashes of him in the deepening murk: sitting in Eichmann's office, sulking and curt; being led from his cell to what may or may not have been death; walking to a waiting car in the freezing night of the Third Reich's downfall, rushed away from the advancing Soviet army, "shackled hand and foot."

And after a certain point, he is no longer even glimpsed. He disappears completely, vanishing in the brutal, impenetrable darkness of the End.

However he died, he died forgotten. How could it have been otherwise, given all the dead? The six million? And the sixty million war dead? What, after all, was his fate compared to theirs? He had been history's pawn, a brave and foolish boy, plucked out of obscurity and played for small moves in the largest and most terrible events in modern history. For a while, fate put him near the heart of the beast. For a while, he could be used—conspicuously used, used both viciously *and* honorably—in the largest moral movements of his time. That done, he was dropped back into oblivion. Sometime after mid-1942, Herschel Grynszpan vanished from history.

There is a certain justice in that. Herschel was always an insignificant young man, a child snared in the incomprehensibly significant events of a world war. That is part of what makes him interesting. He experienced the Second World War and its Holocaust as no one else experienced it. That fact alone endows his very insignificance with a certain power and pathos, giving his entry into history a kind of startling éclat and bestowing a nameless melancholy on his vanishing.

He may have been partly hero and partly fool, yet there is something tragic in his little destiny. When he went to the German embassy that morning, he had a mission. It was a brave, coherent mission, and in its mistaken way, even intelligent. He was determined to do something flamboyant enough to make the world *see*. And he was quite right. It was a month after Munich, and most of the world did not see. Not yet. Looking at Hitler, most of the world did not see how evil the man and his regime really were. They did not see the threat Nazism posed to civilization. Not yet. Of course for many, the menace was obvious, but most of an unseeing world, or so it seemed to Herschel, was looking the other way. Nothing could shatter their complacency, so it seemed to him, except five pistol shots. His pistol shots.

Rash, foolish, fearless boy. To his adolescent mind, breaking the world's complacency lay somewhere between an act of suicide and an act of heroism. I doubt that during the ten seconds it took to shoot down Ernst vom Rath he could distinguish between the two. He hoped, he believed, that he might be an agent of God's will. But who can foresee his fate? Certainly not seventeen-year-old boys. His action, his crime, his hubris—all three were swallowed into a tragic and savage irony when some of the most evil human beings history has known took him up as their pawn and used him for destruction on a scale that was previously unimaginable. *That*, and not his foolish heroics, is what made the world see.

God, oh my God! I didn't want that. Listen to me. I'll explain how it happened so you can explain it to people who might call down God's curse on me.

Such was his lament after the Kristallnacht. He had good reason to lament. Yet if he feared God's curse, he was also proud. During the time that he was famous, his very tragedy made him an emblematic figure for that part of world opinion that understood the Nazi menace. In their eyes, even if he was rash, he was understandably, courageously rash. As Dorothy Thompson put it, there must be some kind of a higher justice for "this boy." In his very youth, recklessness, and even in his foolishness, he had at least seen the threat and tried to warn the world. Thompson's hope for a higher justice was never tested—not in a court at any rate—but while he was waiting to be tried in Paris, delusion and the media made their headway with him. After the war, his attorney Serge Weill-Goudchaux wrote: "Yes, Grynszpan was the first 'resister' in the terrible and abject struggle the Nazis created." That doubtless exaggerates, but the fact remains that he did, at least, fight back, and he was one of the first. When the atrocities committed in his name became known to the world, he did begin to glow in a heroic albeit bizarre light. The anti-Nazi press wanted to find some higher justice for him. He began to speak to reporters about his "mission"; his signature became elaborate and pretentious; to his attorneys' dismay, he became convinced that he would never be convicted. The world, he thought, was on his side. He was deluded, and yet if his crime had been understandable, so were his delusions understandable. After all, he was a child.

Yet the child won, and won in an act of secret self-transcendence. Rather than let himself be used once again as a weapon against his people, he decided to die for them—not heroically, but invisibly, in obscurity. It would be a sweet thing to say that his was an unqualified victory, and sweeter still to say that he lived to relish it and see the defeat of his enemies. But that, too, was denied him. On November 7, 1938, he had stepped into the spotlight of history. But once he was Hitler's prisoner, Herschel saw with clairvoyant intelligence that his task was to remove himself from that spotlight forever. Some strategy to disentangle himself from great events was necessary to complete his destiny. He had to return to the insignificance from which he had emerged. That strategy required great ingenuity and even greater courage in the face of death. He had both, and in that, at least, he succeeded. While the six million of the Holocaust and the sixty million war dead were perishing, he too perished, somewhere, somehow, unseen. There is something heroic in his invisibility. Facing the full forces of evil arrayed against him, he outsmarted them all. It was a victory that required him to vanish from history, but hidden in that vanishing, he died for his people, forgotten and alone.

EPILOGUE

Two Brothers

Herschel Grynszpan's older brother, Mordecai, and Ernst vom Rath's younger brother, Günter, never met—but this singular and unlikely encounter really did almost take place. Both men survived the war; both spent years obsessed with the fate of their famous siblings. In 1952, a former Nazi, anti-Semitic propagandist, and all-round con man who called himself Michael Alexander Graf von Soltikow published an article in a popular German weekly, *Wochenend*, entitled "Top Secret" ("Geheime Reichssache"). The "top secret" that the article purported to reveal was that there had indeed been a homosexual relationship between Herschel and vom Rath; that the homosexual defense had been genuine; and that various major players, from Goebbels to Bonnet, were fully aware of that fact when they tried to portray Herschel as a pawn of "world Jewry." The article was fraudulent in essence. A German court had recently convicted Soltikow of writing anti-Semitic propaganda.[1] His reason for writing "Top Secret" was somehow to show that instead of being the anti-Semite he'd been proven in court to be, he was in fact an anti-anti-Semite, eager to reveal that Herschel had not been the pawn of "world Jewry" after all.

Such was the sleazy motivation behind an article that was a pack of falsehoods. At this point, Günter vom Rath decided he had had enough. He had been a teenager when he stood with his parents beside Ernst's deathbed in Paris; he had grown up to be a distinguished attorney in Wiesbaden. Under German law, unlike Anglo-Saxon common law, it is possible to libel the dead. Outraged, Günter sued both the magazine and Soltikow for defamation of a deceased person. A court was convened in Munich. As one who was perpetually in trouble with the law, Soltikow was himself litigious, and he did his best to turn the defamation trial into a circus, threatening to call literally hundreds of witnesses proving there had been a homosexual affair. At one point, he even insisted he was in touch with Herschel himself, whom he claimed was once actually present in the courtroom, though in secret since he still feared arrest over the murder. Soltikow's legal maneuvers may have been exercises in futility, but they went on ad nauseam, with the European press eagerly following them all. Nonetheless, after a sequence of proceedings that lasted several wearisome years, Soltikow was found guilty of defamation. In all that time, he had been unable to produce even one scrap of legally credible evidence suggesting that either Herschel or vom Rath had been gay.[2]

It was over the Soltikow trial that Mordecai and Günter almost encountered each other. At some point, Günter invited Mordecai to be a witness in the proceedings. The two of them were divided by everything—divided by history, divided in their love of their brothers. They did, however, share one common interest: the discrediting of this lie.

For reasons best known to himself, Mordecai declined.[3]

Yet Mordecai would soon enough be a witness in a vastly more important trial: the 1961 trial of Adolf Eichmann for crimes against humanity. The Grynszpan family was curiously enmeshed in the Eichmann trial. It is a striking fact that the very first witness called was Sendel Grynszpan. Speaking at length, and with quiet eloquence, he told the court about his family's experience in the Polish deportations. After Sendel testified, the next witness called was Mordecai. He, too, told about the Polish deportations.

He confirmed his father's testimony. He explained how his family—Berta excluded—had escaped the reach of the advancing German armies, and how he himself had come to join the Red Army.

And as the court listened, he ended his testimony with the story of his search for his famous but vanished brother.

When the war ended, Mordecai returned to Poland and began a search for Herschel, using the various institutions that had been set up in the postwar chaos to ransack the ruins looking for concentration camp victims, displaced persons, political prisoners, and all the war's lost. It is unlikely that Mordecai knew anything about "Otto Schneider," but even if he had known that name, the search would have been fruitless. Every organization set up to find the vast hosts of the disappeared came back to Mordecai with the same negative answer. Herschel had vanished in the fog of war.

Then in 1947 and 1948, before he moved to Israel, Mordecai lived in Paris, where he continued the search. He met with Moro-Giafferi and Herschel's legal team. He wrote letters to the newspapers. He interviewed anyone he could find who might have known anything about his brother's fate. He learned a lot about his brother, but nothing about what had become of him in the end.[4]

Yet by 1947, rumors about Herschel's supposed survival of the war began to fill the void with fiction. It was asserted with assurance that the American army had liberated Herschel from Magdeburg, though there was no record of that. Rumors proliferated that he was living—sometimes in Germany, sometimes in France—in secret, under an assumed name. Mordecai tracked down as many of these rumors as he could. None had substance. Then in 1948, Mordecai moved to Israel, where he rejoined his parents, married, and had a family.[5]

Mordecai died in Tel Aviv in 1996 at the age of seventy-seven. "Our main proof that [Herschel] did not live," Mordecai's daughter Malka said in an interview, "is that he did not make contact with us. He was so attached to his family that it is unreasonable to think he would not have looked for us."[6]

But the survival rumors did not stop when Mordecai left Paris for Israel.

In 1957, a German scholar named Helmut Heiber concluded what was the first serious scholarly article on the Grynszpan case with an offhand and unsubstantiated claim that Herschel was "living under an assumed name in Paris." Questioned about his source, Heiber later admitted that the claim had come to him as hearsay, and from what source he could no longer recall. Yet the story of Herschel's secret life in Paris was loose in the world; it was elaborated elsewhere. One widely disseminated theory held that under his assumed name, Herschel was working as a garage mechanic in Neuilly, that he had married and had a family.[7]

None of these rumors withstand examination. I know of no informed student of the case who believes that Herschel Grynszpan survived the war.

Other myths, above all the homosexual defense, have been slower to die. It can now be said with confidence that the story of a sexual relationship between Herschel and vom Rath is wholly fictitious. Yet some legitimate uncertainty on the subject persisted until around 2013. Herschel's otherwise forgotten name appears for a few lines in every respectable history of the Second World War, but after 2000, even historians of the highest repute give some glancing, usually incredulous reference to the possibility of the *crime passionel*. This is odd: One would think that the Soltikow verdict of 1960 would have put the homosexual defense to rest once and for all.

It did not. The reason for this persistent uncertainty comes from the work of a distinguished German scholar, Hans-Jürgen Döscher, who in the 1990s consulted all the relevant archives for his important study, *Reichskristallnacht: Die Novemberpogrome 1938* (2000). Among the archives that Döscher examined were the records of the Soltikow trial itself. He seems to have been taken in by the smoke and mirrors of innuendo and gossip about gossip that were typical of Soltikow's method. In any case, Döscher somehow reached the conclusion that Soltikow had been right.[8]

This aspect of Döscher's work was greeted with a certain amount of perplexity. Even scholars who hold a high opinion of *Reichskristallnacht*—the

American authority Alan E. Steinweis, for example—pulled back in mildly
surprised uncertainty. "Most historians who have written about Grynszpan," Steinweis writes, "have tended to regard the homosexual story as a
clever defense." He concludes his analysis of Döscher with a shrug. "We
will probably never know for certain what, if anything, actually happened
between Grynszpan and vom Rath in Paris before November 7, 1938."[9]

Other writers have taken Döscher's dubious conclusion seriously. Under
his influence, in 2005 a writer named Andreas Friedrich Bareiss published
Herschel Feibel Grynszpan: Der Attentäter und die Reichskristallnacht—a sophisticated if sentimental work of fiction that carries as part of its bona fides
extensive quotation from the real archives in Berlin and elsewhere. These references are all seemingly genuine, and some (if true) are very interesting—
nuggets of solid fact in a rather too-sweet pudding of fiction. In 2003, an
American writer named Harlan Greene produced a novel about the supposed affair, *The German Officer's Boy*. This novel does not even pretend to
be based in historical fact, and is, if anything, even more sentimental than
the Bareiss book.[10] In a time of gay liberation, I suppose it is a touching fantasy that in the Nazi era there was an erotic—even loving—bond between
a Jewish boy and a German aristocrat.

But the misty-eyed fantasy of such a liaison is exactly that: fantasy.
Ten years later, perplexed by Döscher's shaky argument, Sidney Smeets, a
brilliant young Dutch lawyer, set out to reexamine all the archives Döscher
consulted, along with the known facts in the Grynszpan case, including
and especially the records of the Soltikow trial. Smeets brought a keen legal
mind to bear on every detail. In 2013, Smeets published his conclusions in
a book entitled *De Wanhoopsdaad* (*Act of Desperation*).

Smeets's analysis of Döscher is devastating. He is relentless. He dissects
and lays before us the long smarmy history of Soltikow's career as a con
man. He scrutinizes every detail of the case. He analyzes each rumor; he
investigates every source. His defense has prosecutorial zeal. In the end,
not one stone of Döscher's argument is left unturned. His conclusion, like
my own, is final. "Apart from the comments of Grynszpan himself, which

he—note well—revoked, and the futile efforts of Soltikow, a crook posing as a reputable journalist, there is no evidence of a homosexual relationship between vom Rath and Grynszpan. In fact, everything seems to indicate that the two men did not know each other until five shots linked them together forever."[11]

In 1960, the year the Soltikow trial ended and a year before Eichmann's trial began, Sendel Grynszpan petitioned a German court in Hanover for a certificate declaring Herschel legally dead. When the petition was made, nobody in the Grynszpan family had heard from their son and brother for over twenty years. There had been no trace of him in any official record since 1942. The postwar search for him had been diligent and fruitless. On June 1, 1960, the Hanover court acted and declared Herschel dead in the eyes of the law. As a matter of form, the court had to supply an official date of death, but since there was no evidence of when or how Herschel met his end, the judges were obliged to choose the date arbitrarily, plausibly, symbolically.[12] They chose May 8, 1945, the last day of the world war in which Herschel played such a singular role.

If he had really survived until that final day, Herschel Grynszpan would have been twenty-four years old.

ACKNOWLEDGMENTS

Writing *Hitler's Pawn* with confidence would not have been possible without generous help on all sides. I am grateful for help from Sidney Smeets, Vicki Caron, Matthew Israel, Lore Segal, Ingeborg vom Rath, Alan Stienweis, Robert Paxton, Susan Hertog, Daniel Smith, James Marcus, and others too numerous to mention. I stumbled onto Herschel's forgotten story one day doing research on Dorothy Thompson, wondering why some notable Americans, like Thompson, were right from the start about Hitler, and others, like Charles Lindbergh and Frank Lloyd Wright, were dead wrong. That night over dinner I told my wife what I'd learned about Herschel's story. Franny listened, gave me a penetrating gaze that is unique to her, and said, "That could be a book."

And so it has.

S.K.

APPENDIX

Herschel Grynszpan's Testament

Dictated in Code
April 24–29, 1942

4.24.42 I herewith declare that my second deposition which I gave to the Gestapo is untrue[.] the reasons for my false testimony are the following[:]

4.25.42 When France extradited me to Germany I thought that there would be no trial in that the Gestapo would murder me

4.26.42 This was naturally more to my liking than a grand propaganda trial whose results would be a death sentence and which undoubtedly would have resulted in bloody pogroms[.] time however proved the exact opposite[.] they did turn me over to the Gestapo as prisoner but they treated me exceptionally very well[.] as I heard there from other prisoners one is treated well by the Gestapo only if one has special plans for that person[.] in my case this could only be a propaganda trial[.] this I wanted to avoid in any event in order to prevent any possible pogroms which could result through my trial and so that I personally as a tool of German propaganda

4.27.42 would not be misused[.] in order to prevent this no means was good enough for me[.] I therefore utilized a touchy phase out of the life of Mr. vom Rath with which my attorney Godcheaux [sic] acquainted me and out of this made up false testimony to the Gestapo[.] I hoped that on the basis of this testimony they would murder me so that no outsider would get wind thereof (several days later I wrote a letter to the Gestapo in which I protested against my illegal extradition and therefore from now on will not testify during interrogations or the trial[.] I did this because I feared that I could contradict myself and would therefore nullify my statements which in any event are so implausible)[.]

4.28.42 Shortly thereafter I received an order for protective custody and was sent to a concentration camp[.] here I was placed in a single cell and was treated quite well[.] almost every wish was fulfilled and I was very curious about this but did not believe that I would again leave the camp alive

4.29.42 Several months later there occurred what I did not expect[.] The Gestapo transferred me to the "UG" [interrogation prison] Moabich[.] one evidently wanted to make a trial with me anyway[.] in order to prevent this I turned to the last available means which remained for me to suicide[.] I did this twice but they were unsuccessful due to the vigilance of Guard Hollmurg[.] I have not given up the hope that I will still succeed[.] in case it should come otherwise I will not defend myself at my trial and refuse the judge all answers in order thereby to prevent perjury[.] I have entrusted this admission to three persons[.] in case they should someday wish to publish it so this is to serve as verification.

—Translated from the German by Gerald Schwab

A NOTE ON SOURCES

The Ur-document on the life of Herschel Grynszpan is a very rare book, *L'Affaire Grynszpan–vom Rath*, by a French physician named Alain Cuénot. Originally written in French, the unpublished manuscript of this text was translated into English by Joan Redmont in 1982 and edited and published as *The Herschel Grynszpan Case* in a limited number of Xeroxed copies by David Rome, in Beverly Hills, California. Copies of this English-language translation are available in some major libraries in both the United States and Europe. The Library of Congress number of the book is 82-237179. All my references to Cuénot are to this translation.

All subsequent studies of Herschel Grynszpan's life rely heavily on Cuénot, who during the 1950s read every document, tracked down every possible source of information, and interviewed every living witness he could find. In the many years that followed his research, almost all the scholarship in Dr. Cuénot's book, especially about Herschel's life in Paris, has proved to be remarkably durable. Every student of this story is indebted to it.

An earlier book in German, *Der Fall des Herschel Grynszpan*, by East German scholar F. K. Kaul (Berlin: Akademie-Verlag, 1965) supplies important information that was available in the archives of the then DDR.

In 1974, Rita Thalmann and Emmanuel Feinermann's *Crystal Night* appeared in English (New York: Holocaust Library; translated from the French by Gilles Cremonesi). Its account of how Herschel was used in the pogrom is much indebted to Cuénot, and though some of its insights have been superseded, the account is generally accurate. It ends with a brief, well-researched account of Herschel's captivity in Germany.

Anthony Read and David Fisher's *Kristallnacht: The Nazi Night of Terror* (New York: Times Books, Random House, 1989) supplied me with much useful information.

The next solid book-length study of Herschel's own life is Gerald Schwab's *The Day the Holocaust Began: The Odyssey of Herschel Grynszpan* (New York: Praeger, 1990). Schwab's book is the most readily available mother lode of information on Herschel. It is deeply indebted to Cuénot, though Schwab is able to supplement Cuénot's account of Herschel's German captivity with detailed knowledge of the German governmental archives that Cuénot does not cite. While subsequent scholarship has added important new information, I am not aware of any significant factual errors in Schwab's book. In *Hitler's Pawn*, whenever Cuénot and Schwab refer to identical facts, I myself cite the more readily available book.

How Gerald Schwab came to have this knowledge is an interesting story.

The Schwab family was victims of the Kristallnacht. Gerald Schwab's father was one of the thirty thousand German-Jewish businessmen who were rounded up and incarcerated in Dachau after the pogrom. His son was thirteen years old. After his father was released from the concentration camp in 1939, young Gerald was sent to Switzerland via the *Kindertransport*. In May 1940 his family acquired visas to the United States, finding refuge on a chicken farm in New Jersey. There Gerald grew up, a bilingual and exceptionally articulate youth, speaking perfect German and American English with a flawless mid-Atlantic accent. In 1944, when he was nineteen years old, Gerald was drafted into the United States Army. In 1944–45, Schwab participated in the U.S. Army's Italian campaign.

Inside the army, Gerald Schwab's linguistic skills were of course quickly recognized, and after Germany's defeat, they became especially useful. Barely out of his teens, the tousle-haired youth was made an interpreter at the Nuremberg Trials. When the trials were over, the army assigned Schwab to Berlin, where he participated in the Allied examination of the Nazi archives. Since the Kristallnacht had driven his family out of Germany, Schwab decided to begin by researching that event. Poring over the files soon led him to Herschel Grynszpan. He became fascinated, asking for more and more material.

At this point, the German Foreign Office functionary who had been excavating the files and bringing them to Schwab's desk took note of his interest in Grynszpan and astonished the young American by telling him that he had been the clerk whom Herschel approached at the front desk that morning in the Paris embassy. He was Wilhelm Nagorka, the very man who had led Herschel to "one of the embassy secretaries," Ernst vom Rath, who then heard the pistol shots, and rushed back to find the wounded vom Rath in the corridor and Herschel in the smoke-filled room. He was the man who led Herschel to the French police. Nagorka is the most reliable of all the eyewitnesses to the assassination. This extraordinary coincidence lends great force to Schwab's account of the event.

Indebted as it is, Schwab's book improves on Cuénot in a number of ways. His view of Herschel's personality differs markedly from Cuénot, who views Herschel in largely negative terms: a feckless, callow, unimaginative if not downright unintelligent youth, who in most of his conduct was something of a fool. Cuénot begins his book with a theory about the psychology of major assassins in history. This theory is not very convincing in the first place; it is even less convincing as the Procrustean bed into which he tries to cram his subject. Schwab is everywhere more sensitive to the real workings of Herschel's adolescent mind, which like many adolescent minds was a very special mix of shallowness and depth.

In 2000, the German scholar Hans-Jürgen Döscher published *Reichs-*

kristallnacht: Die Novemberpogrome, 1938. This study is generally viewed as the definitive work on the Kristallnacht in German, written after close examination of all the relevant files and vast literature.

Döscher's book has been much admired, but it does have one significant flaw: As has since been demonstrated, its analysis of the relation between Herschel and vom Rath is in error. A number of works of fiction have since appeared, based on Döscher's mistaken hypothesis that they had some sort of homosexual connection. None are reliable accounts of the story.

Döscher was followed in 2009 by the most trustworthy twenty-first-century account of the pogrom in English, *Kristallnacht 1938*, by Alan E. Steinweis. Steinweis is a careful scholar who has worked extensively in the archives and who is conscious throughout of Döscher's work. Much that can be learned from Döscher can also be learned from Steinweis.

But after 2000, Döscher's theory about the relationship between Herschel and vom Rath stood uncorrected. Then 2013 saw the publication of *De Wanhoopsdaad (Act of Desperation)*, by a brilliant young Dutch lawyer named Sidney Smeets. *De Wanhoopsdaad* brings crucial new material to the story. In order to write his book, Smeets retraced every step through the archives that Gerald Schwab discovered in 1946, adding the many other archival records examined by Döscher. This involved examining all of the abundant material in the Bundesarchiv in Berlin; the state archives of Bayern and of Munich; and the State Archives of Nordrhein-Westfalen in Düsseldorf. Unlike Schwab, Smeets had access to the full archive of the Soltikov trial, along with the advantage to having had access to the full text of Goebbels's diaries. The details of the relevant archival material are cited in the apparatus of his book. *De Wanhoopsdaad* is especially notable for its systematic and convincing refutation of the supposed homosexual relation between Herschel and vom Rath. Since Smeets, the homosexual hypothesis is no longer tenable.

The Short, Strange Life of Herschel Grynszpan by Jonathan Kirsch also appeared in 2013. It is a readable account of the story, laying special emphasis on Herschel's anomalous place in Jewish history. It was written without the advantage of knowing Smeets's work and does not present new information. It is curiously reticent on the role of Georges Bonnet at every stage of Herschel's odyssey.

In 2015, a French scholar, Corinne Chaponnière, published *Les Quatre Coups de la Nuit de Cristal: Paris, 7 Novembre 1938; L'Affaire Grynszpan–vom Rath*. Chaponnière further discredits the theory of a sexual relationship between Grynszpan and vom Rath.

I must gratefully acknowledge the New York Public Library, in particular its Dorot Jewish Division, which gave me quick, courteous access to any number of rare publications that otherwise would have been very difficult, if not impossible, to find.

A final word on Gerald Schwab: After the army and graduate school, Gerald Schwab began what became a distinguished lifelong career in the State Department. When I began doing research for this book, he very graciously granted me a lengthy interview, escorted me to the library of the United States Memorial Holocaust Museum, and was kind enough to supply me with a great deal of Xeroxed material from his own personal archives. This material included his typed notes made immediately after his 1947 interview with Vincent de Moro-Giafferi, a large number of letters between Alain Cuénot and Günter vom Rath, memoranda and correspondence with Walter Hammer, and extensive documentation of many other aspects of his book. This material was indispensible. I could not have written this book without him. I only regret that since his death in 2014, the moment has passed for me to thank Gerald Schwab publically. He was an impressive man and a generous spirit.

S.K.

VISUALS

Herschel Grynszpan was an exceptionally photogenic adolescent. Yet almost all his known photographs were taken shortly after the shooting and are images of an adolescent in agony. These press photos can be seen in abundance by Googling "Herschel Grynszpan—Images." Many searches will also pull up photographs of Abraham and Chawa.

Inexplicably, the street vendor's photograph of the boy, described on pages 16–17, rarely appears in Google searches. It is reproduced in the front matter.

A Google search of "Ernst vom Rath—Images" will pull up many images of the diplomat, usually accompanied by photographs of his funeral. Some searches find very rare press pictures, such as Count Johannes von Welczeck escorting Ernst's mother to a car.

Interested readers can easily Google such figures in the drama as Vincente de Moro-Giafferi, Friedrich Grimm, even Wolfgang Diewerge. Georges Bonnet makes many appearances on both Google and YouTube.

To capture the frenzy of relief in Paris and London after Munich, YouTube has revealing newsreel footage searchable under "Daladier Arrives Home-Sound."

BIBLIOGRAPHY

Adamthwaite, Anthony. *France and the Coming of the Second World War.* London: Frank Cass, 1977.

———. *The Making of the Second World War.* 1977. Reprint, New York: Routledge, Chapman and Hall, 1992.

Arendt, Hannah. *Eichmann in Jerusalem: A Report on the Banality of Evil.* New York: Viking Press, 1963.

Associated Press. "Noted Paris Lawyer to Defend 17-Year-Old Killer of vom Rath." *New York Times,* November 18, 1938.

———. "Paris Slayer Weeps at News from Reich." *New York Times,* November 10, 1938.

Bareiss, Andreas Friedrich. *Herschel Feibel Grynszpan: Der Attentater und die "Reichskristallnacht."* Geissen: Haland & Wirth, 2005.

Caron, Vicki. *Uneasy Asylum: France and the Jewish Refugee Crisis 1933–1942.* Palo Alto, CA: Stanford University Press, 1999.

Döscher, H. J. *Reichskristallnacht: Die Novemberpogrome, 1938.* Munich: Econ-Ullstein-List-Verlag, 2000.

Dumolin, Pierre [psued.]. *L'Affaire Grynszpan: Un Attentat Contre La France.* Paris: Editions Jean-Renard, 1942.

Evans, Richard J. *The Coming of the Third Reich.* 3 vols. New York: Penguin Books, 2004–2009.

Faber, David. *Munich: The 1938 Appeasement Crisis.* New York: Simon & Schuster, 2008.

Feinermann, Emmanuel, and Rita Thalmann. *Crystal Night.* Translated by Gilles
　　Cremonisi. New York: Holocaust Library, 1974.

Fisher, David, and Anthony Read. *Kristallnacht: The Nazi Night of Terror.* New
　　York: Random House, 1989.

Fry, Varian. *Surrender on Demand.* Boulder, CO: Johnson Books, 1997. First pub-
　　lished 1945 by Random House (New York).

Gilbert, Martin. *The Holocaust: A History of the Jews of Europe During the Second
　　World War.* Paperback ed. New York: Henry Holt, 1986.

―――. *Kristallnacht: Prelude to Destruction.* New York: Harper Perennial, 2007.
　　First published 2006 in hardcover.

Heiber, Helmut. "Der Fall Grunspan." *Vierteljahrshefte fur Zeitgeschicte*, no. 5
　　(1957): 154–72.

Kaul, F. K. *Der Fall des Herschel Grynszpan.* Berlin: Akademie Verlag, 1965.

Kershaw, Ian. *Hitler: 1936–1945; Nemesis.* New York: W. W. Norton, 2000.

Kirsch, Jonathan. *The Short, Strange Life of Herschel Grynszpan.* Paperback ed. New
　　York: Liverright, an imprint of W. W. Norton, 2013.

Klemperer, Victor. *I Will Bear Witness: A Diary of the Nazi Years, 1933–1941.* Pa-
　　perback ed. Translated by Martin Chalmers. New York: The Modern Library,
　　1999.

Le Figaro. "L'Agresseur de M. vom Rath a ete Longuement Interroge." November
　　9, 1938.

Le Matin. "Attentat Politique a Paris." November 9, 1938.

Le Temps. "Un Attentat a l'ambassade d'Allemagne." November 8, 1938.

L'Humanite. "Un Attentat Trouble." *L'Humanite*, November 8, 1938.

―――. "Vom Rath a succombé." November 10, 1938.

Lifton, Robert Jay. *The Nazi Doctors: Medical Killing and the Psychology of Genocide.*
　　1986. Reprinted with preface by the author. New York: Basic Books, an im-
　　print of Perseus Books, 2000.

Marrus, M. R. "The Strange Story of Herschel Grynszpan." *The American Scholar*
　　(Winter 1988): 69–79.

May, Ernest R. *Strange Victory: Hitler's Conquest of France.* New York: Hill and
　　Wang, an imprint of Farrar, Straus and Giroux, 2000. Published 2001 in
　　paperback.

NANA, Inc. "Will Defend Assassin." November 27, 1938.

New York Times. "Berlin Foreign Office Aide Leaves Paris with Slain Diplomat."
　　November 16, 1938.

―――. "Diplomat's Condition Critical." November 9, 1938.

———. "Grynszpan Kin Sentenced." November 30, 1938.

———. "Reich Embassy Aide in Paris Shot to Avenge Expulsions by the Nazis." November 8, 1938.

Paxton, Robert. *Vichy France: Old Guard and New Order*. New York: Columbia University Press, 2001. First published 1972 by Alfred A. Knopf (New York).

Reynolds, Quentin. "Portrait of a Murderer." *Collier's*, February 25, 1939.

Roizen, Ron. "Herschel Grynszpan: The Fate of a Forgotten Assassin." *Holocaust and Genocide Studies*, 217–28.

Schmidt, Uif. *Karl Brandt: The Nazi Doctor; Medicine and Power in the Third Reich*. New York: Hambldon Continuum, 2007. 2nd ed. published 2008.

Schwab, Gerald. *The Day the Holocaust Began: The Odyssey of Herschel Grynszpan*. New York: Praeger, an imprint of Greenwood, 1990.

Shengold, Mordecai. *The Shengold Jewish Encyclopedia*. Lanham, MD: Taylor Trade, 2011.

Shirer, William L. *The Collapse of the Third Republic*. Paperback ed. New York: Da Capo Press, 1994. Originally published 1969 by Simon & Schuster (New York).

———. *The Nightmare Years: 1930–1940*. Boston, MA: Little, Brown, 1984.

Smeets, Sidney. *De Wanhoopsdaad: Hoe een zeventienjarige de Kristallnacht ontkende*. Amsterdam: Uitgeverij Balans, 2013.

Steinweis, Alan E. *Kristallnacht: 1938*. Cambridge, MA: Belknap Press, an imprint of Harvard University Press, 2009.

Taylor, Telford. *Munich: The Price of Peace*. Garden City, NY: Doubleday, 1979.

Weill-Goudchaux, Serge. "L'Affaire Grynszpan." *L'Arche* (January 1960): 11.

Young-Bruehl, Elisabeth. *Hannah Arendt: For Love of the World*. New Haven, CT: Yale University Press.

NOTES

Chapter 1: La Paix! La Paix! La Paix!

1. Ernest R. May, *Strange Victory: Hitler's Conquest of France* (New York: Hill and Wang, 2000), 168. These pages also present a general summary of Daladier's mood returning from Munich.

2. For a detailed analysis of Daladier's leadership, see *Munich: The Price of Peace*, by Telford Taylor (Garden City, NY: Doubleday, 1979), chapter 21: "Édouard Daladier—Man of Indecision," 504–34.

3. William Keylor, "France and the Illusion of American Support, 1919–1940," in *The French Defeat of 1940 Reassessments*, ed. Joel Blatt (Providence: Berghahn Books, 1998), 234.

4. William Shirer, *The Collapse of the Third Republic: An Inquiry into the Fall of France in 1940* (Cambridge, MA: Da Capo Press, 1969), 339–40.

5. Shirer, *Collapse*, 407.

6. Anthony Adamthwaite, *France and the Coming of the Second World War* (London: Frank Cass, 1977), 332.

7. Shirer, *Collapse*, 403.

8. Taylor, *Munich*, 58–59.

9. William L. Shirer, *The Nightmare Years: 1930–1940,* vol. 2 of *Twentieth Century Journey* (Boston: Little, Brown, 1984), 362.

10. There are numerous newsreels of Daladier's return available on the Internet. For example, from the Associated Press newsreel archive: www.aparchive.com /metadata/youtube/386f8a05fc9e455f80226c9261f5ab82.

11. A. P. J. Taylor, *Origins of the Second World War*, paperback ed. (New York: Simon & Schuster, 2005), 191.

12. David Faber, *Munich: The 1938 Appeasement Crisis* (New York: Simon & Schuster, 2008), 5–7.

13. Shirer, *Nightmare Years*, 402. See also Taylor, *Munich*, 58–59.

14. Jean-Paul Sartre, *Le Sursis* (Paris: Gallimard, 1945). See also Taylor, *Munich*, 58–59.

Chapter 2: The Child

1. For the general survey of Herschel's life, see my "A Note on Sources" at the end of this book. Adolf Eichmann referred to Herschel as a "*Knabe*" or "lad" during his 1961 trial in Jerusalem.

2. It is unwise to attempt diagnosis of people who have never been medically examined. Nonetheless, some speculation is inevitable. What we know of Herschel's psychological state is that he was a bright, pleasant young man who was nonetheless subject to flamboyant irrational rages, flights of grandiosity, and crushing clinical depression. These traits are consistent with the traits of bipolar 1 syndrome, and it is at least possible that Herschel's emotional dilemmas were located somewhere on that spectrum.

3. Alain Cuénot, M. D. *The Herschel Grynszpan Case*, ed. David Rome, trans. Joan Redmont (Beverly Hills: D. Rome, 1982), 11.

4. Serge Weill-Goudchaux, "L'Affaire Grynszpan," *L'Arche* (January 1960): 11.

5. Ian Kershaw, *Hitler: 1936–1945; Nemesis* (New York: W. W. Norton, 2000), 136.

6. Martin Gilbert, *The Holocaust: A History of the Jews of Europe During the Second World War* (New York: Henry Holt, 1986; Holt Paperbacks Edition, 1987), 66–68. Herschel Grynszpan was under the mistaken impression that twelve thousand Polish Jews had been forced to leave Germany during these deportations. The actual number was eighteen thousand.

7. While it is not quite true that "all governments" were closed to him, the two countries to which he wished to emigrate—Israel and the United States—were. Israel did not accept immigrants under the age of eighteen—though there was a busy underground railway importing youthful illegal Jews. The United States was effectively closed by the quota system.

8. Gerald Schwab, *The Day the Holocaust Began: The Odyssey of Herschel Grynszpan* (New York: Praeger, an imprint of Greenwood, 1990), 46–47.

9. See Mordecai Shengold, *The Shengold Jewish Encyclopedia* (Lanham, MD: Taylor Trade, 2011).

10. This claim was made after his arrest in his psychiatric interview conducted by a social worker: Mlle. de Loustelle. The anecdote may be factual; it may have been a bit of the youth's grandiosity.

11. The reasons for Herschel's difficulty entering France remain murky. Both Schwab and Sidney Smeets accept without further question that the boy had to enter France illegally because he was without funds.

12. Herschel traveled under a Polish passport, and though he had been born in Germany, the law saw him as Polish—though he had never been in Poland and could not speak its language. He thus had a legal Polish passport with a German exit visa. The Belgians, however, required an entry visa, which they would not issue unless the bearer had an authorized visa for a return to Germany. The Belgians wanted to be free to expel anyone they pleased without legal obstacles. Herschel applied to the German government in Hanover for this re-entry visa, and it was granted—though at the time, neither Herschel nor the German emigration authorities expected it to be used. Illegal entry into France by German refugees was very common at this time, and the Popular Front government of the time took a rather lenient approach to it. Two months after arriving in Paris, in late September 1936, the boy was granted a legal French visa. In the weeks after that, he used an organization called the "Central Committee for Aid to Immigrant Jews" to help him prepare a strong application for a French *carte d'identité* and a *permis des séjour.*

    On the strength of this receipt, Herschel's position in France was regularized and his subsequent time in France legalized.

13. Whether Abraham did or did not meet his nephew in Valenciennes is unclear. When the police made an effort to establish this simple fact, Abraham was evasive. He could not appear to have assisted Herschel's illegal entry for fear of further criminal charges being leveled against him. Nonetheless, the probability that he met his nephew at the Villeneuve station is very high.

14. Herschel's abdominal affliction is mentioned in every biography. See Schwab, 52–53.

15. Schwab, *The Day the Holocaust Began*, 52.

16. After committing the crime, Herschel was subjected to a lengthy psychological examination by a certain Mlle. de Loustal, a social worker. In this court-ordered report, Mlle. de Loustal describes in detail Herschel's depressive collapse upon arriving in Paris. Abraham's assessment of Herschel's depression was made before the examining magistrate.

17. In a good week, Abraham earned around 600 French francs, or approximately

$18 in 1938, the equivalent of about $285 in the early twenty-first-century United States. Dramatic differences in the cost of living mean that these numbers are misleading. Abraham's poverty was real but not crushing. Note, for example, that over the years he had managed to accumulate some savings.

18. Schwab, *The Day the Holocaust Began*, 61.

19. Schwab, 58.

Chapter 3: Hunted

1. Once he was in Paris, Herschel had to regularize his otherwise illegal entry into France, paying a fine of 100 francs. This done, he was entitled to submit his application for a residence permit (*permis de séjour*) and an identity card (*carte d'identité*) to the Ministry of the Interior. While this application was under consideration, the ministry issued a receipt that allowed Herschel to remain in France pending its approval or disapproval.

    The ministry took nineteen months to reach its negative decision. During this time, both Herschel's Polish passport and his reentry visa permitting his return to Germany expired. Despite various efforts to renew these documents, neither was in effect when the ministry refused his application. Thus, when he was ordered out of France, he could neither return to Germany nor take refuge—if refuge it can be called—in Poland. In the eyes of the law, he was an illegal immigrant in France and internationally a stateless person, or as Gerald Schwab put it, "the proverbial wandering Jew." Through no fault of his own, France, Israel, Germany, Poland, and the United States were closed to him. Ordered to leave France, he had nowhere to go.

2. Schwab, *The Day the Holocaust Began*, 56, 73–74, 87.

3. The definitive work on Jewish refugees in Paris during this period is *Uneasy Asylum: France and the Jewish Refugee Crisis*, by Vicki Caron (Palo Alto, CA: Stanford University Press, 1999).

4. Schwab, *The Day the Holocaust Began*, 78.

5. Caron, *Uneasy Asylum*, 186.

6. Caron, 186.

7. Caron, 3.

8. Caron, 173–76.

9. Caron treats the complex legal and social maneuvers of the anti-immigration "decree laws" with exacting detail, especially in chapters 8 and 9 (pp. 171–205). These pages also identify the senior figures most responsible: Daladier himself; his minister of the interior, Alfred Sarraut; and Sarraut's close confed-

erate in the Daladier cabinet, Georges Bonnet. These chapters also include an interesting and notably accurate account of the Grynszpan affair.

10. Caron, 174.
11. Caron, chapter 11, "The Missed Opportunity," 240–67.
12. Caron, 181, 186.
13. Adamthwaite, *France and the Coming of the Second World War*, 98.
14. Adamthwaite, 332.
15. Adamthwaite, 269–70. See also Caron, *Uneasy Asylum*, 194.
16. Schwab, *The Day the Holocaust Began*, 55.
17. Caron, *Uneasy Asylum*, 213.
18. Schwab, *The Day the Holocaust Began*, 56.
19. Schwab, 56.
20. Schwab, 57.
21. *L'Humanite*, "Un Attentat Trouble," Paris. November 8, 1938.
22. Schwab, *The Day the Holocaust Began*, 54.
23. The contents of Herschel's hideout appeared in contemporary news reports.

Chapter 4: Dispossession

1. For lucid accounts of the Polish deportations, see Richard J. Evans, *The Third Reich in Power* (New York: Penguin, 2006), 578–79; Martin Gilbert, *Kristallnacht: Prelude to Destruction* (New York: Harper Perennial, 2006), 23–27; Alan E. Steinweis, *Kristallnacht: 1938* (Cambridge, MA: Belknap Press, an imprint of Harvard University Press, 2009), 16–25; Schwab, *The Day the Holocaust Began*, chapter 8, "The Deportation of the Grynszpan Family," 59–69. For an interesting eyewitness account of the deportations from Berlin, see *The Author of Himself*, by Marcel Reich-Ranicki (Princeton, NJ: Princeton University Press, 1999), 106–9.
2. *Sicherheitspolizei*, or *SiPo*. A branch of the German national police, later absorbed into the Gestapo.
3. This account derives from Berta's postcard to Herschel (Schwab, *The Day the Holocaust Began*, 4) and the testimony of Sendel Grynszpan at the 1961 trial of Adolf Eichmann in Jerusalem.
4. Rita Thalmann and Emmanuel Feinermann, *Crystal Night*, trans. Gilles Cremonisi (New York: Holocaust Library, 1974), 35.
5. Schwab, *The Day the Holocaust Began*, 62–69.
6. Thalmann and Feinermann, *Crystal Night*, 27.
7. Hannah Arendt, *Eichmann in Jerusalem: A Report on the Banality of Evil* (New York: Viking Press, 1963), 229.

8. Testimony of Zindel Grynszpan, Eichmann Trial, April 25, 1961, session 14. See also Thalmann and Feinermann, *Crystal Night,* 35–36.

9. Arendt, *Eichmann in Jerusalem,* 229.

Chapter 5: The Assassin's Night

1. Schwab, *The Day the Holocaust Began*, 4.

2. Schwab, 56–57.

3. Schwab, 63–64.

4. *Pariser Haint*, November 4, 1938, as quoted in *Kristallnacht: The Nazi Night of Terror*, by David Fisher and Anthony Read (New York: Random House, 1989), 40.

5. Schwab, *The Day the Holocaust Began*, 63.

6. Schwab, 64.

7. The best information on the quarrel between Abraham and Herschel comes from a personal message sent to the anti-Nazi journalist Dorothy Thompson from Herschel's prime lawyer, Vincent de Moro-Giafferi, via a member of the Journalists' Defense Fund, Oswald Villard. Moro-Giafferi explained how the 3,000 francs had been sent illegally to Abraham, how Herschel had demanded that this money be sent to Poland immediately to relieve the Hanover Grynszpans, and how Abraham had agreed that the money should indeed be sent, but only after it would be secure to do so. Moro-Giafferi is therefore the source for my account here, which is summarized by Schawb, *The Day the Holocaust Began*, 115–16.

8. Schwab, 116.

9. Schwab, 115.

10. In November 1938, Herschel had been in Abraham and Chawa's care for more than two years. How, and how much, of the 3,000 francs from Sendel had been spent for his care during that time is unknown. Perhaps Abraham had reserved the money and defrayed Herschel's expenses from his own pocket, or perhaps he had savings of his own. In any case, he intended to send financial relief to the Hanover Grynszpans. The argument was not over whether to send relief, but when.

11. Schwab, *The Day the Holocaust Began*, 71–73, 116.

12. Schwab, 73–74.

13. Schwab, 73–74.

14. Schwab. 74–75.

15. Herschel's dreams were recorded during interrogations made by medical au-

thorities and in the presence of Moro-Giafferi. Cuénot, *The Herschel Grynsz-pan Case*, 46.

16. Cuénot, 45.

Chapter 6: The Assassin's Day

1. Schwab, *The Day the Holocaust Began*, 4.

2. My account of the assassination is primarily indebted to Schwab's version, the first chapter of *The Day the Holocaust Began*, which (so far as I can see) is somewhat incomplete, but error-free. I am also indebted to Sidney Smeets, *De Wanhoopsdaad: Hoe een zeventienjarige de Kristallnacht ontkende* (Amsterdam: Uitgeverij Balans, 2013), 53–56. Smeets is more concise and in virtually complete agreement with Schwab, though he supplies important new material about the vom Rath family. Numerous details, culled from newspaper reports and various other sources, are cited *passim*.

3. The Parisian press interviewed M. and Mme. Carpe extensively.

4. Fisher and Read, *Kristallnacht: The Nazi Night of Terror*, 5.

5. Schwab, *The Day the Holocaust Began*, 75–76.

6. Smeets, *De Wanhoopsdaad*, 49–51.

7. Schwab, *The Day the Holocaust Began*, 15–17.

8. Thalmann and Feinermann, *Crystal Night*, 57. Maddeningly, Thalmann and Feinermann do not supply their source for this anecdote. My own search for a source traced Magnus Davidsohn to Great Britain, where he was associated with an organization known as the "Association of Jewish Refugees." He was interviewed by the journal of this organization, but this interview does not seem to be the source.

9. Martin Gilbert, *The Holocaust: A History of the Jews of Europe during the Second World War* (New York: Henry Holt, 1985), 117. Why Gustav vom Rath, who may have believed the Gestapo killed his son, would have accepted employment of this kind is unclear. He certainly did not need the income.

10. Smeets, *De Wanhoopsdaad*, 43.

11. Otto Abetz, *Franco-German Political History 1930–1950* (Paris: Editions Stock, 1953).

12. Smeets credits as possible Herschel's later claim that he said something more elaborate: "It is not enough that the Jews have to suffer in Germany and be thrown into concentration camps; now it expels them as if they were vicious dogs." Schwab credits Herschel's earlier statement as the correct one.

13. Cuénot, *The Herschel Grynszpan Case*, 53.
14. Schwab, *The Day the Holocaust Began*, 2–3.
15. Schwab, 3.

Chapter 7: Hitler's Luck

1. We know that Ambassador von Welczeck returned from his morning constitutional around 10:20, and that soon after his return, certainly before eleven o'clock at the latest, he received a telephone call from Hitler. The news of the shooting seems to have reached Berlin very shortly after ten o'clock, Paris time.
2. There is no documentary evidence of Hitler's communication with Goebbels at this time, though it undoubtedly took place, almost certainly by telephone.
3. Bräuer's transcribed telephone call is reproduced in Andreas Bareiss's *Herschel Feibel Grynszpan: Der Attentäter und die "Reichkristallnacht"* (Geissen: Haland & Wirth, 2005). Though this book is a work of fiction, the author insists that the documentary material he supplies is authentic. Bareiss says the transcription here is to be found in the German Foreign Ministry's personal file on Ernst vom Rath. See page 13.
4. Bareiss claims the transcription was sent simultaneously to Goebbels and Hitler direct from the Foreign Office.
5. Steinweis, *Kristallnacht: 1938*, 19–20.
6. *The [London] Telegraph*, November 7, 1938.
7. Kershaw, *Hitler*, 171.
8. Kershaw, 162.
9. Kershaw, 157–68.
10. Kershaw, 136.
11. Kershaw, 136.
12. It is difficult to believe that Goebbels would have embarked on the major anti-Semitic propaganda campaign that he set in motion on the morning of November 7 without Hitler's knowledge and explicit consent and order. At this moment, Goebbels's position in Hitler's esteem was shaky; he would never have risked Hitler's displeasure by launching a major governmental demarche without permission. He was entirely subservient to the Führer.
13. Schwab, *The Day the Holocaust Began*, 20.
14. Steinweis, *Kristallnacht: 1938*, 20.
15. Steinweis, 20–21. See also Schwab, *The Day the Holocaust Began*, 80.
16. Steinweis, *Kristallnacht: 1938*, 21–22.

17. A standard biography of Goebbels is by Peter Longerich, *Goebbels: A Biography* (New York: Random House, 2015).

18. Longerich, 21–22.

19. Longerich, 32.

20. Longerich, 95–96.

21. See Sinclair Lewis, *It Can't Happen Here* (New York: Doubleday, 1935), as well as Tim Bouverie, "Goebbels by Peter Longerich, review: 'meticulous and highly readable,'" review of *Goebbels* by Longerich, *The [London] Telegraph*, January 8, 2011.

22. Longerich, *Goebbels*, 21.

23. See Kershaw, *Hitler*, 171.

24. Longerich, *Goebbels*, 224.

25. Longerich, 392.

Chapter 8: Arrest and Fame

1. Schwab, *The Day the Holocaust Began*, 3–4.

2. Schwab, 3.

3. "Reich Embassy Aide in Paris Shot to Avenge Expulsions by the Nazis," *New York Times*, November 8, 1938, p. 1.

4. Schwab, *The Day the Holocaust Began*, 3. See also Friedrich Karl Kaul, *Der Fall des Herschel Grynszpan* (Berlin: Akademie Verlag, 1965), 18–19.

5. "Une Déclaration de M. Georges Bonnet," *Le Monde Juif* (April–June 1964).

6. The claim that Herschel's true target was the ambassador has enjoyed a long afterlife. It is still treated as fact in more than one canonical history of the war. There *is* some ambiguity. It is possible—it is even likely—that in his fantasies before the shooting, Herschel mused on gunning down the top man. He may later have told people that he would have liked to assassinate the ambassador. His own lawyers, Weill-Goudchaux and Moro-Giafferi, claimed as much. Nonetheless, it is clear that when he arrived in the embassy, Herschel did not ask to see the ambassador. He asked to see "one of the embassy officials."

7. "Diplomat's Condition Critical," *New York Times*, November 9, 1938.

8. Steinweis, *Kristallnacht: 1938*, 27.

9. Adamthwaite, *France and the Coming of the Second World War*, 265–66.

10. Schwab, *The Day the Holocaust Began*, 8–9.

11. Cuénot, *The Herschel Grynszpan Case*, 57.

12. Ulf Schmidt, *Karl Brant: The Nazi Doctor; Medicine and Power in the Third Reich* (New York: Hambldon Continuum, 2007), 109–10. The quotation from

Brandt was recorded by Otto Brautigam, *So hat es sich zugetragen . . . Ein Leben als Soldat und Diplomat* (Wurtzberg: Holzer, 1968), 344.

13. Schwab, *The Day the Holocaust Began*, 10.
14. "Un Attentat Trouble," *L'Humanité*, November 8, 1938.
15. Schwab, *The Day the Holocaust Began*, 56–57.
16. German Ministry of Propaganda files, vol. 991, pp. 54–55, as cited by Schwab, *The Day the Holocaust Began*, 5.

Chapter 9: Two Speeches

1. Cuénot, *The Herschel Grynszpan Case*, 53. The quotation is taken from confiscated French files held in the archives of the German Ministry of Propaganda.
2. Schwab, *The Day the Holocaust Began*, 77.
3. Schwab, 78.
4. Newspaper account, *L'Ouevre*, November 9, 1938.
5. "Un Attentat a l'ambassade d'Allemagne," *Le Temps*, November 10, 1938, cited by Schwab and Cuénot.
6. Schwab, *The Day the Holocaust Began*, 79.
7. Serge Weill-Goudchaux, in a letter to the editor of *L'Arche* (January 1960): 11.
8. Richard Breitman, *The Architect of Genocide: Himmler and the Final Solution* (New York: Alfred Knopf, 1991), 50–55.
9. Peter Longerich, *Heinrich Himmler*, trans. Jeremy Noakes and Lesley Sharpe (New York: Oxford University Press, 2012), 409.
10. Kershaw, *Hitler*, 130.
11. Breitman, *The Architect of Genocide*, 50.
12. Breitman, 51.
13. Breitman, 51.
14. Breitman, 51.

Chapter 10: The Whole World Hears

1. Schwab, *The Day the Holocaust Began*, 9; Steinweis, *Kristallnacht: 1938*, 42.
2. For an excellent summary of British official reaction to vom Rath's death and the Kristallnacht, see Taylor, *Munich*, 937. When German propaganda claimed that Churchill, Clement Atlee, and Duff Cooper were among the instigators of the shooting, the British government closed ranks with its critics.
3. Quoted from a letter to Sam [Sal] Shenkier, written from prison December 2, 1938. Cited in Bareiss, *Herschel Feibel Grynszpan*, 143 (Bundesarchiv R55/20991).

4. Schwab, *The Day the Holocaust Began*, 11–12.

5. Steinweis, *Kristallnacht: 1938*, 37.

6. Steinweis, 24–25.

7. Steinweis, 57.

8. Fisher and Read, *Kristallnacht: The Nazi Night of Terror*, 61.

9. Steinweis, *Kristallnacht: 1938*, 38.

10. Steinweis, 39–43, 46–55.

11. Goebbels to Tagebücher, part I, volume 6, November 10, 1938.

12. Goebbels to Tagebücher.

13. Goebbels's role as the instigator of the pogrom, with Hitler almost passive, and even "taken aback" by its violence and illegality, has been widely debated. In *Hitler: 1936–1945; Nemesis*, pp. 143–53, Ian Kershaw provides an excellent summary of this debate, with a persuasive and highly informed resolution. See also Steinweis, *Kristallnacht: 1938*, 3, 42.

14. Goebbels's speech is cited in Fisher and Read, *Kristallnacht: The Nazi Night of Terror*, 62. Their source is *Der Stürmer*, November 15, 1938. Annals of the International Military Tribunal at Nuremberg, vol. X evidence of Julius Streicher and Joachim von Ribbentrop.

15. The course of the Kristallnacht has been traced many times. In English, a classic description can be found in *Crystal Night*, by Thalmann and Feinermann (translated from the French by Gilles Cremonesi). A popular account, one that is especially rich in detail, is *Kristallnacht: The Nazi Night of Terror*, by Read and Fisher. At the summit of scholarship about the Second World War is Gilbert's *Kristallnacht: Prelude to Destruction*. A more recent scholarly study is Steinweis's *Kristallnacht: 1938*. The bibliography of German scholarship on the November pogrom is voluminous. Among the most noteworthy is Hans-Jurgen Döscher's *"Reichskristallnacht;" Die Novemberpogrome, 1938* (Munich: Econ-Ullstein-List-Verlag, 2000), though as we shall see, certain problems attend that work.

16. Fisher and Read, *Kristallnacht: The Nazi Night of Terror*, 68.

17. Fisher and Read, 68.

18. Schwab, *The Day the Holocaust Began*, 31.

19. Schwab, 32.

20. Schwab, 31.

Chapter 11: Grief and Grandiosity

1. Associated Press, "Slayer of vom Rath Weeps Over Nazi Fine," *New York Times*, November 13, 1938.

2. *La Journée Parisienne*, no. 4314 (December 2, 1938), Bundesachiv R55/20991, quoted in Bareiss, *Herschel Fiebel Grynszpan*, 143.

3. Schwab, *The Day the Holocaust Began*, 106. Schwab points out that Herschel wrote this to an uncle in a letter clearly not intended for publication. Nonetheless, that Herschel intended only to wound and not kill his victim may be doubted.

4. Schwab, 88.

5. Schwab, 88.

6. Schwab, 89.

7. Schwab, 94–95.

8. Discussion of Dorothy Thompson's involvement in the case, and the account of the founding of the Journalists' Defense Fund, is indebted throughout to Schwab, 35–41, 90–95.

9. Schwab, 39.

10. Schwab, 91.

11. Schwab, 80. See also Smeets, *De Wanhoopsdaad*, 108–12. In 1953, Grimm published a memoir, *Politische Justiz* (Bonn: Bonner Universitaets-Buchdruckerei).

12. For insight into Grimm's role in France after 1940, see Robert O. Paxton, *Vichy France: 1940–1944* (New York: Columbia University Press, 1972, 2001), 14, 28, 65–66.

13. Cuénot, *The Herschel Grynzpan Case*, 93–96.

14. Schwab, *The Day the Holocaust Began*, 10–12; Smeets, *De Wanhoopsdaad*, 103–7.

15. Schwab, 10.

16. Schwab, 12.

17. Schwab, 82–85.

18. Schwab, 84.

19. Schwab, 79–80.

20. Schwab, 58.

21. This account is taken from Schwab's typewritten notes from an interview with Vincent de Moro-Giafferi, January 23, 1947.

22. Schwab, 188.

Chapter 12: The Phony War

1. Moro-Giafferi expressed this opinion in an interview with Schwab, January 23, 1947. Weill-Goudchaux, "L'Affaire Grynszpan," *L'Arche* (June 1960): 16.

2. Schwab, 96, and chapter 11.

3. Weill-Goudchaux is quoted in Friedrich Grimm's book written under the pseudonym Pierre Dumoulin, *L'Affaire Grynszpan: Un Attentat Contre la France* (Paris: Editions Jean Renard, 1942), 33.

4. Dumoulin, 33.

5. Schwab, *The Day the Holocaust Began*, 104.

6. Schwab, 102.

7. Schwab, 100–2.

8. Schwab, 117–18.

9. Schwab, 117–18.

10. See Paxton, *Vichy France* (2001 ed.), 65–66, 143. Paxton does not mention Herschel in his assessment of Grimm's activities, but Grimm's role in arranging for Bonnet's testimony in the planned show trial is covered in Schwab, *The Day the Holocaust Began*, 136–46.

11. See Paxton, *Vichy France* (2001 ed.), especially the chapter entitled "The French Civil War 1934–1937," 243.

12. Schwab, *The Day the Holocaust Began*, 116.

13. Schwab, 117.

14. See "Grynszpan Seeks Release to Kill Some More Nazis," an Associated Press dispatch from Paris of October 4, 1939. *New York Times*, October 5, 1939.

15. Schwab, *The Day the Holocaust Began*, 118.

16. Schwab, 119.

17. Schwab, 119.

18. Schwab, 120.

19. I rely on Schwab's account of the two Guinand missions in *The Day the Holocaust Began,* 116–21. Schwab also reports that Herschel's first request for release in order to join the French army was submitted in a letter to Bonnet's predecessor as Minister of Justice—a Bonnet ally—on August 28, 1939, four days before the invasion of Poland and the outbreak of war. Since there was little hope that Herschel's request would be granted, it seems that this move, like the later one in October, was as much intended for newspaper consumption and general propaganda purposes as it was in the unlikely expectation of a favorable outcome.

Chapter 13: "I'm Herschel Grynszpan! Arrest Me!"

1. May, *Strange Victory*, 324.

2. See Paxton, *Vichy France*, 12.

3. It is true that Bonnet's membership on the National Council was inactive. The

council itself was to draft a constitution only after the armistice of June 1940 was replaced by a fully developed peace treaty, something that the Germans would not permit until the surrender of Great Britain—an event Bonnet avidly hoped would take place. (See Paxton, *Vichy France*, 91.) Since Britain did not surrender, the National Council never acted. Nonetheless, membership meant full agreement with Vichy policy. Meanwhile, it is not quite correct to say that Bonnet was inactive during Vichy. He was in regular contact with the senior leadership, and as late as 1943, he was angling for a diplomatic appointment. (See Paxton, 322n.)

4. Paxton, 91.
5. Schwab, *The Day the Holocaust Began*, 121.
6. Schwab, 124–25.
7. Schwab, 124–25. See also Smeets, *De Wanhoopsdaad*, 125–26.
8. Cuénot (*The Herschel Grynszpan Case*, 123) asserts that Herschel was one of the six prisoners taken from the wreck to Bourges. Schwab, citing a German report (p. 125), claims that the six inmates were taken to Bourges by their guards, and that Herschel followed on his own, making a surprise appearance at the Bourges prison upon their arrival.
9. Schwab, 125.
10. Cuénot, *The Herschel Grynszpan Case*, 126–30.
11. Schwab, *The Day the Holocaust Began*, 128.
12. Varian Fry, *Surrender on Demand* (Boulder, CO: Johnson Books in conjunction with the United States Holocaust Memorial Museum, 1997), 52. In 1951, Gerald Schwab approached Varian Fry asking for the source of his information. Fry replied that he could not remember with certainty, but that he thought it was probably the historian Konrad Heiden, one of the refugees whom Fry helped cross the border.
13. Schwab, *The Day the Holocaust Began*, 129–30.
14. Schwab, 128.

Chapter 14: Herschel the Captive

1. Serge Weill-Goudchaux, "La fin de Gruenspan," *Evidences* (Paris) 1 (May 1949): 19–20. See also Henry Torres, *Accuses hors serie* (Paris: Gallimard, 1957), 9.
2. Cuénot, *The Herschel Grynszpan Case*, 130.
3. Cuénot, 130.
4. *New York Times*, September 8, 1940.

5. Smeets, *De Wanhoopsdaad*, 172, 174; Schwab, *The Day the Holocaust Began*, 179–80.

6. The English translation of Herschel's testament can be found complete in Schwab, 181, and in the appendix to this book.

7. Various writers have questioned the authenticity of Herschel's testament, leaning toward the suspicion that it was a Nazi forgery. Their reasoning is strictly circumstantial: They notice that in disavowing the homosexual strategy, the testament served Nazi purposes—ergo, the Nazis must have written it. This logic is unpersuasive. Gerald Schwab addresses it directly in *The Day the Holocaust Began* (189–91) and provides a number of convincing reasons discrediting the theory.

8. Schwab, 187.

9. Schwab, 181. The full text of Herschel's final testament is translated in Schwab. I have made minor alterations in the word order of that translation for the sake of clarity.

10. Schwab, 145.

11. Schwab, 134–35.

12. Steinweis, *Kristallnacht: 1938*, 140.

13. Marrus, 72.

14. Schwab, 181.

15. Schwab, 83, 196.

16. Schwab, 40.

17. This tract was published in 1942 under Grimm's French pen name, Pierre Desmoulins, as *L'Affaire Grynszpan, un attentat contre la France*. The same material appeared in German, as *Denkschrift über die in Paris im Juni-Juli 1940 Von der Deutschen Feldpolizei in Der Grünspan-Sache beschlagnahmtem Akten*. n.d. See Schwab, 220.

18. Otto Abetz made this statement in his book *Franco-German Political History 1930–1950. Memoirs of an Ambassador* (Editions Stock, 1953).

19. Schwab, 131. See also Cuénot.

20. Michael Marrus, "The Strange Story of Herschel Grynszpan." *The American Scholar* (Winter 1988), 73.

21. Schwab, *The Day the Holocaust Began*, 134.

22. This list of goals appears verbatim in Schwab, 134.

23. Schwab, 135–36.

24. Schwab, 136.

25. Schwab, 138, 136.

26. Schwab, 139.

27. Schwab, 143, 146.

28. Ted Morgan, *Maugham: A Biography* (New York: Simon & Schuster, 1984).

29. Adamthwaite, *France and the Coming of the Second World War*, 332.

30. Schwab, *The Day the Holocaust Began*, 139.

31. William Irvine, "Domestic Politics and the Fall of France in 1940," in *The French Defeat of 1940 Reassessments*, ed. Joel Blatt, 85–99.

32. Schwab, *The Day the Holocaust Began*, 142–45.

33. Paxton, *Vichy France* (2001 ed.), 192–93.

34. Paxton, 193.

35. Adamthwaite, *France and the Coming of the Second World War*, 101.

36. Adamthwaite, 101.

37. Adamthwaite, 101.

38. Schwab, *The Day the Holocaust Began*, 136.

Chapter 15: The Homosexual Strategy

1. Corinne Chaponnière in *Les Quatre Coups de la Nuit de Cristal: L'Affaire Grynszpan–vom Rath* (Paris: Albin Michel, 2015) has discredited the claim that Gide wrote about Herschel in his diary.

2. Smeets, *De Wanhoopsdaad*, 191–92.

3. Schwab, *The Day the Holocaust Began*, 16–17.

4. Schwab, 73; Cuénot, *The Herschel Grynszpan Case*, 21.

5. This version of the homosexual defense is recounted in Cuénot, pp. 136–37. Cuénot's source is Grimm's memoir, *Politische Justiz*.

6. Cuénot, 136. Oddly, Cuénot notes: "In truth, this incredible story did not even merit verification."

7. Schwab, *The Day the Holocaust Began*, 132.

8. Schwab, 170.

9. Schwab, 170.

10. Schwab, 142. Schwab is quoting Goebbels's diary entry of January 24, 1942.

11. Schwab, 142.

12. Schwab, 180.

13. Schwab, 181.

14. Schwab, 180.

15. As to the dating of the trial, Schwab, 141–43; as to Bonnet's testimony, Schwab, 144.

16. This betrayal was one of long duration. The informer probably had been with

Herschel in Moabit from the beginning, and everything Herschel told him had been noted and filed in a set of Gestapo documents called the *Grüne Hefte,* or "Green pamphlets." The chief prosecutor kept everything in the *Grüne Hefte* in absolute secrecy, and every scrap of it was there to be used against Herschel in the trial. The informer posed as a dissident imprisoned for his activities against the regime; he had been promised his freedom after Herschel's execution. See Schwab, 179, 180, 183.

Chapter 16: Victory Unaware
1. Steinweis, *Kristallnacht: 1938,* 144.
2. Steinweis, 144.
3. Schwab, *The Day the Holocaust Began,* 172.
4. Schwab, 176. See also Steinweis, *Kirstallnacht: 1938,* 144–45.
5. Joel Colson, *Léon Blum: Humanist in Politics* (Durham, NC: Duke University Press, 1987), 405.
6. See chapter 16.
7. Schwab, *The Day the Holocaust Began,* 174.
8. Schwab, 183.
9. Schwab, 177. Schwab suggests that Admiral Leahy's departure and the heavy symbolism it involved may have been the instrument through which Bonnet decided to reconsider.
10. Jonathan Kirsch, *The Short, Strange Life of Herschel Grynszpan.* Paperback ed. (New York: Liveright, an imprint of W. W. Norton, 2013), 248. Kirsch does not give his source.
11. Stanley Hoffmann, *New York Times Book Review,* November 1, 1981. This quotation is from Hoffmann's review of *Vichy France and the Jews,* by Robert O. Paxton and Michael Marrus, Basic Books, New York, 1981.

Chapter 17: Oblivion
1. Schwab, *The Day the Holocaust Began,* 199.
2. Schwab, 184.
3. See Schwab, 199. See also Steinweis, *Kristallnacht: 1938,* 146. Steinweis relies on Döscher, *Reichskristallnacht,* 172. Steinweis and Döscher estimate the execution as taking place in the late summer; Schwab, citing the testimony of another prisoner in Sachsenhausen, places the date of the transfer in late September.
4. Schwab, 200–1.

5. Schwab, 200. My italics. In 1942—shortly after the trial was postponed—Grimm published a compilation of what he saw as evidence of Jewish complicity in vom Rath's assassination. The German edition of his book was called *Der Grünspan Prozess*. Grimm also published a translation into French under the pseudonym Pierre Dumoulin: *L'Affaire Grynspan: Un Attentat Contre la France*. It seems likely that the ministerial memorandum and these two publications were linked. If so, the phrase "for the time being" indicates that Grimm believed that Herschel was still alive at the time the material was published.

6. Schwab, 198–99. Schwab's sources here are a letter from Walter Hammer to Alain Cuénot, MD, dated April 11, 1957, and a memorandum for general distribution dated July 7, 1959. Copies of these documents are in my possession, a gift from Gerald Schwab.

Epilogue: Two Brothers

1. Smeets, *De Wanhoopsdaad*, 181.
2. For the basic facts of the Solitkow case, see Schwab, *The Day the Holocaust Began*, 197–200. For a full discussion, see Smeets, 179–97.
3. Riva and Malka Grynszpan, interview by Yotam Feldman, *Haaretz*, November 13, 2008.
4. Smeets, *De Wanhoopsdaad*, 204.
5. Smeets, 204.
6. Riva and Malka Grynszpan, interview by Feldman.
7. For the rumors of Herschel's survival of the war, see Schwab, *The Day the Holocaust Began*, 197–201.
8. Smeets, *De Wanhoopsdaad*, 204. Döscher, *Reichskristallnact*, 74.
9. Steinweis, *Kristallnacht: 1938*, 142–44.
10. Harlan Greene. *The German Officer's Boy* (Madison: The University of Wisconsin Press, 2005).
11. Smeets, *De Wanhoopsdaad*, 197.
12. Schwab, *The Day the Holocaust Began*, 201.

INDEX

Abetz, Otto, 28, 69, 130–31, 143, 151, 168, 196
  Nazified France, 143
Achenbach, Ernst, 72
Aktion, 35–36, 43
A la Fine Lame (shop), Paris, 60–62, 98, 99, 168, 187
Arendt, Hannah, 40, 42
Auer, Herr, 180
Auschwitz, 164, 200, 201
Austria, 12, 55, 141, 169
  Anschluss, 98
  anti-Semitic propaganda, 105, 106, 116, 117–19, 169
Autret, François, 64, 73, 75, 90

Baarová, Lída, 87–88
Bareiss, Andreas Friedrich, 216
Batestini, M. M., 146
Battle of Britain, 176, 177, 196
Baumgartner, Amédée, 95, 96, 111

Beer Hall Putsch, 81–82
Belgium, 18, 107, 108, 143
Berenbaum, Mina, 46
Bismarck, Otto von, 64
Blum, Léon, 175, 195
Bonaparte, Napoleon, 8, 63–64, 124
Bonnet, Charles, 146
Bonnet, Georges
  Herschel Grynszpan, 90, 91, 93, 95, 132, 133, 146, 151–52, 163, 172–77, 190, 194, 196, 198–200, 212
  Nazi appeasement, 6, 8, 12, 25, 26, 27–29, 77, 112, 113, 142–43, 145, 149–50, 197
Bonnet, Odette, 28
Bormann, Martin, 195, 203
Brandenburg, 206, 207
Brandt, Karl, 94–95, 96–97, 111, 180
Bräuer, Curt, 74, 75–76, 78, 93
Buchenwald, 119

Café Heck, Munich, 114

Caron, Vicki, 30

Casablanca (film), 157

Catholics, 107

Cavarroc, Pierre, 154, 155, 156

Céline, 163

Chamberlain, Neville, 5–6, 7–8,
11–12, 113

Chicago Tribune, 127

Chichery, Albert, 177

Churchill, Winston, 28, 113

Claas, Dr., 74–75, 95

Clinique de l'Alma (hospital), Paris,
95–96, 99, 103, 111

Cooper, Duff, 113

Crystal Night (Thalmann, Feinermann), 68–69

Cuénot, Alain, 152–53

Czechoslovakia, 6, 8, 78, 79, 106, 107,
132, 142

Dachau, 80, 119

Dahms, Fritz, 204, 207

Daladier, Édouard, 5–11, 12–13, 25,
27, 30, 98, 175, 195

De Wanhoopsdaad (Act of Desperation)
(Smeets), 216–17

Diewerge, Wolfgang
anti-Semitic propaganda campaign, 83, 128–29, 163
Herschel Grynszpan, 166–67,
168, 170–71, 177, 186, 187,
193, 194, 204, 208

Döscher, Hans-Jürgen, 203, 215–17

Dreyfus affair, 32, 154

Dupuich, Victor, 146

Eden, Antony, 113

Eichmann, Adolf, 14, 16, 40–42, 69,
79, 80, 163, 171, 177
Herschel Grynszpan, 204–6,
207–8
trial, 213–14, 217

Emergency Rescue Committee, 156

Evian Conference, 29

Feinermann, Emmanuel, 68–69

First World War, 7, 20, 64, 81, 107,
109

Fitzgerald, F. Scott, 127

Flossenbürg, 170, 185

France, 3, 5–11, 14, 16, 17, 130–31
anti-German sentiment, 113,
146–48
Foreign Legion, 30
German embassy, 63–73, 74–76,
82, 99, 168
German invasion, 142, 143, 144,
146–47, 150–55, 157
German refugees, 98
immigration laws, 25–27, 29, 141
Jewish deportation, 200–201
Jewish refugees, 19–20, 23,
24–25, 26–27, 28, 29–30
National Assembly, 64
National Council, 175–76
Nazi collaborators/sympathizers,
143, 146, 149–50, 156, 197
Nazi fugitives, 158
Ostjuden, 33–42
Popular Front, 25, 175
Riom trial, 175, 194, 195–96, 197
Sûreté, 102

Vichy government, 143, 144, 150,
156–57, 159, 161, 174–75,
176, 177, 195, 196–97,
198–99, 200, 201
Frankel, Isidore, 158, 160
Frankfurter, David, 83
Freemasons, 107
Fresnes prison, Paris, 101, 151, 158
Fry, Varian, 156–57

Gaulle, Charles de, 177
General Electric Hour (radio program),
125
George VI, King of England, 12
Géraud, André, 127
German Officer's Boy, The (Greene),
216
Germany, 4, 7, 8, 12, 23, 76–77, 105,
129–30
anti-German sentiment, 113,
163
Austria, 98, 105, 106, 116, 117–19,
169
Czechoslovakia, 6, 8, 78, 79, 106,
107, 132, 142
France, 93–94, 128, 132, 142,
143, 146–47, 175–76
Great Britain, 11, 176, 177, 196
Jewish expulsion, 16, 17, 24,
33–42, 43, 79
Munich, 112–14, 115–16, 117
National Socialism, 69, 87, 88, 94,
107, 174
Nuremberg Laws, 15, 79
Poland, 94, 131–32, 174, 200
See also Hitler, Adolf

Gide, André, 179
Goebbels, Joseph
anti-Semitic propaganda campaign, 3, 4, 78, 80, 89, 90,
95, 97, 101, 112, 117–18,
123–24, 128–29, 160–78,
171, 172, 198
Herschel Grynszpan, 69, 74, 75,
76, 84, 89, 160–78, 179, 184,
188, 190–91, 192, 193–95,
198, 202, 212
sex life, 87–88
Goebbels, Magda, 87–88
Göring, Hermann, 78, 113, 116
Great Britain, 5, 7, 8, 11–12, 107,
113
Battle of Britain, 176, 177, 196
Greene, Harlan, 216
Grimm, Friedrich
anti-Semitic propaganda, 128–29,
143–45, 176–77, 204
Herschel Grynszpan, 130–32,
140, 142, 147, 151, 153, 161,
163, 166–68, 170–71, 172,
173, 184–85, 186, 187, 194,
199, 208
Nazified France, 143
Gruber, Heinrich, 69
Grynszpan, Abraham and Chawa, 14,
18, 20, 23, 30–31, 43, 45, 46–47,
48–51, 54, 90, 97, 98, 103, 125,
158, 201
arrest and conviction, 141–42
Grynszpan, Berta, 33–34, 36, 37–38,
42, 43–44, 45, 49, 90–91, 138,
200, 214

Grynszpan, Herschel, 3–4, 14–22, 40
  asylum, 29–30
  capture by Gestapo, 157–59
  celebrity, 102–3, 164
  chance for escape, 151–53
  coded personal testament,
      162–63, 165, 181, 189–90,
      191, 195
  concentration camps, 101,
      168–69, 170, 177, 182, 185,
      202, 203
  death, 202–11, 217
  defense, 123–25, 127, 131–37,
      139–40, 144–45, 160,
      169–70, 179–91, 192–95,
      197–200, 212
  depression, 30–31, 44–45
  disappearance, 153–55
  Dorothy Thompson, 125–27, 131
  dossier, 155–56
  Ernst vom Rath murder, 42, 45,
      46, 70–73, 74–89, 90–100,
      112, 115, 118–20, 121–23,
      161, 163, 164, 167, 168, 200,
      209
  France, 14–22, 46–58, 59–68,
      69–73, 74–76, 90–100,
      121–23, 138–40, 164, 165
  Germany, 14, 16, 17–18, 160–78,
      186, 202
  Hôtel de Suez, 54–58, 59
  indictment, 150–51
  interrogation, 103–6, 110, 114
  persecution, 30, 31–32, 44–45, 48,
      92–100, 97, 101, 122–23, 151
  prison in France, 101, 138–41,
      142

  prison in Germany, 160–78, 186,
      202
  suicide, 189–90, 192
  trial, 162–64, 170–73, 175,
      177–78
Grynszpan, Mordecai, 15, 34, 36,
  37–38, 200, 212, 213–14
Grynszpan, Salomon, 124
Grynszpan, Sendel and Rivka, 14, 34,
  36, 37–38, 40–42, 45, 47–48,
  200, 213, 217
Grynszpan, Wolf, 18
Guinand, Marcel, 145–48, 174
Gurs, 201

Halter, Heinrich. *See* Grynszpan,
  Herschel
Hammer, Walter (pen name), 206–7
Haus Elephant (hotel), Munich, 77
Heiber, Helmut, 215
Herriot, Édouard, 124
*Herschel Feibel Grynszpan: Der At-
  tentäter und die Reichskristallnacht*
  (Bareiss), 216
Himmler, Heinrich, 35, 113, 114, 117,
  167
  anti-Semitic propaganda cam-
      paign, 106–10
Hitler, Adolf
  anti-Semitic propaganda cam-
      paign, 3, 12–13, 14, 15, 16,
      17, 19, 21, 23–25, 24, 32,
      33–35, 47–48, 69, 74–89,
      90, 93–95, 97, 101, 107–10,
      112–16, 127–28, 129–30,
      131, 141, 144, 160–78, 172,
      209

Beer Hall Putsch, 81–82
Ernst vom Rath murder, 74–89,
    91–100, 111, 127–28, 129–31,
    132–33, 134–35, 142–43,
    144, 150–51, 163
  Gestapo, 4, 33, 36, 39, 40, 49, 69,
    75, 122, 129, 151, 157–59,
    161, 166, 177, 203
  Herschel Grynszpan, 4, 28, 29,
    75, 76–77, 160–78, 181, 192,
    195, 198, 203, 204, 210
  Holocaust, 79–80, 81, 105–8,
    111–12, 114–20, 121, 126,
    129, 130, 131–32, 144,
    163–64, 171–72, 177, 186,
    192, 198, 199, 200–201, 205
  money, 78–79, 120
  rise to power, 81–82
  Third Reich, 17, 28, 39, 107, 131,
    159
  See also Kristallnacht
Hoffmann, Stanley, 200
Holocaust, 3, 11, 12, 14, 16, 29, 32,
    45, 68, 74, 79, 82, 105, 106, 110,
    112, 115–16, 117, 120, 121, 122,
    124, 129, 142, 144, 160, 163, 164,
    167, 171–72, 177, 186, 198, 199,
    200–201, 205, 209, 210
Hôtel Beauharnais, Paris, 63–64, 70
Hôtel de Suez, Paris, 54–58, 59, 98, 99

Israel, 16, 18, 40, 200, 214
Italy, 107

Jagusch (interrogator), 182, 184
Jewish refugees, 19–20, 23, 24–25,
    26–27, 28, 29–30

Kaufmann, Nathan, 21, 30, 44–45,
    46, 47, 48, 49, 51–53, 54, 99
Kershaw, Ian, 80
Kirsch, Jonathan, 200
Köster, Roland, 67–68, 69, 70
Kristallnacht, 3, 4, 12, 16, 29, 45, 68,
    74, 79, 82, 105, 112, 115–16, 117,
    121, 122, 124, 129, 142, 144, 163,
    164, 167, 177, 209
Krueger, Herr, 71, 72, 73

L'Affaire Grynszpan (Grimm), 140
Landru, Henri, 124
La Santé prison, Paris, 101–2, 103
Laval, Pierre, 143–44, 174, 176, 177,
    197, 199, 200, 201
Leahy, William, 197
Le boeuf sur le Toit (gay bar), Paris, 180
Le Figaro (newspaper), 98
Leger, Alexis, 13
Le Temps (newspaper), 104
Lorz, M., 91, 92, 93, 97

Magdeburg, 207
Magnus, Dr., 111
Marrus, Michael, 165, 171
Maugham, Frederic, 173
Maugham, Somerset, 173–74
Mein Kampf (Hitler), 82
Menegaud, M., 155–56
Mizrachi Youth Organization, 18
Moabit (prison), Berlin, 186, 189, 202
Monneret, M., 92, 97, 98, 99, 102
Moro-Giafferi, Vincent de, 124–25,
    127, 131–32, 133, 134–37, 138,
    141, 145, 147, 151, 158, 160, 164,
    169, 170, 180, 181, 182, 187, 214

Mowrer, Edgar, 127
Mueller-Hass, Victor, 186
Munich Agreement, 5, 6, 8, 11, 12, 13, 16,
    28, 30, 64, 78, 93, 94, 106, 112, 132
Mussolini, Benito, 5

Nagorka, Wilhelm, 66, 70–72, 73
Nazi Party, 3–4, 7, 8, 11, 14, 15, 25,
    26, 27, 28–29, 30, 33–34, 45, 47,
    48, 49, 65, 68, 83, 86, 92, 97, 101,
    103, 112, 114, 115, 124, 131
    Movement Day, 81, 82, 106,
        112–13, 115–16
    Sturmabteilung (SA), 69, 105–6,
        112–13, 115–16, 118
New York City, 20
New Yorker, 40
New York Herald Tribune, 125
New York Times, 93, 161
Night of Long Knives, 69
North Africa, 175

Pariser Haint (newspaper), 44
Pertinax. *See* Géraud, André
Pétain, Philippe, 144, 151, 156, 200
Pirie, A. R., 140
pogroms. *See* Holocaust; Kristallnacht
Poland, 16, 24, 33–42, 45, 94, 107,
    140, 174, 200, 214

Rath, Ernst vom, 67–73, 74–89,
    90–100, 103, 104–5, 111–12, 114,
    116, 117, 131, 166
    homosexuality rumors, 133–37,
        140, 169–70, 179–91, 192–
        93, 194–95, 200, 212–13,
        215, 216, 217

Nazi hero, 170
Rath, Günter vom, 111, 136, 212–13
Rath, Gustav vom, 67, 68–69, 111, 131
*Reichskristallnacht: Die Novemberpo-
    grome* (Döscher), 215–16
Reynaud, Paul, 195
Rhysselberghe, Maria van, 179
Ribbentrop, Joachim von, 130, 171,
    173
Ribeyre, Paul, 154–55
Roberts, Andrew, 84
Röhm, Ernst, 88
Roosevelt, Franklin, 12, 29, 30, 122,
    197
Russia, 196, 200, 206

SA. *See* Sturmabteilung (SA)
Sachsenhausen, 119, 168–69, 170, 177,
    182, 185, 202, 203, 206
Schenkier, Sal, 21, 30, 121
Schlumberger, Jean, 179
Schneider, Otto. *See* Grynszpan,
    Herschel
Schuschnigg, Kurt, 169
Schwab, Gerald, 124, 131, 136, 138,
    143, 153, 162, 163, 203, 204
Second World War, 4–12, 75, 132,
    140, 142, 143, 144, 149, 160–78,
    176–77, 196, 197, 210, 215
Smeets, Sidney, 68, 203, 216–17
Soltikow, Michael Alexander, 136,
    212, 213, 215, 216, 217
Sonnenburg, 206, 207
Soviet Union, 108
Sportsclub Aurore, Paris, 98, 131
Steinweis, Alan, 113–14, 115, 163–64,
    203, 216

Sturmabteilung (SA), 69, 105–6

Surrender on Demand (Fry), 157

Switzerland, 143, 158, 177

Szwarc, M., 125, 127

Tesnière, Judge, 103–4, 110, 131, 144

Thalmann, Rita, 68–69

Thompson, Dorothy, 3–4, 14, 125–27, 131, 146, 167, 210

    Journalists' Defense Fund, 127, 167

Tout Va Bien (café), Paris, 21–22, 62–63, 99

Treaty of Versailles, 65

United States, 107, 196, 197, 199

University of Münster, 128

Vésine-Larue, M., 125, 127

Völkischer Beobachter (newspaper), 114

Wagner, Richard, 64

Wannsee Conference, 163, 171, 186, 193

Weill-Goudchaux, Serge

    Herschel Grynszpan, 15, 105, 125, 132–33, 134, 135, 139, 140, 151, 160, 169, 210

Welczeck, Johannes Graf von, 28–29, 65, 68, 77, 90, 91, 92–93, 94, 163

Wiesäcker, Ernst von, 130

Wilhelm II, Kaiser of Germany, 64, 81, 113

Wochenend (magazine), 212, 213

Wollenberg, Erich, 136–37

World Jewish conspiracy, 166–68, 171–73, 199

Zionism, 16, 18

STEPHEN KOCH is the author of two novels and many books of nonfiction on subjects ranging from Andy Warhol to World War II. After serving as chairman of the Creative Writing Division in the School of the Arts at Columbia University, he wrote a classic text on writing, *The Modern Library Writer's Workshop*. The director of the Peter Hujar Archive, he lives with his wife in New York and has one daughter.